Minority Nations in Multinational Federations

Multinational federations rest on the coexistence of two or more nations within a single polity. Within these federations, minority nations play a significant role as their character differs from the other building blocks of the federation.

This edited volume offers a comprehensive comparison of two such minority nations – Quebec in Canada and Wallonia in Belgium – that exemplify many dimensions, themes and issues highly resonant to the study of federalism and regionalism across the globe. Quebec and Wallonia have experienced several decades of federal dynamics where both regions have had to find their way as a minority nation in a multinational federation. For those studying federalism and regionalism their importance lies in a number of characteristics, but principally in the fact that these minority nations have transformed into mini-states with fully fledged legislative powers within their federation. This book seeks to study the specific dynamics within these small worlds, and between them and the rest of the federation.

This text will be of key interest to students and scholars of federalism, nationalism and regionalism, comparative politics and policies, political ideas and social movements.

Min Reuchamps is Professor of Political Science at the Université catholique de Louvain, Belgium.

Routledge Series in Federal Studies
(Formerly The Cass Series in Regional and Federal Studies)
ISSN 1363–5670

Series Editor: Michael Burgess, Centre for Federal Studies,
University of Kent, UK
Formerly edited by John Loughlin, Cardiff University, UK

This series brings together some of the foremost academics and theorists to examine
the timely subject of regional and federal studies, which since the mid-1980s have
become key questions in political analysis and practice.

Minority Nations in Multinational Federations

A comparative study of Quebec and Wallonia

Edited by
Min Reuchamps

Routledge
Taylor & Francis Group

LONDON AND NEW YORK

First published 2015
by Routledge
2 Park Square, Milton Park, Abingdon, Oxfordshire OX14 4RN

and by Routledge
711 Third Avenue, New York, NY 10017

First issued in paperback 2016

Routledge is an imprint of the Taylor & Francis Group, an informa business

British Library Cataloguing in Publication Data
A catalogue record for this book is available from the British Library

Library of Congress Cataloging in Publication Data
   Minority nations in multinational federations : a comparative study of Quebec and Wallonia / edited by Min Reuchamps.
      pages cm
   Includes bibliographical references and index.
   1. Minorities--Case studies. 2. Nationalism--Case studies. 3. Regionalism--Case studies. 4. Federal government--Case studies. I. Reuchamps, Min.
   JC312.M58   2015
   320.4493'049--dc23
                2014022743

ISBN 13: 978-1-138-23837-4 (pbk)
ISBN 13: 978-1-138-79632-4 (hbk)

Typeset in Times New Roman
by Taylor & Francis Books

Contents

List of illustrations

Figures

Tables

Notes on contributors

Sandra Breux is a professor at the Institut National de la Recherche Scientifique, Urbanisation Culture Société (INRS-UCS) in Montreal, Canada. Her research interests are municipal elections, local governance and territorial representations. She has published several books and her work has appeared in *International Journal of Urban and Regional Research, Canadian Journal of Political Science, Geography Compass* and *Annales de géographie.*

Michael Burgess is Professor of Federal Studies at the Centre for Federal Studies, School of Politics and International Relations, University of Kent, United Kingdom. He has published widely on comparative federalism, European integration and constitutional politics in Canada. His most recent book is *In Search of the Federal Spirit: New Comparative Empirical and Theoretical Perspectives* (Oxford University Press, 2012).

Jean-François Caron holds a PhD from the Université Laval and is currently Assistant Professor in Political Science at the Université de Moncton, New Brunswick, Canada. His research focuses on federalism and nationalism. He has published articles in *National Identities,* the *Journal of Intercultural Studies,* the *International Journal of Canadian Studies* and *Politique et Sociétés.*

Jérémy Dodeigne is a research fellow of the Fonds de la Recherche Scientifique-FNRS at the Université de Liège and at the Université catholique de Louvain, Belgium. His research interests are career patterns and legislative recruitment in multi-multilevel systems. He is currently working on a doctoral thesis on the political representation of minority nations in multi-multilevel systems (Catalonia, Scotland and Wallonia).

Philippe Hambye is Professor of French Linguistics at the Université catholique de Louvain, Belgium. His research mainly includes works in sociolinguistics regarding the variation of linguistic norms and practices in the French-speaking world, language practices in education and work, and language policies. His work aims to discover the role language plays in issues of legitimacy, power and social inequalities.

Vincent Jacquet is a PhD student in political science at the Université catholique de Louvain, Belgium. His research interests are participatory and deliberative democracy, political participation, local politics and democratic theory. He has published several articles on democratic innovations.

Marine Kravagna holds a Masters in political science from the Université de Liège, Belgium. Her research interests include the study of European institutions, democracy, local policy analysis as well as language and politics.

Heidi Mercenier is a PhD student in political science at the Centre for European Studies at the Université Saint-Louis Bruxelles, Belgium. Her research interests include political legitimacy, multilevel governance and citizenship as well as European and Belgian politics.

Stéphane Paquin is a full professor at the École nationale d'administration publique (ÉNAP), Montréal, Canada, where he is the holder of the Canada Research Chair in International and Comparative Political Economy (CRÉPIC). He has authored or co-authored nine books, including, *Théories de l'économie politique internationale* (Presses de sciences po, 2013) and *International Policy and Politics in Canada* (Pearson Canada, 2010). He has published upwards of 100 articles, including several that have appeared in academic journals such as the *International Journal, Canadian Foreign Policy Review, the Hague Journal of Diplomacy, Nationalism & Ethnic Politics*, the *Canadian Journal of Political Science, Canadian Public Administration* and *Guerres mondiales et conflits contemporains*.

Julien Perrez is an assistant professor at the Department of Modern Languages of the Université de Liège, Belgium, where he teaches Dutch linguistics. His research interests include foreign-language learning (especially French-speaking learners of Dutch), the expression of spatial relations in typologically different languages and the study of metaphors in political discourse. His work has been published in *Cognitive Linguistics, Cognitextes* and *Review of Cognitive Linguistics*.

Maxime Petit Jean is a PhD student in political and social science at the Université catholique de Louvain, Belgium. His PhD research concerns the processes of emergence and development of foresight in public management and public governance. His research interests are mainly public management, public policy analysis and comparative politics.

Min Reuchamps is Professor of Political Science at the Université catholique de Louvain, Belgium. His teaching and research interests are federalism and multi-multilevel governance, comparative politics and democratic innovations as well as participatory and deliberative methods. He has published several books and his work has appeared in *Acta Politica, Party Politics, Politics, Politique et Sociétés, Regional and Federal Studies, Res Publica, Territory, Politics, Governance* and *West European Politics*.

Luc Turgeon is an assistant professor of political science at the School of Political Studies, University of Ottawa, Canada. His recent work focuses mostly on federalism, nationalism, the bureaucratic representation of minorities, and public opinion toward immigration and ethnic pluralism. His work has been published in the *Canadian Journal of Political Science, Canadian Public Administration, Regional and Federal Studies, Nations and Nationalism* and the *Journal of Canadian Studies.* He recently published two co-edited books at UBC Press: *Segmented Cities: How Urban Contexts Shape Ethnic and Nationalist Politics* and *Comparing Canada: Methods and Perspectives on Canadian Politics.*

Acknowledgements

This book owes much – if not everything – to its contributors who have taken up successfully the challenge to offer an appraisal – in English – of Quebec and Wallonia for each of the issues at stake within one single comparative chapter. This comparative dialogue started from a workshop organized at the Université de Liège in Belgium with the support of the Association internationale des études québécoises (AIÉQ) and the Centre d'études québécoises (CÉQ) of the Université de Liège. Michael Burgess, the editor of the Routledge Series in Federal Studies, has always been extremely supportive of this enterprise from its very beginning. His continuing support, in addition to the insightful comments from the two anonymous reviewers, has definitely contributed to the book's current form. At Routledge, Heidi Bagtazo and Alexander Quayle initially and then Charlotte Endersby, Jennifer Harding, Sabrina Lacey and Andrew Taylor have offered a highly professional support throughout and above all have always believed in the potential of this book, despite the limited size of its targeted market. It is now up to the readers to continue this story.

Min Reuchamps

Introduction
Quebec and Wallonia in comparative perspective

Min Reuchamps

Among the genus of federal designs, multinational federations stand out because of their very special nature. Their federal dynamics rests on the coexistence of several – at least two – nations within a single polity. Such a multinational dynamics implies specific federal relations within and between the constituent units, its building blocks. Nonetheless, in the comparative study of federalism, while scholars have paid increasing attention to multinational federations as a whole (for instance, Gagnon and Tully 2001; Keating 2001; McRoberts 2001; Gagnon, Rocher, and Guibernau 2003; Burgess and Pinder 2007), less research has been devoted to the "small worlds" inside them (Simeon and Elkins 1974; Elkins and Simeon 1980; Burgess 2013), with some important exceptions, particularly on the grounds of subnational constitutional politics (Tarr 1998; Burgess and Tarr 2012). When these small worlds are minority nations in a multinational federation, the comparative study of their character is even more relevant to apprehend the federal dynamics in such polities. A few notable cases have received attention in the past decades: the Basque Country and Catalonia in Spain, Bavaria in Germany, Flanders in Belgium, Quebec in Canada and, more recently, Scotland in the United Kingdom. Yet the considerable attention paid to these minority nations has mostly been focused on their politics of difference and, more specifically, on the question of their breaking away or not, leaving aside a view from within and how these minority nations have transformed into (mini-)states with fully fledged legislative powers within their federations.

This need to study more closely the small worlds follows the "meso" turn in social science as a consequence of the rise of the meso-level or region throughout the world and in Europe in particular (Keating 2013). Too often the focus is on national politics and policies and as such regions are seen as mere consequences of these dynamics. This common approach of regional and federal dynamics suffers, however, from "methodological nationalism" (Jeffery and Schakel 2013). One typical example is the "second-order election" theory that posits all but national elections to be of second-order nature (Reif and Schmitt 1980). They are subordinate to first-order national elections because there is less at stake in the other elections, and this implies for these second-order elections: lower turnout, less votes for government parties and more votes for small, new and opposition parties. But recent scholarship that focuses specifically on regional elections has demonstrated that the issues at stakes are much more complex than this dichotomy assumes (Dandoy and Schakel 2013; Schakel and Jeffery 2013). An effort to understand fully the regional dynamics is thus highly needed.

This book therefore seeks to study the specific dynamics *within* these small worlds – since they are too often considered as monolithic blocks – and *between* them and the rest of the federation; that is, both the federal order and the other constituent units – since both so-called vertical and horizontal interactions deserve a comprehensive grip to understand fully the dynamics of minority nations in multinational federations. In the concert of minority nations within multinational federal systems, Quebec and Wallonia, despite their differences, share specific features that make their comparison insightful and important, albeit understudied by the students of federalism across the world, beyond the typical comparison between Belgium and Canada (for instance, Karmis and Gagnon 2001; Poirier 2004; Béland and Lecours 2005, 2007; Erk 2008; Fournier and Reuchamps 2009; Poirier 2009b; Reuchamps 2011; Hambye and Richards 2012).

First, Quebec and Wallonia have experienced for several decades a federal dynamics where both regions have had to find their way as a minority nation in a multinational federation. While, in this regard, the comparison between Quebec and Flanders has often led to an interesting and meaningful comparison because of their similar history of grievance and nationalism (Erk 2002), the latest development of Canadian and Belgian federalism has brought Quebec and Wallonia closer to each other, re-emphasising their minority status. Indeed, in their recent history these two minority nations had a momentum – a critical juncture – the very same year, 1995: the second referendum in Quebec and the first direct election of the Walloon parliament. These two episodes can be considered as the founding moment of contemporary politics in Quebec and Wallonia, and fostered their transformation from minority nations to (mini-)states with fully fledged legislative powers.

With the defeat of the "no" camp in the second referendum, Quebec and the Québécois had to find their way back into Canadian federalism despite the grievances of the past and the political turmoil following the referendum and its results. From there, the struggle for recognition took a more legislative power-oriented path than sovereignty *per se*, and increasingly Quebec reinforced both its internal and external powers within the Canadian federation (Gagnon 2006). In Wallonia, the minority status was not so much felt on political grounds (given the consociational nature of Belgian federalism), but rather on socioeconomic grounds (Quévit 1978, 2010), in contrast to an increasingly self-confident politically (with its majority status) and economically (with its ever-flourishing economy) Flanders (Deschouwer 2012). Nonetheless, in the 1990s the devolution process, which had started in the end of the 1960s, enabled Wallonia to become a fully fledged region with state-like powers. The last state reform of 2011 allocates even more powers and more fiscal responsibilities to the Belgian regions and thus to Wallonia (Deschouwer and

Reuchamps 2013; Reuchamps 2013). As such, both Quebec and Wallonia put aside their minority status to embrace a state-like status within their own federation.

Quebec and Wallonia provide thus a very fertile ground to reflect on minority nations in multinational federations. In fact, their comparative study sheds light on federalism (in terms of both politics and policies) and also on territorial, identity and party politics in two regions that have politically changed in the last 20 years and which are likely to experience further transformations. Nonetheless, the research on comparative federalism has hitherto largely ignored the comparison between these two interesting cases. When students of federalism have devoted some attention to the comparison of Quebec and Wallonia, they have focused on specific topics and issues mainly related to substate nationalism (Erk 2002), intergovernmental (Poirier 2002, 2009a) and international (Massart-Piérard 2008; Paquin 2009) relations or specific public policies like language (De Coster 2007).

To fill this gap, the aim of this book is to offer a comprehensive appraisal of the comparison between Quebec and Wallonia. This endeavour brings about three important questions for the study of minority nations in multinational federations. First, what is the nature and the role of these two minority nations within their multinational federation? This relates to nationalism, substate nationalism and subregion nationalism, as well as to federalism and intergovernmental relations. Secondly, what is their political dynamics? Or, more specifically, what is specific with their politics? Thirdly, what kinds of policy are designed and implemented in Quebec and in Wallonia? These are the very questions of their political, economic, social and cultural development.

The nature and the role of minority nations in multinational federations is a key – albeit understudied – question in the comparative study of federalism. This is even more so when minority nations form federated entities of a federation. Such federated entities are then often "viewed as recipients and receptacles of national state loyalties, national political priorities and national policy preferences", but, as Michael Burgess continues, "they are hugely significant both *individually* and *collectively* as distinct diverse political communities in their own right" (2013: 8, emphasis in the original). It is therefore important to analyse minority nations through the lenses of nationalism, substate nationalism and also subregion nationalism because this threefold dynamics has to be captured in order to understand the nature of the minority nations. That is, in short, their political identity, or, as a question: are they nations *per se* or just linguistic communities? Above all, what is behind their name? Indeed, minority nations are not monolithic blocks facing the majority block, but are shaped by internal and external dynamics that define what they are. What is more, federalism and intergovernmental relations also shape these two types of dynamics and thus the specific role and place of minority nations within the larger whole that is the federal system.

In fact, provinces, cantons, landers, regions and other federated entities are not only constituent units or "building blocks", as they are often referred to in the mainstream literature (Watts 2008: 71), of a given federation, but also they are political actors with their individual destinies and, above all, with their own politics. The second encompassing question that this book brings about calls for the investigation of the political dynamics in Quebec and in Wallonia. Indeed, it is often studied how the small worlds operate in the whole federal system, but not so much how they operate themselves as a political entity in its own right. In other words, political actors and actions should be analysed for themselves. Such endeavours enables an insightful comparative approach that can be divided into two parts, namely the *within* and the *between* perspectives. The former calls for a close examination of the political dynamics within one single case, that of its subnational policy and politics. The latter brings a comparative perspective of the two small worlds under investigation and draws from such an exercise insights about their cultural and ideological differences as well as their socioeconomic differences and, above all, their political differences.

The third question derives from the first two questions: what kinds of policy are designed and implemented? A bridge between the study of politics and of policies is often neglected in the mainstream literature on comparative federalism. Yet politics and policies are closely interrelated and even more so when minority nations form a federated entity. Indeed, because of this minority position, it might be felt that policies are adopted by and for the majority groups. Therefore, the policies designed and implemented in the territory of the entity might be more suited for its specific public. Above all, policies can also be instruments of politics through some forms of nationalism or substate nationalism. Thus, a comprehensive study of Quebec and Wallonia implies a close attention to the political, economic, social and cultural development of these two small worlds and how they use their development in the construction of their state within the larger federation.

To appraise these three questions, which is a challenging exercise in comparative politics, the book is divided into three self-reinforcing parts of two to three chapters, each covering both cases. The first part sets the stage of the comparison with two chapters that show the similarities and the differences between Quebec and Wallonia, and endeavours to explain them in light of history, sociology and politics. The second part digs into the politics of Quebec and Wallonia with three chapters on, respectively, their political parties, their members of parliament and their local politics. The third and last part deals with the public-policies realm in Quebec and Wallonia with, on the one hand, one chapter discussing their public administration and, on the other hand, two chapters reflecting on two prominent public policy areas: language and international relations. The conclusion brings the analysis of Quebec and Wallonia back into a comparative federalism perspective and explains why their comparison sheds light on current trends in federalism throughout the world and, in particular, on minority nations in multinational federations.

The first chapter by Luc Turgeon investigates intergovernmental relations and constitutional reforms in Canada and in Belgium. Over the past 40 years, they have been at the forefront of the political life of both countries, impacting directly on Quebec and Wallonia respectively. But there is a difference in the ability of these two political entities to ensure the enactment of constitutional or quasi-constitutional measures to protect or further their interests. While some of the difference may be explained by the difference in political weight, this chapter argues that two other factors are of crucial importance: institutions and critical junctures. In order to assess these two factors, a conceptual framework, inspired by neo-institutionalist works on policy feedback, is presented and applied in the analysis of the evolution of constitutional politics of both cases since the 1960s. So doing, the chapter deciphers the political implications of the different approaches to constitutional politics and intergovernmental relations in Canada/Quebec and Belgium/Wallonia and thus sets the stage for the rest of the book.

As a starting point of the second chapter, Jean-François Caron observes that it may seem irrelevant to compare the challenges associated with the Quebec and Walloon identities, since both societies are facing different historical and institutional realities. Indeed, as a national minority within the Canadian federation, Quebec identity is affirmed and further claimed than in the Walloon case that is historically associated with the Belgian government itself. However, the changes of identity that Quebec has experienced in the 1960s during the Quiet Revolution have several elements in common with Wallonia, which has long been torn by tension between an ethnic identity that would be characterised by the use of French and civic identity that is primarily territorial. The aim of this chapter is to show the similarities between the cases of Quebec and Wallonia, and also to discuss the pitfalls of identity that can occur when a society seeks to define itself through an identity that is more political.

The second part on politics in Quebec and Wallonia begins with an examination of political parties manifestos by Heidi Mercenier, Julien Perrez and Min Reuchamps. Political parties are indeed one of the main political actors in both Quebec and Wallonia. As their main ambition is to govern their region, they contribute to shape Quebec and Wallonia. Therefore, this chapter aims at exploring their vision of their region. To do so, the more standardised (and thus comparable) source of information is their electoral manifestos. This chapter analyses the electoral manifestos for each of the main political parties in Quebec (ADQ and then CAQ, PLQ and PQ) and in Wallonia (CDH, Ecolo, MR and PS) for every election over the last 20 years. Through a quantitative and qualitative politico-linguistic approach, the analysis of this massive load of information sheds light on the political parties' views of their region and its future, and how it has evolved over time in their recent history. So doing, this chapter links the first part of the book to the second, and guides the reader into the study of politics in Quebec and Wallonia.

In the fourth chapter, Jérémy Dodeigne investigates political representatives and brings to the fore their different opportunity structures, and their similar political class. In Western advanced democracies, where parliaments are at the centre of politics, studying the representatives – "the nucleus of a political class" – has always fascinated political scientists. Who are the representatives? How are they recruited? And, why do they decide to enter parliaments? Those are core questions for students of legislative recruitment. The aim of this chapter is to offer a picture of representatives in Quebec and Wallonia along these three lines of research. Based on an original dataset of all the individual political careers since the 1990s, the chapter comes back briefly to the sociological profiles of representatives while it extends on representatives circulation. Career maintenance and career advancement of representatives are specifically examined in the two federations. Overall, despite large differences in the Canadian and Belgian opportunity structures, it concludes that Québécois and Walloon representatives share more than they differ in terms of political class.

The analysis of the local elections through the figure of the mayors by Sandra Breux and Vincent Jacquet is the next step of this comparative endeavour. In the 2000s, local electoral systems have experienced deep changes, notably with the strengthening of the mayor's role within municipalities. These changes also occurred in Quebec and Wallonia. Nonetheless, despite this strengthening of the mayor's role, its function and its position remain quite ambivalent within an increasingly multilevel environment. To explore the local political dynamics in Quebec and Wallonia, this chapter studies the career of mayors in both regions. To do so, it relies on new empirical data from the 2005 local elections in Quebec and the 2006 local elections in Wallonia. With this background, the aim of this chapter is to understand more finely the specific nature of local political dynamics within the two federations.

Building on the first two parts, the third part on policies starts with a chapter by Maxime Petit Jean on public administration. More specifically, this chapter tackles recent public-management reforms that are mainly related to the central administration in Quebec and Wallonia. Therefore it respectively and diachronically covers the evolution of their administrations, with a particular focus on the last 15 years, with reforms such as the Public Administration Act in Quebec and the creation of a unique central ministry in Wallonia, the *Service public de Wallonie*. These two reforms are emblematic of a change in the orientation given by their own governments to the public management of these substate administrations towards a more efficient and more responsive public action. The chapter gives also comparative insights on the trajectories of reform, notably on factors supporting or not the administrative reforms. Finally, it assesses how these reforms could contribute or not to the strengthening of the autonomy of Quebec and Wallonia.

This comparative book had to cover the – often hotly debated – field of language policy. Philippe Hambye reminds us that the aims of language policy are, in general, non-directly linguistic: through the regulation of a language and of its uses, such policies try to organise access to other resources or public goods. As a consequence, languages policies are related to several domains of public policy: education, immigration, culture and international relations, to name but a few. Within these different domains, political measures taken in Quebec and Wallonia since their emergence as major political entities within their respective countries, present some similarities due to their common situation of peripheral French-speaking communities, but also deep divergences. To understand them, this chapter analyses the main orientations of language policy in Quebec and Wallonia, and tries to relate them to their founding principles in terms of political philosophy.

In the eighth chapter, Stéphane Paquin, Marine Kravagna and Min Reuchamps tackle the key issue of Quebec's and Wallonia's international relations. While both nations are minority nations, they are very active on the international scene. In this chapter, the authors assess how these two minority nations – that will have to be qualified, especially in the case of Belgium – try to consolidate their position through their international relations. More specifically, they assess their treaty-making capacity and its underlying dynamics both internally – notably their relation with the federal government – and externally – with the other international actors. This chapter is therefore less about parallel diplomacy and more about the growing influence of substate governments in foreign-policy making.

Finally, the conclusion of the book by Michael Burgess assesses the overall significance of what this comparative study of Quebec and Wallonia tell us about minority nations in multinational federations in terms of politics, policies and polities. As he draws the book to a close it becomes more obvious how far this specific comparison sheds light on current trends in federalism, and contributes to our understanding of regional and federal dynamics throughout the world.

References

Béland, Daniel and André Lecours (2005). "The politics of territorial solidarity: nationalism and social policy reform in Canada, the United Kingdom, and Belgium", *Comparative Political Studies*, 38(6): 676–703.

Béland, Daniel and André Lecours (2007). "Federalism, nationalism and social policy decentralization in Canada and Belgium", *Regional and Federal Studies*, 17(4): 405–19.

Burgess, Michael (2013). "The Character, Role and Significance of Constituent Units in Federations and Federal Political Systems", *L'Europe en Formation*, (3): 7–19.

Burgess, Michael and John Pinder (2007). *Multinational Federations*, New York: Routledge.

Burgess, Michael and G. Alan Tarr (2012). *Constitutional Dynamics in Federal Systems: Subnational Perspectives*, London and Montreal: McGill-Queen's University Press.

Dandoy, Régis and Arjan H. Schakel (2013). *Regional and National Elections in Western Europe. Territoriality of the Vote in Thirteen Countries, Comparative Territorial Politics*, Houndmills: Palgrave Macmillan.

De Coster, Michel (2007). *Les enjeux des conflits linguistiques: Le Français à l'épreuve des modèles belge, suisse et canadien*, Paris: L'Harmattan.

Deschouwer, Kris (2012). *The Politics of Belgium: Governing a Divided Society*. 2nd edn, *Comparative Government and Politics Series*, Houndmills: Palgrave Macmillan.

Deschouwer, Kris and Min Reuchamps (2013). "The Belgian federation at a crossroad", *Regional and Federal Studies*, 23(3): 261–270.

Elkins, David J. and Richard Simeon (1980). *Small Worlds: Provinces and Parties in Canadian Political Life*, London and Toronto: Methuen Publications.

Erk, Jan (2002). "Le Québec entre la Flandre et la Wallonie: une comparaison des nationalismes sous-étatiques belges et du nationalisme québécois", *Recherches sociographiques*, 48(3): 499–516.

Erk, Jan (2008). *Explaining Federalism. State, Society And Congruence in Austria, Belgium, Canada, Germany and Switzerland*, Routledge Series in Federal Studies. London and New York: Routledge.

Fournier, Bernard and Min Reuchamps (2009). *Le fédéralisme en Belgique et au Canada. Comparaison sociopolitique, ouvertures sociologiques*, Bruxelles: De Boeck Université.

Gagnon, Alain-G. (2006). *Le fédéralisme canadien contemporain: fondements, traditions, institutions*, Montréal: Presses de l'Université de Montréal.

Gagnon, Alain-G., François Rocher and Montserrat Guibernau (2003). *The Conditions of Diversity in Multinational Democracies*, Montréal: Institute for Research on Public Policy.

Gagnon, Alain-G. and James Tully (2001). *Multinational Democracies*, Cambridge and New York: Cambridge University Press.

Hambye, Philippe and Mary Richards (2012). "The paradoxical visions of multilingualism in education: the ideological dimension of discourses on multilingualism in Belgium and Canada", *International Journal of Multilingualism*, 9(2): 165–88.

Jeffery, Charlie and Arjan H. Schakel (2013). "Editorial: towards a regional political science", *Regional Studies*, 47(3): 299–302.

Karmis, Dimitrios and Alain-G. Gagnon (2001). "Federalism, federation and collective identities in Canada and Belgium: different routes, similar fragmentation". In *Multinational Democracies*, ed. Alain-G. Gagnon and James Tully, 137–75. Cambridge: Cambridge University Press.

Keating, Michael (2001). *Plurinational Democracy: Stateless Nations in a Post-Sovereignty Era*, Oxford and New York: Oxford University Press.

Keating, Michael (2013). *Rescaling the European State: the Making of Territory and the Rise of the Meso*, Oxford: Oxford University Press.

Massart-Piérard, Françoise (2008). *L'action extérieure des entités subétatiques. Approche comparée Europe Amérique du Nord*, Louvain-la-Neuve: Presses universitaires de Louvain.

McRoberts, Kenneth (2001). "Canada and the multinational state", *Canadian Journal of Political Science/Revue canadienne de science politique*, 34(4): 683–713.

Paquin, Stéphane (2009). "Fédéralisme et système de gouvernance à paliers multiples en matière de politique étrangère: Une comparaison entre le Canada et la Belgique". In *Le fédéralisme en Belgique et au Canada. Comparaison sociopolitique*, ed. Bernard Fournier and Min Reuchamps, 197–205. Bruxelles: De Boeck Université.

Poirier, Johanne (2002). "Formal mechanisms of intergovernmental relations in Belgium", *Regional and Federal Studies*, 12(3): 27–32.

Poirier, Johanne (2004). "Fédéralisme en Belgique et au Canada: parallèles, dissonances et paradoxes", *Septentrion: arts, lettre et culture de Flandre et des Pays-Bas*, 26–32.

Poirier, Johanne (2009a). "Le partage des compétences et les relations inter-gouvernementales: la situation au Canada". In *Le fédéralisme en Belgique et au Canada. Comparaison sociopolitique*, ed. Bernard Fournier and Min Reuchamps, 107–22. Bruxelles: De Boeck Université.

Poirier, Johanne (2009b). "Les fédérations belge et canadienne: essai de comparaison synthétique et systématique", *Revue de droit de l'ULB*, 1–2: 13–32.

Quévit, Michel (1978). *Les causes du déclin wallon*, Bruxelles: Vie ouvrière.

Quévit, Michel (2010). *Flandre – Wallonie: quelle solidarité ? De la création de l'Etat belge à l'Europe des Régions*, Charleroi: Couleurs livres.

Reif, Karlheinz and Hermann Schmitt (1980). "Nine second-order national elections: a conceptual framework for the analysis of European election results", *European Journal of Political Research*, 8(1): 3–44.

Reuchamps, Min (2011). *L'avenir du fédéralisme en Belgique et au Canada. Quand les citoyens en parlent*, Bruxelles: P.I.E.-Peter Lang.

Reuchamps, Min (2013). "The current challenges on the Belgian federalism and the Sixth Reform of the state". In *The Ways of Federalism in Western Countries and the Horizons of Territorial Autonomy in Spain*, ed. Alberto Lopez Basaguren and Leire Escajedo San-Epifanio, 375–92. Berlin: Springer-Verlag.

Schakel, Arjan H. and Charlie Jeffery (2013). "Are regional elections really 'second-order' elections?", *Regional Studies*, 47(3): 323–41.

Simeon, Richard and David J. Elkins (1974). "Regional political cultures in Canada", *Canadian Journal of Political Science/Revue canadienne de science politique*, 7(3): 397–437.

Tarr, G. Alan (1998). *Understanding State Constitutions*, Princeton, NJ: Princeton University Press.

Watts, Ronald L (2008). *Comparing Federal Systems*, 3rd edn. Montreal and Kingston: McGill-Queen's University Press.

Part I
Setting the stage

1 Critical junctures, feedback effects and constitutional change

A comparison of Quebec/Canada and Wallonia/Belgium

Luc Turgeon

Constitutional politics and state reform have been at the forefront of the political life for both Quebec and Wallonia over the past 40 years. Negotiations over constitutional change or state reform, acrimonious intergovernmental relations and referendums (in Quebec) have often been the norm rather than the exception. Both communities continue to be preoccupied, or even obsessed, with the conditions of their participation with the Canadian and Belgian political communities. It is sometimes said in Canada that constitutional politics is the country's second national sport after hockey.

While high-stake negotiations have preoccupied the political class and the citizens of both Quebec and Wallonia, there are important differences between the two communities. Quebec has asked that its unique character be recognised in the constitution to reflect Canada's multinational nature and that it be given unique powers in the federation to face its distinctive challenges in the North American context. While it has failed to see this unique character recognised in the constitution, *ad hoc* intergovernmental agreements have nonetheless led to the adoption of non-constitutional reforms to respond to some of Quebec's demands. Broader reforms of the Canadian federation, however, have proved to be elusive. Wallonia, on the other hand, has been involved, and, in recent years, increasingly unwillingly, in a continuous process of constitutional change that has transformed a once unitary state into a federation. Some of those reforms have been driven by Wallonia's desire for greater autonomy in Belgium, especially with regards to the management of its economy. In short, as argued by Reuchamps (2011: 36), Canada's constitutional immobility is in contrast with Belgium's constitutional "hypermobility".

Such a difference in the ability of those two political entities to ensure the enactment of quasi-constitutional or constitutional measures to protect or further their interests could be seen as solely the result of differences in their political weight. Quebeckers, after all, represent less than 25% of the Canadian population. Residents of Wallonia, conversely, constitute 32% of the Belgian population. Moreover, approximately between 40 and 45% of the Belgian population is French speaking.[1] However, while demography is indeed an important factor, it is not sufficient to understand the trajectory of both regions. This chapter argues that two other factors are of crucial importance. The first one is institutional. Wallonia could not have defended its interest without the consociational system that, in effect, provides the French-speaking Belgians with a veto on important state reforms. As for Quebec, the majoritarian nature of Canadian political institutions has limited its capacity to bargain for important changes to the federation in exchange for the support of the central government.

The second factor has to do with critical junctures. Key reforms in the 1970s and 1980s have had a distinct impact in both countries. In Belgium, reforms adopted in 1970 to placate growing regional demands have instead had negative feedback effects, accelerating the transition towards a federal state through a series of constitutional changes. In Canada, the Constitution Act of 1982 had positive feedback effects, reinforcing the status quo and making more difficult any attempt at reforming Canada's constitution to satisfy Quebec's demands. As such, Quebec and Wallonia are fighting different constitutional dynamics. On the one hand, Quebec has been incapable of convincing the rest of Canada to modify the Canadian constitution so that it reflects the province's unique status in Canada. On the other hand, Wallonia is faced with continuous demands for constitutional change by Flanders, demands that the institutional setting of Belgium makes almost impossible to ignore.

To structure the comparison between these two minority nations, the chapter is divided into four sections. In the first, I present a short conceptual framework inspired by neo-institutionalist works on policy feedback. In the following two sections, I present an overview of the evolution of constitutional politics of both countries and regions since the 1960s. Finally, in the conclusion, I discuss the political implications of the different approaches to constitutional politics and intergovernmental relations.

1 Critical junctures, feedback effects and institutions: a framework

An important contribution of the neo-institutionalist approach has been to stress the central importance of key historical events or moments, some of which have been labelled as critical junctures. According to Pierson (2004: 135), "junctures are 'critical' because they place institutional arrangements on paths or trajectories, which are then difficult to alter". The adoption of a new constitution or major constitutional changes, for example, can establish a critical juncture in a country's history. For neo-institutionalists, critical junctures are especially important because they constitute the starting point for many path-dependent processes. Decisions made during such critical junctures have self-reinforcing or positive feedback effects, which account for why countries stay on a certain path.

Two types of positive feedback are especially important. The first one may be referred to as political feedback. In this context, certain political decisions empower particular groups with a stake in the maintenance of a policy or an institution over others. These groups are likely to protect a policy or institution against attacks and push for its maintenance over time. As Pierson (2004: 73) suggests, once they reach a certain size, these groups become politically powerful and policy-makers may feel pressured to avoid any reform that alienates them. Such groups may include political actors, bureaucrats or societal actors such as interest groups or social movements. A second type of positive feedback is what might be called ideational feedback. Ideas embedded in early policy or political decisions can have long-lasting effects, independent of the changing power of the groups promoting these policies, and as such, some scholars have emphasised the normative or ideational dimension of policy feedback. For example, in his work on the Scandinavian model of the welfare state, Cox (2004) argues that its resilience is the product of a commitment by policy-makers and citizens to the idea of a Scandinavian model of welfare.

While neo-institutionalists have tended to focus on positive feedback – that is, feedback that is likely to contribute to institutional continuity, a growing body of literature has focused on negative feedback, which Weaver (2010: 137) defines as "consequences of policy that tend to undermine rather than reinforce the political, fiscal or social sustainability of a particular set of policies". For example, a number of scholars have argued that welfare regimes that privilege means-tested social programmes are more likely to experience welfare backlash and retrenchment than those that privilege universal social programmes (Korpi 1980; Esping-Anderson 1990). Negative policy feedback does not mean that past choices do not matter. Such choices will have undoubtedly closed some options. Nevertheless, they make the status quo unlikely. For Weaver, all reform measures have both positive and negative effects. Whether an institutional or policy regime is changed, then, depends "on the balance of positive and negative feedback, the availability of incremental reform options that make the negative effects of the current policy regime more bearable, and the availability of paradigmatic reform options (or regime transition options) that are feasible in both political and policy terms" (2010: 138).

In Weaver's formulation, these three aspects are cumulative. First, the negative balance between negative and positive feedback is likely to place reform on the policy agenda. That means that before adopting major reforms – such as major state reforms – policy-makers are more likely to explore the possibility of incremental reform. In federal states, this may involve non-constitutional reform through intergovernmental agreements. However, if more incremental reform options cannot be found, "restructuring reform" becomes a likely option. The success of such reforms can still be blocked "because no alternative policy regime is perceived to be available, because alternatives are politically unfeasible or too expensive, or because those who would lose from a transition are well placed politically to block it" (Weaver 2010: 143).

As a point of clarification, the notions of "positive" and "negative" feedback are analytical, not normative concepts. In other words, they do not imply that the lack of change resulting from the existence of positive feedback is, from a normative or moral standpoint, a desirable result. In fact, the incapacity of institutions to change or adapt as a result of positive feedback can be viewed as problematic. What "positive" and "negative" mean, then is more concerned with whether a decision or juncture creates its own reinforcing mechanisms – positive feedback – or whether it opens the doors for its own contestations – negative feedback.

The next sections will demonstrate how the distinct institutional setting of both countries, especially Canada's majoritarian and Belgium's consociational institutions – combined with the feedback effects associated with the adoption of important constitutional reforms – have either contributed to piecemeal, incremental reforms in the former, or formal, important state reforms in the latter.

2 Positive feedback and Canada's constitutional immobility

2.1 A brief history of constitutional politics in Canada[2]

Canada became a federal state in 1867, when three former British colonies (the provinces of Canada, New Brunswick and Nova Scotia) joined to form a federal union. The province of Canada was divided into two separate provinces, Ontario and Quebec, which meant that the French-speaking minority would, in effect, constitute a majority in one province. As such, for French Canadians, confederation constituted a compromise: while they joined a federal state in which their demographic weight would be reduced further, they gained exclusive control over institutions that they viewed as essential to their cultural survival in a continent increasingly dominated by English speakers (Silver 1997). The British North American Act (BNA) of 1867, now referred to as the Constitution Act, 1867, (re)-established a legislative assembly,[3] which would later be named the National Assembly of Quebec. The province's distinct legal system, the civil code, was confirmed and the official status of the French language and Catholic institutions was recognised, gaining exclusive control over sectors such as education, which were considered essential to the reproduction of the unique character of the province.

The BNA Act focuses especially on the division of powers between the two levels of government, while guaranteeing certain rights for the religious minorities of the different provinces. Section 92 of the BNA Act outlines 16 areas that are the prerogative of provincial governments, including control over social policy, municipal institutions, property and civil rights. The provinces have the power to raise direct taxes. The act does not have a similar preamble to certain constitutions, which provide a clear definition of the nature of the political community, and it is very much what Janet Azjenstat (1995) has called a "procedural constitution"; that is, a constitution as the rulebook of the political game, devoid as much as possible of normative considerations. In fact, one of the striking elements of the federal settlement is that different political actors have interpreted it very differently. For some of the fathers of confederation,[4] one of the BNA's key objectives was to create a strong federal government that could sustain a strong political nationality. A second interpretation of confederation is what has come to be referred to as the "compact theory of provincial rights". This perspective viewed confederation as a compact entered by the provinces and the United Kingdom. As such, the creation of the federal government was the creation of the provinces. This interpretation was used to denounce the intrusion of the federal government in areas of provincial jurisdictions. A third perspective, a compact of peoples, is associated with the French-Canadian journalist and intellectual Henri Bourassa. The compact of provinces came to be seen as inadequate because several provinces used it as a justification to restrict the rights of francophone minorities. This led Bourassa to argue that Canada was also the product of a compact between French and English Canadians.

Constitutional ambiguity was, as such, a defining element of the Canadian constitution. In the first 50 years of the federal settlement, the country evolved in a decentralist fashion, the result not so much of significant constitutional changes, but a series of judicial decisions of Britain's Judicial Committee of the Privy Council, Canada's last court of appeal until 1949, as well as a party system that largely rested on regional rather than cross-class alliances (Turgeon and Wallner 2013). Three key reasons explain why constitutional reform ended up back on the policy agenda in the 1960s and 1970s. First, as an act of the British parliament, the BNA Act did not have a Canadian amending formula. Second, the prime minister of Canada, Pierre Elliott Trudeau, wanted to add a Charter of Rights to the Canadian constitution. And third, the decade saw also the rise of a new form of Quebec nationalism, largely driven by the French Canadians' lower socioeconomic position and their exclusion from key institutions in the federal government. Whereas nationalism before the Quiet Revolution was conservative and focused on the defence of French Canadians throughout Canada, the new post-1960 nationalism favoured greater state intervention and focused mostly on the defence of Quebec's interests. A key demand of Quebec nationalists was for the province to be granted special status within the constitution in order to recognise its unique challenges.

The 1970s were marked by different constitutional proposals that would have incorporated into the constitution all these three: an amending formula, a Bill of Rights, and some form of recognition of Quebec's special status. Following the election of the pro-independence *Parti Québécois*, the debate over Quebec independence intensified. Public discourse focused on either convincing Quebeckers of the benefits of remaining in Canada or, conversely, the potential benefits of independence. As a result of the increasingly polarised debate, a referendum was held in May 1980. It called for a mandate to negotiate with the rest of Canada a new relationship called "sovereignty association". While it is probable that the majority of French-speaking Quebeckers voted "yes" to independence, the proposal was ultimately defeated, with 60% voting "no" to independence. At the end of the referendum campaign, Prime Minister Trudeau promised that a no vote would be followed by a commitment to a "renewed federalism". For Quebeckers, the promise entailed greater powers for the Quebec government. That would ultimately not be the result of the negotiation that ensued to "repatriate" the constitution from the United Kingdom.

Following a series of failed constitutional talks and appeals to the Supreme Court of Canada in light of the federal government's threat to act unilaterally, the nine predominantly English-speaking provinces and the federal government led by Trudeau came to a compromise that left out Quebec. The compromise, which became the Constitution Act, 1982, following its signature, contains a Charter of Rights and Freedoms and an amending formula. The charter includes a series of rights that recognise or protect a number of groups: women, aboriginal and multicultural groups, and linguistic minorities – anglophones in Quebec and francophones in the rest of Canada. Some of those rights, however, are subject to a "notwithstanding clause", following provincial demands, which permits any government to set aside certain sections of the charter for a limited period of time.[5] As for the amending formula, to make most changes to the constitution it requires the approval of the federal parliament and seven of the provinces, representing over 50% of the Canadian population. For other amendments, including revoking the country's monarchical system, it requires unanimity.

Even though Quebec did not sign the Constitution Act, 1982, it is bound by it. Nevertheless, many political actors in the province, whether partisan of Quebec independence or not, have questioned its legitimacy. As a result of the protests within the province, the conservative government of Brian Mulroney, elected in 1984, proposed a constitutional package that would allow Quebec to sign the constitution with "honour and dignity". The result of this process was the Meech Lake Accord of 1987, in which the main proposal was to add to the constitution an interpretative clause that would recognise Quebec as a "distinct society" within Canada. It also would have granted Quebec a veto over any future constitution changes, including a constitutional guarantee of Quebec's representation on the Supreme Court of Canada, restriction on the federal government's spending power (see below) and a constitutionalisation of existing agreements granting Quebec a key role in the selection of immigrants. The accord was never implemented, as two provinces failed to ratify it before the three-year deadline, set out in the 1982 Constitution, expired. Following the failure of the Meech Lake Accord, another attempt was made at reforming the Canadian constitution, in part by addressing the demand of aboriginal Canadians for greater representation as well as from western Canadians for a reform of the Canadian Senate. That accord, the Charlottetown Accord of 1992, was ultimately rejected by a majority of Canadians (including by a majority of Quebeckers, who viewed it as a diluted version of the Meech Lake Accord).

The failure of those attempts to reform the Canadian constitution reinvigorated the Quebec independence movement. In October 1995, a second referendum on Quebec independence was held. The "yes" option obtained 49.4% of the vote, 50,000 votes less than the "no" option. Despite the shock associated with such a close result, no constitutional reform was adopted to respond to Quebec's demand for greater recognition. Since the 1995 referendum, politicians and public opinion outside Quebec have become increasingly opposed to any attempt at reforming the constitution. As shown next, the incapacity to reform the Canadian constitution, despite the dissatisfaction of many Quebeckers with the status quo, can be traced back to feedback effects of the Constitution Act, 1982.

2.2 Feedback effects and constitutional politics in Canada

Three positive feedback effects associated with the adoption of the Constitution Act, 1982, have made constitutional reform to respond to Quebec's demands especially difficult, and have been more determinant than the negative feedback associated with the fact that the Quebec government did not sign the Constitution Act, 1982. The first one is institutional. The amending formula makes constitutional reform almost impossible. In certain cases, twelve actors must authorise a constitutional reform (the ten provincial legislatures, the House of Commons and the Senate). Moreover, two provincial legislatures (British Columbia and Alberta) have adopted legislations that require that they hold a referendum on any proposed constitutional change. Those two provinces are also the ones where the population has been the most hostile to the recognition of Quebec as a distinct society. It is not surprising, then, that many Quebec politicians and intellectuals have argued that the amending formula is a constitutional straightjacket.

The second feedback effect is related to the numerous groups that defend the Charter of Rights and Freedom. The adoption of the Constitution Act, 1982, led to the creation of, or reinforcement of, what some analysts have called "charter groups" (Morton and Knopff 2000), which include groups who defend the multicultural definition of the country,[6] women's groups and other groups who defend section 15 of the charter, the equality rights section. These groups have tended to oppose the recognition of Quebec's distinct status, seeing it as a threat to their interests and vision of the country. For example, English-speaking feminists have, at times, opposed the recognition of Quebec as a distinct society on the grounds that such a clause could be used to put limitations on the equality rights of Quebec women.[7] Those groups have not only acted independently, but have joined forces. During the debates over the Meech Lake Accord, they formed the Canadian Coalition on the Constitution to defeat the accord. The chairperson of the coalition, Deborah Coyne, presented the nature of such a coalition:

> The charter's appeal to our non-territorial identities – shared characteristics such as gender, ethnicity and disability – is finding concrete expression in an emerging power structure in society. ... This power structure involves new networks and coalitions among women, the disabled, aboriginal groups, social reform activists, church groups, environmentalists,

ethno-cultural organisations just to name a few. All these new groups have mobilised a broad range of interests that draw their inspiration from the charter and the constitution.

(Coyne, quoted in Morton and Knopff 2000: 27–28)

The third feedback effect, related to the second one, is ideational. The Constitutional Act, 1982, has promoted a certain view of the Canadian political community that is not conducive to the recognition of Quebec's specificity in Canada nor of the multinational character of the country. Many commentators in Quebec and Canada have argued that the charter promotes a view of Canada as composed of citizens as bearers of individual rights, rather than as members of specific communities, living in one of ten equal provinces. Kenneth McRoberts succinctly presents Quebec's case against many of the changes adopted under the leadership of Pierre Eliott Trudeau:

The Charter of Rights and Freedom may offer support for the francophone minorities outside Quebec, but in the eyes of many Quebeckers it was above all a threat to Bill 101[8] and the continuation of francophone life in Quebec. Multiculturalism denied the cultural dualism that has always defined the basic structure of Canada and will continue to do so. The principle of equality of the provinces is a repudiation of Quebec's centrality to francophone life. And Ottawa's claim to be a national government imposing national standards seems to deny the historical status of a distinct francophone community and the Quebec government's responsibility for it.

(McRoberts 1997: 248–49)

Considering the incapacity of Canada's constitution to be modified to respond to some of the demands of the Quebec government, and in light of the strength of the secessionist movement, the federal government has mostly used non-constitutional means to respond to such demands. It has done so mostly in an *ad hoc* fashion, a reflection of the fact that intergovernmental relations in Canada are not specially institutionalised. Contrary to other federal systems, there is no mechanism of representation of the constituent units in federal institutions. The Canadian Senate is not an institution that represents provincial interests. It functions mostly as a patronage body for the federal government. While a complex network of intergovernmental institutions has been established to deal with policy issues, this machinery is also weakly institutionalised. It does not appear in the constitution and has no legislative basis.

Two mechanisms have been used to respond to some of Quebec's demands. First, the federal government has allowed for *de facto* asymmetry in the distribution of power to exist, even though political actors have opposed formal or constitutional asymmetry. In the 1960s, when the federal government used its controversial "spending power" to develop national programmes, despite the fact that welfare is a provincial responsibility, the Liberal prime minister Lester B. Pearson allowed provinces to opt out of those programmes with financial compensation so that Quebec could start its own programme.[9] In the 1970s, Pierre Eliott Trudeau, who strongly opposed a special status for Quebec, signed in the 1970s a first agreement on immigration with the Quebec government, allowing Quebec to select a significant proportion of immigrants to the province. It must be stressed that immigration, in the Canadian constitution, is a concurrent jurisdiction. Other provinces have, so far however, declined to play a role in the immigration sector similar to the one played by the Quebec government. In the wake of the Quebec referendum, the federal government also agreed to devolve power over manpower training, a long-lasting demand of Quebec, to the provinces.

Second, the Canadian House of Commons has also adopted a number of largely symbolic resolutions and motions to recognise Quebec's distinctiveness. In the wake of the 1995 referendum, which came in the aftermath of two failed constitutional reforms to recognise Quebec's special status in Canada, parliament passed a resolution acknowledging Quebec as a distinct society within Canada. A regional veto law was also adopted, which stipulated that the federal government could not propose a constitutional change without the prior consent of five Canadian regions (Quebec, Ontario, British Columbia, the Prairies and the Atlantic). This, in effect, made any constitutional amendments even more difficult. In the mid-2000s, following another surge in support for independence and growing demands from Quebec politicians, intellectuals and citizens that Quebec be recognised as a nation in Canada, the conservative minority government introduced in parliament a motion, which was adopted, that stipulated "that this House recognises that the Québécois form a nation within a united Canada".

In most cases, attempts at responding to Quebec's demand for recognition of its distinct status or for greater powers have come in the wake of a rise in support for Quebec independence or when parties have tried to make electoral inroads in Quebec, Canada's second largest province. Because of Canada's majoritarian institutions, contrary to the cases of Belgium and Spain that have proportional representation and coalition governments, Quebec nationalists have not had the power to negotiate support for a government at the federal level in exchange for concessions to Quebec.

In short, the adoption of the Constitution Act, 1982, has created positive-feedback effects that have made difficult the adaptation of the Canadian constitution to respond to Quebec's desire for constitutional recognition of its special status. Other non-constitutional avenues have been used to respond to Quebec's demand, whether through bilateral agreements to devolve responsibilities to Quebec or to withdraw from sectors in which both levels of government had been active, or through unilateral motions that did not require any formal negotiations either with the provinces, or because of Canada's strong majoritarian institutions, with other political actors. Paradoxically, while federal government intrusions in areas of provincial jurisdictions at times

contributed to increased tensions between Quebec and the federal government, later withdrawal from those jurisdictions were presented as attempts to
respond to Quebec's demands for more autonomy and asymmetrical federalism. As we will see in the following section, however, this is in sharp contrast
to Belgium, where the first state reform of 1970 and the country's consociational
arrangements have contributed to numerous episodes of constitutional changes.

3 Negative feedback and the constitutional hypermobility in Belgium

3.1 A brief history of constitutional politics in Belgium

In order to understand the distinct constitutional dynamic between Belgium
and Canada, it is essential to stress that federalism has come to both countries
differently. To use Alfred Stepan's (1999) dichotomy, Canada constitutes a
case of "coming together" federalism; that is, previously autonomous or semi-
autonomous regions coming together to form a federal state; Belgium constitutes
a case of "holding together" federalism, in which a previously unitary state
has devolved powers to newly created regions. As argued by Kris Deschouwer
(2009b: 69), "typical for these more recent federal or regionalised states are
institutions *à la carte*, adapted to sometimes widely varying demand from
different parts of the national territory". In the Belgian case, such *à la carte*
institutions are a reflection of the different demands that came to be articulated
over time by intellectuals, politicians and civil society organisations, foremost
in Flanders, but also in Wallonia.

Considering the recent "hypermobility" of the Belgian constitution, it is
important to stress that it changed very little in its first 140 years. Originally
adopted in 1831, the Belgian constitution was only significantly modified
twice over the following century and a half, first, in order to officially recognise the adoption of universal suffrage and, second, to adopt the new electoral
system of proportional representation. Constitutional stability does not mean
that Belgium politics was similarly stable. Political conflicts abounded, pitting
secular liberals and Catholics, as well as workers and employers, against each
other. To resolve such tensions, Belgium resorted to the use of consociational
mechanisms, which ensured that the main mobilised groups would have as much
autonomy as possible and that governance would occur in a consensual
manner. Political elites especially played a key role in negotiating compromises
as representatives of key segments of the population.

Prior to the 1970s, linguistic groups were not directly represented in the
party system, although the Socialist Party was much more popular in Wallonia
and the Catholic/Christian Democratic Party in Flanders. Small parties emerged
sporadically throughout the twentieth century, pursuing a more regionalist, or
even sometimes nationalist, agenda. Moreover, in the inter-war period, the
Catholic Party was, in effect, divided into two different linguistic sections
(Gerard 2006). Responding to the political and administrative dominance of
the French language, the Flemish (and more powerful) wing of the party

pushed for linguistic legislations that would increase the representation of Dutch speakers in public administration and ensure that Dutch would be the only language of public communication in the Flemish Region, with the exception of Brussels and areas with linguistic – French-speaking – minorities. Such changes were made without modifying the unitary structure of the state.

Interestingly, it was not so much Flemish militants mobilising for either greater representation in federal institutions or to limit what they viewed as the creeping "Frenchification" of the Brussels periphery that first promoted the idea of transforming Belgium into a federal state. Rather, the challenge first came from the Walloon movement. In 1945, at a conference bringing together the main Walloon leaders of the country, a majority voted in favour of an autonomous Wallonia in a federal Belgium (Hooghe 2004: 60). The growing Walloon militancy was the product of the region's economic decline and fears over the perceived growing power of the Flemish majority. Nevertheless, in the immediate post-war period, this proposal did not gain traction, as debates about the future of the monarchy and the school question were at the forefront of political debates.

By the 1960s, however, the linguistic and regional question was back on the political agenda. Three regionalist parties were founded or gained seats during this decade: the *Rassemblement wallon*, the *Front démocratique des francophones* (a Brussels-based party) and the *Volksunie*, which had been formed in 1954. All three parties came over time to promote federalism (Van Haute and Pilet 2006; Deschouwer 1997). Such pressures would lead the traditional parties, liberals, Christian democrats and socialists, to embark on a series of constitutional reforms that would eventually transform Belgium into a decentralised federal state. It would involve four key constitutional moments.

First, in 1970, the constitution was modified to recognise the existence of cultural communities and of regions in Belgium, although there was really no clear consensus on what would be their roles. The creation of those two distinct types of subnational entities – communities and regions – reflected different perceptions of a potential post-unitary Belgium (Deschouwer 2009a: 68). For Dutch speakers, Belgium is composed of two linguistic communities, and Brussels is considered part of the Flemish Community, largely due to its geographical presence in the historically Dutch-speaking northern part of the country. For Walloons, the country is composed of three regions, in which Brussels is a separate, mainly francophone region. In effect, however, only the community aspect was first developed. Cultural councils were created and charged with responsibility over culture, language and certain aspects of education policy (Uyttendaele 1997: 38). Those councils consisted of Dutch-speaking and French-speaking members of the national parliament, and monitored small executives composed of ministers who were accountable to the national government (Hooghe 2004: 71).[10]

As will be seen in the following section, of crucial importance in 1970, besides the creation of regions and communities, was the adoption of a number of institutional reforms to deal with growing linguistic tensions. Both houses of the parliament were divided into language groups (Dutch and French). The measure was a necessary condition to the realisation of three other measures. First, when it came to the cabinet, the parity rule was adopted, an equal number of ministers having to come from each linguistic group.[11] Second, the "alarm-bell procedure" was instituted. This measure entails that when 75% of parliamentarians of one language group state that a proposal being discussed is potentially harmful to their community, parliamentary procedures must be stopped. Third, a new category of laws was created: "special majority laws". Those laws, which are constitutional in nature, do not have to go through the usual constitutional amendment procedure to be adopted. They can be used to fill in the principles laid out in the constitution; for example, with regard to the responsibilities of communities and regions, provided that a majority within each linguistic group supports them (Deschouwer 2009b: 50).

The second important constitutional revision occurred in 1980. It extended the powers of the communities, who were now made responsible for "personal matters" (*personnalisables/persoonsgebonden*), which allowed the Flemish Community to organise Flemish health and social services in Brussels (Uyttendaele 1997: 38). Regions were formally created and charged with responsibility over urban planning, environment, housing and employment policy. Formal institutions were created for the Flemish-, French- and German-speaking communities, as well as for the regions of Flanders and Wallonia. The status of Brussels was still not resolved and the region was still governed by the national government. The parliamentary assemblies created were not directly elected by the population, but based on the existing language groups in the national parliament. Flemish parliamentarians decided at this stage to merge the institutions of region and community in order to form one single political entity with only one government and one parliament.

The third reform came in the wake of more linguistic tensions, which brought the government down in 1987. Forming a new government after the election required a new agreement on a number of issues that had risen on the political agenda since the last constitutional reform. The reforms adopted in 1988–89 continued to push Belgium towards a federal system. The new constitutional revision transferred more responsibilities to communities (over education) and to regions (over public work, economic development and transport). The revision also addressed the question of the status of Brussels, as it received the status of a region. It also became the first assembly to be directly elected by the population.

It is with the Saint Michael Agreement of 1993, however, that Belgium officially became a federal state. The agreement put in place the institutions and mechanisms associated with a modern federation (Hooghe 2004: 73): the direct election of subnational councils; a senate in which subnational interests are represented; mechanisms to ensure a certain degree of fiscal autonomy of subnational entities; the granting of residual competencies to subnational units (although not yet applicable); guaranteed constitutional autonomy for both levels of government; and unique amongst most federal states, international competencies and treaty powers in their areas of jurisdiction, as discussed in Chapter 8 of this book.

While the 1993 Accord consecrated the creation of a federal regime, it did not stop the transformation of Belgium's state architecture. Reforms have since pursued the federalisation of the country, first in 2001 and more recently in 2011, with the transfer of further responsibilities to both regions and communities. Moreover, in 2011, the Senate was fully transformed into an assembly of regional parliaments, ending as such the direct election of some senators. Those recent reforms have thus contributed to the further decentralisation of Belgium and the continuing hollowing out of the centre (Hooghe 2004).

3.2 Negative feedback effects, consociationalism and constitutional politics in Belgium

The adoption of a federal system in Belgium could be seen as simply the logical conclusion of the first wave of reforms in 1970. Such an interpretation would be misleading, however. For as argues Kris Deschouwer:

> The federal result was however not deliberate. On the contrary, the first reforms – especially those of 1970 – were attempts to contain the ethnolinguistic tensions and to avoid a movement towards federalism. Only radical regionalist parties saw federalism as a desirable solution for the Belgian linguistic division.
>
> (Deschouwer 2006: 903)

While the 1970 reform did not have as an objective the adoption of a federal constitution, it had negative feedback effects that made the maintenance of purely non-territorial mechanisms for managing linguistic conflict unlikely. More specifically, the use of the consociational approach, which historically had been used to deal with non-territorial class and religious conflicts, to deal with the territorial cleavage had negative feedback effects that favoured significant changes over time.

Before exploring negative feedback, it is essential to understand why it did not create significant positive feedback that could, as in the Canadian case, outweigh any negative feedback. First, while the 1970 reform modified the unitary structure of the state, it remained unclear what was the ultimate objective of such a reform in terms of the transformation of the Belgian political system. The ambiguity of the reform was evident in the vague declaration of the prime minister at the time, Gaston Eyskens:

> The unitary state, at least as its structures and functions are legally stipulated, has been replaced by its own practical realities. The communities and regions must have a place in new state structures, which will be more appropriate to deal with the specific situation of the country.
>
> (Eyskens, quoted in Uyttendaele 1997, our translation)

Without a clear endpoint or ultimate objective for this reform, it is perhaps not surprising that so many reforms were adopted after 1970. As Jan Erk (2013: 287) argues in his comparison of Canada and Belgium, "ambiguity in interpreting what already exists is different from ambiguity as a way forward". While in the former it contributes, as it did for a long time in Canada, to constitutional stability as all actors can argue that their vision is embodied in existing institutions, the opposite is the case for the latter since communities push for institutions to be created to embody their vision of the country.

While there was little positive feedback associated with the 1970 reform, there were significant negatives ones. These negative effects are mostly associated with the adoption of consociational mechanisms to deal with community relations at the centre. A first negative effect has to do with the nature of consociationalism itself. In short, one of the defining characteristics of consociationalism is that issues in which consensus cannot be obtained should be dealt with by each segment or community. In the case of the religious and class pillars, this mostly involves granting responsibility to private organisations representing those different pillars (the Church or unions) for a number of policy sectors. In the context of territorial conflict, however, it essentially involves taking existing competencies of the centre and transferring them to subnational governments who do want to use the power of the state, for example in Wallonia, to improve the economy of the region (Hooghe 2004: 81). Consequently, there is a (continuous) decentralist tendency inherent to the consociational model when applied to territorial conflicts. This decentralist logic, however, was even further reinforced by the parity principle, which means, in effect, that the Flemish majority could not ensure that its policy preferences would prevail at the central level.[12] As such, it made sense for Flemish politicians to push for further decentralisation. Another element favouring decentralisation is the fact that while the Flemish attached greater importance to the communities, the francophone populations of both Brussels and Wallonia paid more attention to the region. This meant that any attempts to extend the powers of the communities also had to be extended to regions (Covell 1993: 70).

Another negative feedback effect is associated with the government parity rule, which requires the formation of an executive in which both linguistic communities are equally represented. In short, the parity rule means that when one of the two linguistic partners wants a constitutional reform, it may block the formation of a government. This phenomenon helps explain why it took more than a year after the 2010 election to form a government. As argued by Deschouwer:

> When one of the language communities – i.e. the governing parties of that community – really wants to put an issue on the agenda and really wants a solution to be found, it can put a lot of pressure on the other community. Refusing to negotiate means either the end of the government coalition or the postponement of the formation of a new coalition.
>
> (Deschouwer 2006: 905–6)

Not only, then, is there a strong incentive to negotiate a new constitutional agreement, but also no other actors can really oppose the changes negotiated by the political elites at the centre. Since, as we explored above, federal Belgium is a classic "holding together federation", regional institutions have not been involved in negotiating their policy responsibilities. Even today, the federal parliament alone decides the competences of the communities and regions, and, therefore, the communities and regions do not have vetoes on constitutional change in Belgium.[13] And contrary to Switzerland, Australia or Canada, constitutional amendments have never been the object of a referendum (Swenden 2005: 195–96).

The federalisation process has also been hastened by the division of parliament into linguistic units, which also furthered the division of political parties along linguistic lines, a process that started in the late 1960s following the split of the Christian democrats and ended with the splitting of the Socialist Party in 1977. These splits meant both that traditional parties had to compete in their respective regions with more radical regionalist parties, and also that previous intra-party mechanisms to deal with linguistic tensions were no longer available. This explains, in part, why the Socialist Party in Wallonia came to support a federal solution in the 1980s. As summarised by Swenden:

> The break-up of the state-wide parties along linguistic lines has enabled the previously unitary parties to harden their electoral profiles on regionalist issues. Indeed, the break-up did not mark the end of Belgian consensual policy making. Rather, consensual decision-making became more visible, as it was no longer primarily intra-party, but rather shifted to the inter-party arenas (coalition-making, decision-making in the national parliament and executive between ideologically related parties drawn from both linguistic groups).
>
> (Swenden 2005: 191)

In short, the constitutional reform adopted in 1970 put in place institutional mechanisms that, far from ensuring the maintenance of the unitary state, facilitated its transformation into a federal state, albeit one that continues to be unstable.

4 Conclusion

This chapter has sought to explain why Canada's constitution has proved to be largely incapable of being modified to respond to Quebec's demands, while Belgium has, and continues to live through, a period of constitutional hypermobility. The response, I have argued, can be found in the feedback effects, positive or negative, of two important "constitutional moments": the adoption in Canada of the Constitution Act, 1982, and, in the case of Belgium, the 1970 constitutional reform.

Differences in terms of feedback effects are both ideational and political. In the Canadian case, the 1982 Constitution proposed a new definition of the political community that has come over time to be embraced and defended by a vast number of Canadians outside Quebec. This vision – one that celebrates the multicultural character of the country and the protection accorded to individuals living in one of the country's ten equal provinces – has proved difficult to reconcile with Quebec's demand for recognition of its special status. Moreover, the Constitution Act, 1982, put in place an amending formula that makes constitutional change extremely difficult. Despite such constitutional immobility, *ad hoc* reforms in the distribution of powers have been adopted and occasional symbolic declarations have been pronounced to respond to political pressures coming from Quebec. In Belgium, contrary to Canada, the 1970 reform did not present a clear objective of such constitutional change. Adopted as a way to ease growing regional tensions, it has instead put in place mechanisms that have, over time, favoured constitutional change over the status quo.

What are the consequences of those reforms on the relationship between linguistic and regional communities in both countries? In the Canadian case, it is clear that the adoption of the Constitution Act, 1982, and the failure of the Meech Lake and the Charlottetown accords are partly responsible for the close result of the 1995 referendum. The fact that previous attempts at reforming the constitution failed and led to increased support for independence is used as an argument, even by those who believed in the past that such reform was necessary, against, again, attempting to get Quebec to sign the constitution. While tensions between the two main linguistic communities have been at a low point over the past decade, it can be argued that it has more to do with a feeling of mutual indifference than improving relations. In Belgium, on the other hand, for long periods of time, the process of federalisation has reduced tension between French speakers and Dutch speakers in Wallonia and Flanders, respectively. Swenden (2005: 199) also argues that the process of federalisation has played a key role in reducing some of the fiscally expensive practices that had been put in place to ensure support for the unitary state, without contributing to a decline in the population's loyalty to Belgium. Nevertheless, the process of constitutional adaption does not seem to have a clear end in sight, as shown by the constitutional crises that continue to shake Belgium.

Notes

1 The French-speaking population of Wallonia is smaller than the overall French-speaking population of Belgium since Brussels, once a Flemish city and located in the Flemish northern half of the country, is nowadays mostly French speaking, albeit increasingly international. As such, in the Belgian context, it is difficult, although important, to distinguish between French speakers and Walloons. See Caron in this book for a discussion of the Walloon identity and the relationship with Brussels' French-speaking community.

2 This section draws on works with Gagnon and Simeon (Gagnon and Turgeon 2003; Simeon and Turgeon 2013).

3 Quebec, which was then known as Lower Canada, was granted its own Legislative Assembly in 1791. However, it was abolished in 1840 following a rebellious upheaval.

4 Although it was a federal and not a confederal settlement, it was referred to as a confederation in reaction to the negative connotation of federalism in the wake of the American Civil War.

5 That clause has rarely been invoked, with the exception of the Quebec government that has used it at times to shield some aspects of its linguistic legislation.

6 In the early 1970s, Trudeau had rejected the bicultural definition of the country favoured by a majority of French-speaking Quebec intellectuals and politicians in favour of a policy of official multiculturalism.

7 Quebec feminists, it must be stressed, rejected the notion that the rights of women in Quebec were in jeopardy because of such a clause.

8 Bill 101 was the province's main linguistic legislation at the time of the Charter's signature. It limited access to publicly funded English education to those whose parents have received their education in Quebec (later changed to Canada following a Supreme Court decision) and it forbade the use of other languages than French in commercial signing (it now requires predominance of French and does not forbid other languages, again following a Supreme Court decision).

9 Such power is not in the constitution, but many constitutional scholars have inferred its existence from the powers to levy taxes, arguing that the federal power must have the power to spend the money its taxes yield. It has been used by the federal government to start national programmes, mostly in the social-policy sector, despite such sector being the responsibility of the provinces.

10 Eventually, a German-speaking community council was also created in 1984 to govern the affairs of the small German-speaking minority living in the eastern part of Belgium.

11 This excludes the prime minister, who, since the adoption of the 1970 reform has almost always been Flemish, with a few exceptions.

12 Although, at time, considering the historical under-representation of the Flemish majority in national institutions, it represented a victory for the Flemish community. Moreover, as shown by Reuchamps (2007), the position of prime minister (which does not count in the distribution of portfolios) has, until recently, always been attributed to a Dutch speaker, and a higher proportion of secretaries of state have been Flemish.

13 Although it could be argued that, since the party system is regionalised, regions are represented through the national party system.

References

Azjenstat, Janet (1995). "Decline of procedural liberalism: the slippery slope to secession". In *Is Quebec Nationalism Just? Perspective from Anglophone Canada*, ed. Joseph H. Carens, 120–136. Montreal and Kingston: McGill-Queen's University Press.

Covell, Maureen (1993). "Political conflict and constitutional engineering in Belgium", *International Journal of the Sociology of Language*, 104(1): 65–86.

Cox, Robert (2004). "The path dependency of an idea: why Scandinavian welfare states remain distinct", *Social Policy and Administration*, 38(2): 204–19.

Deschouwer, Kris (1997). "Une fédération sans fédérations de partis". In *La réforme de l'État ... et après? L'impact des débats institutionnels en Belgique et au Canada*, ed. Serge Jaumain, 77–83. Brussels: Éditions de l'Université de Bruxelles.

Deschouwer, Kris (2006). "And the peace goes on? Consociational democracy and Belgian politics in the twentieth-first century", *West European Politics*, 29(5): 895–911.

Deschouwer, Kris (2009a). "La dynamique fédérale en Belgique". In *Le fédéralisme en Belgique et au Canada*, ed. Bernard Fournier and Min Reuchamps, 65–72. Brussels: De Boeck Université.

Deschouwer, Kris (2009b). *The Politics of Belgium: Governing a Divided Society*, Houndmills: Palgrave Macmillan.

Erk, Jan (2013). "'Two Souls, alas, reside in my chest': the constitutional foundations of Belgium between a popular democracy and a multination federation", *The Political Quarterly*, 84(2): 278–88.

Esping-Anderson, Gosta (1990). *Three Worlds of Welfare Capitalism*, Princeton, NJ: Princeton University Press.

Gagnon, Alain-G. and Luc Turgeon (2003). "Managing diversity in eighteenth and nineteenth century Canada: Québec's constitutional development in light of the Scottish experience", *Commonwealth and Comparative Politics*, 41(1): 1–23.

Gerard, Emmanuel (2006). "La Démocratie rêvée, bridée et bafouée, 1918–39". In *Nouvelle Histoire de Belgique*, vol. 2: 1905–50, ed. Michel Dumoulin, Emmanuel Gerard, Mark van den Wijngaert and Vincent Dujardin. Brussels: Éditions Complexe.

Hooghe, Liesbet (2004). "Belgium: hollowing the center". In *Federalism and Territorial Cleavages*, ed. Ugo M. Amoretti and Nancy Bermeo, 55–92. Baltimore, MD: Johns Hopkins University Press.

Korpi, Walter (1980). "Social policy and distributional conflict in the capitalist democracies: a preliminary comparative framework", *West European Politics*, 3(3): 296–316.

McRoberts, Kenneth (1997). *Misconceiving Canada: the Struggle of National Unity*, Toronto: Oxford University Press.

Morton, F.L. and Rainer Knopff (2000). *The Charter Revolution and the Court Party*, Peterborough, ON: Broadview Press.

Pierson, Paul (2004). *Politics in Time: History: Institutions, and Social Analysis*, Princeton, NJ: Princeton University Press.

Reuchamps, Min (2007). "La parité linguistique au sein du conseil des ministres", *Res Publica*, 49(4): 602–27.

Reuchamps, Min (2011). *L'avenir du fédéralisme en Belgique et au Canada. Quand les citoyens en parlent*, Brussels: Peter Lang.

Silver, A.I (1997). *The French-Canadian Idea of Confederation, 1864–1900*, Toronto: University of Toronto Press.

Simeon, Richard and Luc Turgeon (2013). "Seeking autonomy in a decentralized federation: the case of Québec". In *Practising Self-Government: A Comparative Study of Autonomous Regions*, ed. Yash Ghai and Sophia Woodman, 32–61. Cambridge: Cambridge University Press.

Stepan, Alfred C. (1999). "Federalism and democracy: beyond the U.S. model", *Journal of Democracy*, 10(4): 19–34.

Swenden, Wilfried (2005). "What – if anything" – can the European Union learn from Belgian federalism and vice versa?", *Regional and Federal Studies*, 15(2): 187–205.

Turgeon, Luc and Jennifer Wallner (2013). "Adaptability and change in federal systems: comparing Australian and Canadian taxation authority". In *The Global Promise of Federalism*, ed. Grace Skogstad, David Cameron, Martin Papillon and Keith Banting, 188–213. Toronto: University of Toronto Press.

Uyttendaele, Marc (1997). "La Belgique: un modèle de fédéralisme panache". In *La réforme de l'État ... et après? L'impact des débats institutionnels en Belgique et au Canada*, ed. Serge Jaumain, 37–44. Brussels: Éditions de l'Université de Bruxelles.

Van Haute, Emilie and Jean-Benoit Pilet (2006). "Regionalist parties in Belgium (VU, RW, FDF): victims of their own success?", *Regional and Federal Studies*, 16(3): 297–313.

Weaver, Kent (2010). "Paths and forks or chutes and ladder? Negative feedbacks and Policy regime change", *Journal of Public Policy*, 30(2): 137–62.

2 Québécois and Walloon identities

The shift from an ethnic to a civic identity

Jean-François Caron

At first glance, it may seem irrelevant to compare the challenges associated with Québécois and Walloon identities, since both societies are shaped by different historical and institutional realities. Of course, as cultural and linguistic groups in an integrated regional federal structure, it is not surprising that their members manifest multiple belongings to their nation (Kesteloot 1997: 181),[1] their region or linguistic community, and the state in which they are most included.[2] Above all, there is the language connexion between Quebeckers and Walloons. But comparisons should stop there. As a national minority within the Canadian federation, Québécois identity is affirmed and further claimed that in the Walloon case, which was historically associated with the Belgian government itself.

It is worth remembering that at the time of the founding of Canada, Quebec was only a minority segment of the federal state that has subsequently transformed into a "national government" for most Anglo-Canadians, while the situation was totally different for Wallonia. From its inception, the Belgian state has been closely associated with the French, in fact so much so that it is not surprising today to find that a vast majority of Walloons identify themselves primarily with Belgium rather than with their other cultural entities (whether the Walloon Region or the French-speaking Community of Belgium).[3] The identity shift between these two societies should not surprise us unduly. In these cases, the element of "domination" of identity has played a significant role in creating the sense of identity of these "minority" nations. In this perspective, it might seem to be more appropriate to compare Québécois identity with Flemish identity, and Walloon identity with the identity of English Canada. But this approach would also be somewhat misleading, as there are indeed parallels between Québécois and Walloon identities.

The changes of identity that Quebec has experienced in the 1960s during the Quiet Revolution have several elements in common with Wallonia, which has long been torn by a tension between a typical ethnic identity and a civic identity that is primarily territorial. My ambition in this chapter is to show the similarities between the cases of Quebec and Wallonia, and also to discuss the pitfalls of identity that a society may face when it seeks to define itself through an identity that is more political.

1 The Walloon identity

It would be wrong to believe that the Walloon identity – like all identities – is an objective and natural state. Rather, it is a political construct built around values, myths, heroes, past traumas or glorious moments that serve to galvanise the group and to unite it in a collective spirit. The perception of this "imagined community" is what helps to give an objective reality, the "we" in this community. In the colourful words of Jean Giraudoux, it is under this political construction that it can be said that a people will get a real life, only if it is able to own a powerful unreal life (Courtois and Pirotte 1994: 14).

Obviously, if one adheres to constitutional and institutional reality, Wallonia is a relatively new political entity that dates back to 1970 when Belgium began its march towards federalisation, as Luc Turgeon explained in the first chapter. The fact remains that its collective psyche is much older and helped the growth of the Walloon movement that emerged in the late nineteenth century. My goal is not to portray a historiographical perspective, which has already been done (Destatte 1997). Rather this chapter proposes a discussion of the contemporary identity tension within the Walloon movement, which tends to oppose a linguistic substratum with an essence that is more political and civic.

1.1 The complexity of identities in Wallonia between linguistic identity and political identity

While the Flemish identity movement, in my opinion, can be assessed relatively simply, the Walloon movement is itself much more complex, since it feeds on an added complexity. Since the 1980 reform, the Flemish have decided to merge the destiny of the Flemish Region with that of the Flemish Community, which are now joined by a single institution, namely Flanders with a single – Flemish – parliament and government. Economic and cultural competences are exercised within the same institution. In Flanders the sense of belonging is therefore usually threefold: Flemish, Belgian and European.[4] This is not quite the case in Wallonia where the Walloon Region and the French-speaking Community remain two separate entities. Obviously, this contributes to complicate the political analysis of the Walloons' identities. However, this duality of structures has the merit of reflecting the tension between two strands of identity that can found inside the Walloon movement. This is why the "we" in the south is much more complex to determine. Is it made of Walloons or francophones? This question is not trivial, since these identities refer to very different philosophies of nationality: territory for the Walloon identity, and language for the francophone identity (Reuchamps 2008). In many ways, this twofold dynamic is very similar to the evolution of identity that Quebec has experienced in the early 1960s with the Quiet Revolution, hence the reason why the comparison between Quebec and Wallonia is appropriate. These are the two currents that will be the focus of my attention in this text.[5]

The contemporary Walloon movement is divided in two trends that emerged in the early twentieth century. One could say that the Walloon movement is a "daughter of events" like the political right in 1789. It would not have appeared in the absence of the Flemish movement, which claimed in the early years of the founding of the Belgian state the recognition of Dutch as an official language. Yet only after 40 years did Belgium begin to adopt legislation that formally recognised the country's linguistic and demographic reality, as the Dutch speakers accounted since the beginning of the country for the majority of its inhabitants. Thus the year 1873 marked the recognition of bilingualism by adopting a law allowing the use of Dutch in the courts of Flanders. This was followed 25 years later by the adoption of the Coremans–De Vriendt law, the so called "law of equality", which established the principle of equality of French and Dutch as official languages. The Walloon movement was born in reaction to these policies that were perceived as a threat to national unity, a waste of money and a threat to the employability of unilingual French-speaking Walloons (Lothe 1976: 192). This message was voiced by various groups, such as the Walloon League of Ixelles, the Hive Walloon Society propaganda or advocacy movement, and francophone Wallonia.

Very quickly, however, the Walloon movement reoriented its discourse after its members realised that the linguistic evolution of Belgium was irreversible. It is generally accepted that 1905 is the date when the Walloons ceased to defend the idea of monolingualism in favour of a new political discourse centred on the need to establish a unilingual French-speaking Wallonia, but a bilingual Flanders. Thus, in 1912, the Walloon congress delegates formed an informal Walloon Assembly whose purpose was to defend such a principle.[6] This re-articulation of the discourse around Wallonia – the territory of the Walloon identity – and around the premises of language – the protection of French in the country – has introduced a major difficulty in the Walloon identity: the status of Brussels. Territorially, the city is historically in Flanders, but it was increasingly inhabited by French-speaking people. This obviously creates tension within the Walloon movement between supporters of a linguistic approach and those of a more political and territorial bent.

1.2 The ideological currents of the Walloon movement

The linguistic current that started in 1905 was primarily driven by the protection of French and francophones in and around Brussels. From a Walloon movement it transformed into a francophone movement. As such it mainly fought not only for the city to be declared officially bilingual,[7] but also that certain municipalities on the outskirts of the city in Flemish Brabant, as the number of their French-speaking inhabitants rose, would be integrated within Brussels' bilingual area. The last three communes that moved in 1950s from the Dutch-speaking region to the bilingual region are Berchem-Sainte-Agathe/Sint-Agatha-Berchem, Ganshoren and Jette. Soon after, at the beginning of the 1960s, the linguistic border was frozen, meaning that communes could no longer change linguistic status. Accordingly, the linguistic current of the Walloon movement subsequently advocated a system of language facilities so that some communes located on the "wrong side of the linguistic border" but made up of a significant proportion of francophones were accorded special rights. Throughout the years, this position has strongly been defended by the *Front démocratique francophone* (FDF) (Francophone democratic front) that recently became the *Fédéralistes démocrates francophones* (Francophone democratic federalists). Its programme is to defend French-language rights in the out-skirts of the capital and in the Flemish Brabant (where some of their judicial and electoral rights are granted),[8] and also to advocate an enlargement of Brussels and an extension of bilingualism in the surrounding communes. This francophone movement – fostered by linguistic identity – is politically focused exclusively around Brussels.

This francophone vision is, however, not shared by all Walloons. As mentioned earlier, there is a historical trend based on the idea of an administrative separation between Wallonia and Flanders so that the French-speaking region is not affected by bilingualism (Joris 1999: 253–59). This territorial current of the Walloon movement owes much to Julien Delaite, Emile de Laveleye and especially to Jules Destrée, who wrote one of the founding texts of the Walloon regional identity and who was a partisan of the federalisation of Belgium. His letter was originally published on 15 August 1912 in the *Revue de Belgique* and was subsequently reproduced in other newspapers. In this letter to the King of Belgium, Albert I, Jules Destrée wrote the now famous sentence "Sire, allow me to tell you the truth, the large and horrifying truth: 'There are no Belgians, but Walloons and Flemings'". For Philippe Destatte, since then the federalist option was the engine of the assertion of Wallonia (1997: 415).

Inevitably, this option had an important consequence: being locked in Flemish territory, the French-speaking Brussels was virtually ignored by par-tisans of a Walloon movement centred on Walloon territory. In this definition of the Walloon, the territorial dimension was of much more central impor-tance than the linguistic dimension. It is therefore not surprising that Destrée had said in 1923 – tinged with some racism – that the people of Brussels were a cluster of "mestizos" who had "added the defects of both races, losing their qualities" (Schreiber 1995: 243–54). Following this logic, since the 1920s proponents of this option have advocated the conversion of the Belgian uni-tary state into a federal system composed of three regions, which gradually came out of the state reforms. In terms of rhetoric and symbolism, we can see that the supporters of this current have somehow "abandoned" their co-national francophone Brussels in favour of the image of an imagined community that is strictly territorial.

The tension between these two currents was manifested concretely in 1983 when 80 prominent Walloons published a Walloon manifesto that required the suppression of the French-speaking Community and the transfer of its competencies to the Walloon Region.[9] The signatories of the manifesto invoked the idea that the development of Wallonia could occur if a project featuring identity and culture was associated with its proposed economic reorganisation. They did not hesitate to support that the Walloon Region is culturally distinct from Brussels and in this sense the French-speaking Community does not represent or define them properly. According to them, Brussels is "a city that is not Walloon and that does not wish to identify [itself] as belonging to the Walloon community".[10] This appeal was heard in 2006 by 100 people in Brussels, who also supported the cultural difference and identity of Brussels compared to the two other – main – communities and, consequently, it that was time to allow it to flourish culturally like the Walloons and the Flemings.[11,12]

The fact remains that at the time of its initial publication, the manifesto for Walloon culture was not unanimously accepted within the Walloon movement, sparking tension between the territorial current and the linguistic current. Many blamed the signatories for wanting to create a movement of withdrawal of Wallonia and end the solidarity with their fellow French-speaking countrymen.[13] This is why the French-speaking communitarian discourse is extremely critical of the concept of Walloon identity that, according to its proponents, does not exist (Jongen 1989: 95–103). On this point, the tension between the two different approaches of Walloon identity is very similar to that which emerged in the early 1960s in Canada when Quebec had redesigned its collective identity around a purely territorial sense. The Québécois were then accused of abandoning the francophones outside Quebec (Langlois 2003: 173).

The opposition between these two visions of Walloon identity allows us to have a better understanding of their respective foundations. One can see very clearly that the francophone approach is based on community membership that relies on an objective criterion, namely the French language, whereas in the second case, nationalism – or, better, regionalism – is what might be termed much more "civic" and territorial. A good illustration of this is a quote from the manifesto of Walloon culture of 1983, which stated:

> The Walloon culture is a minority one, but alive, tolerant and pluralist. We are aware of our local peculiarities but we live the historical moment where our diversities must shape our strengths together. All those who live and work in the Walloon region are undeniably part of Wallonia. All beliefs and thoughts which are respectful of humans, without any reserve, are at home in Wallonia.
>
> (Centre d'études wallonnes et de République 1983)

This tension of identity seems to have many points in common with Quebec, which in the 1960s made a fundamental identity shift in turning from a French-Canadian nationalism centred mainly on the French language to a nationalism giving priority to the territorial reference. This is what I analyse in the next section.

2 From French-Canadians to Québécois

Following the failed rebellions of 1837–38 and the merger of Upper and Lower Canada within the same state structure (United Canada), Canada's francophones were organised around what most Quebec historians call the "nationalism of survival". Until that time, French Canadians were living mainly in the territories of Lower Canada, while English Canadians lived in Upper Canada, which stood to the west. Being thus divided, the inhabitants of these territories had the opportunity to establish their own laws. It goes without saying that they were established in the interests of the majority group. However, after the rebellions of 1837–38 by the patriots, the British government sent an inspector, Lord Durham, to North America to investigate the events that had happened and to propose solutions. A key recommendation of the Durham Report was to merge the two territories into one. The latter did not fail to say that French Canadians formed "a people without a history" and it was in their best interest "to be assimilated as soon as possible". Thus, French Canadians were seen as victims of the new constitution. With this union, they lost several of their rights: only the English language was now recognised in institutions, despite their demographic weight, which was larger than that of English speakers at the time, they obtained an equal number of members in the new assembly. The future became extremely obscure to them and their main objective was to save what remained of their identity.

Referred to the heart of its culture, language and traditions, French-Canadian nationalism quickly became an exaltation of the traditional values of their ancestors and the Catholic clergy were the catalyst for this "nationalism of survival". Inevitably, this new form of nationalism found itself subject to the Catholic Church. As indicated by Quebec political scientist Louis Balthazar:

> This framework will come to religious influence on the lives of so many French Canadians that the idea of a French-Canadian nation appears as inseparable from the Catholic faith. Indeed, it is the clerics themselves who will undertake to define the nation and promote nationalism. They will do much in terms of traditional doctrine based on reactionary motives deflected against all modern ideas: the rationalism of the 18th century, the French Revolution, liberalism. Being French Canadian, it means to be true to the faith of his ancestors, keep the family and parish intact, remain rooted in the ancestral land and resist industrialisation.
>
> (Balthazar 1986: 72)

However, whereas initially this type of nationalism tended to gather all the French Canadians of Canadian territory, some elements from the late nineteenth century and the early twentieth century favoured the decline in Quebec.

As mentioned by theologian Gregory Baum, a professor of religious studies at McGill University:

> But as we dismantled the system of French schools in provinces other than Quebec, and what was growing assimilation of French Canadians by English-speaking populations, few French-Canadian leaders finally were convinced that their national culture could survive in Quebec, where French Canadians made up the vast majority of the population and controlled the Legislature.
>
> (Baum 1998: 142)

This decline of French-Canadian nationalism in Quebec caused serious repercussions on the identity framework and gave rise to a true ethnic nationalism. For many authors, such as Lionel Groulx, a citizen residing in Quebec must inevitably share the Catholic religion, and the French language and traditions as a family. Those who did not fit into these elements were seen as a potential threat to the survival of the French-Canadian nation. It is therefore not surprising that several contemporary Québécois authors, such as Gérard Bouchard, have seen in this type of xenophobic nationalism that pressure from abroad would compromise the interests of the French-Canadian nation (2001: 307–28). Blood ties, membership in the Catholic religion and respect for ancestral traditions constitute the essence of the French-Canadian nation. It was therefore seen as a mainly ethnic reality and this definition continued to prevail, even in the second half of the twentieth century.[14]

However, the 1960s marked a watershed in the evolution of identity in Quebec that abandoned its design and exclusive ethnic nationalism in favour of a more varied ideology set mainly around land and legal references, which resulted in the granting of citizenship status to all residents of Quebec, notwithstanding their cultural heritage. Several factors contribute to explain such a change. On the one hand, while the old nationalism valued the idea of a rural and agricultural society, it was clear that this ideal was not a sociological reality since the 1920s when Quebec had become a predominantly urban and industrial society. On the other hand, this time the new identity coincided with a marked decline in religious influence on Quebec society. In sum, although these aspects are not exclusive to the explanation of this change, the fact remains that they represent how well the old conception of the nation was judged to be highly anachronistic.

From this perspective, as recalled by Kenneth McRoberts (1999: 58), "To survive, French Canada was to become a modern society. But that was only in Quebec, where francophones made up the overwhelming majority, that all economic institutions, social and cultural context of a modern society could function in French". Specifically, it had become clear to many that the survival of French culture in America was through the presence of institutions and state resources (Balthazar 1986: 126). It is this need that really explains the new identity in Quebec: the Quebec government was now to be the guarantor of the survival of Quebec' language and culture. Quebeckers *had* dissociated themselves from the French-Canadian diaspora, which still lived in the rest of Canada (particularly in Ontario, Manitoba and New Brunswick). In the eloquent words of Balthazar, the year 1960 has marked the "Quebecisation of French Canadian nationalism" and the replacement of French-Canadian nationalism by the ethnic territory as a theoretical framework of this new nationalism. Thus, neo-Quebec nationalism has come to be decidedly inclusive, and redefined the exercise of citizenship in an essentially territorial way in which all individuals living there have come to enjoy the same rights and privileges.

The "we" has become the national "Quebec" rather than "French Canadian", even if that legacy has remained at the heart of the political culture of its citizens through the use of a common language (French), particular representations of the past, with its symbols (the flag with lilies), its customs, rituals, festivals, its values and its way of seeing the world. Inevitably, like Wallonia, this reformulation of identity has had the effect of excluding the sense of Quebec by some individuals who previously left the imagined community (in the case of Quebec, francophones living outside Quebec, and in the case of Wallonia, francophones living in Brussels).

3 The contemporary Quebec nation: a return to essentialism of identity through the political

By its transformation, it is clear that neo-nationalism in Quebec came out of the rug of ethnic essentialism in its definition of "Quebecitude". Membership criteria are now based on political determination and a willingness by its intellectual and political elites to be open to ethno-cultural pluralism so that the idea of Quebec citizenship would be able to address all citizens of the province.[15] However, having ceased to identify membership in Quebec in ethnic terms does not mean that an essentialist discourse of another type does not develop.

Under the new definition of Québécois identity, this contemporary essentialism is no longer built around ethnic, but rather gravitates around policies that contribute to give a unique flavour to Quebec citizenship. It is clear that any individual or collective-identity movement is largely conditioned by otherness. Individuals and communities need an "other" that acts as a mirror and against which they are able to see what sets them apart. It is often by the close presence of another group of individuals that another community of people is able to assert itself in terms of an identity giving the context for its collective psyche.

It is this dynamic that has helped English Canada to assert its collective existence for much of the twentieth century. It is important to remember that, at the beginning, Canada was closely associated with a British identity. With the gradual extinction of links with the British Empire that started in the first half of the twentieth century, this assertion of identity has rearticulated itself around an anti-Americanism that has become the catalyst for the collective assertion of English Canada. As the historian J.N.S. Careless wrote in his essay *Limited Identities* in 1969, the imagined English-Canadian community would not exist without the United States (Gwyn 1985: 195). Being two societies, with an Anglo-Saxon heritage, the English language and a Protestant religion in common, the distinction drawn by the intellectual elites of English Canada has revolved around political differences. So while the USA is a society affected by a nativist discourse, political and social conservatism, anti-unionism or unilateralism in international relations, English Canada has built a collective psyche marked by openness to ethno-cultural pluralism, the importance of social democracy, labour and concerted multilateral international relations (Granatstein 1996: 283). This analysis is well documented in Canadian literature (Bashevkin 1991; Brown 1967; Russell 1966; Stairs and Winham 1985).

The problem with this is how to create a dynamic movement of exclusion, since identity is found by political criteria based around specific objectives. As such, there is nothing that can distinguish between this form of nationalism and with what is usually criticised for ethnic nationalism – apart from the fact that through democratic agony, members of a political community have the possibility of reorganising the imagined community around new political principles. Under this model, an individual will be considered Canadian if he/she promotes social-democratic values, advocates multilateralism internationally and shows openness to ethno-cultural pluralism. It is clear that this identity is marked by a form of identity essentialism. The political definition of the Canadian essence is rooted in objective factors that may exclude those people who do not share these values.[16]

Obviously, one can question whether such a consequence is not an inescapable fate of all civic nationalism, which, by nature, lacks identity density. To exist, a people must be able to show its uniqueness on its own.[17] This distinction is easy to operate through ethnicity – although this may be difficult in the case of similar societies on the cultural level, such as English Canada and the USA – but more problematically through civic lenses. The construction of an imagined community around general political principles may not allow community members to feel their distinctions, while, on the other hand, organising principles around too specific ideas and ideals runs the risk of generating a political essentialism that is to be exclusive for some who, for reasons that are personal to them, do not adhere to these political values.

It can be argued that a similar movement occurred in Quebec, notably through the *Bloc Québécois* – whose political representation in the Canadian parliament has been reduced to a trickle since the election of 2 May 2011. Following the failed 1995 referendum, the party has made a political realignment. While at its inception its objective was to promote Quebec's sovereignty at the federal level, it instead adopted in the post-referendum period a discourse defending the interests of Quebeckers under the leadership of Gilles Duceppe. He was, however, criticised for having amalgamated the ideals of the political left to its definition of Quebec identity (Caron 2008, 2013; Béland and Lecours 2011: 37–52). But when one looks closer, it is neither more nor less than persuasive essentialist fiction, as several polls have shown that Quebeckers share values similar to those found in English Canada.[18] This way of thinking regarding the collective psyche of Quebec is increasingly criticised in Quebec, and has recently led to incredible rhetorical excesses since the ascension of Stephen Harper's Conservative Party as a majority government.[19]

As a comparative point, it may be useful to see how the Walloon region-alist movement is confronted by the dangers of essentialism. This question is particularly relevant as the prime minister of the region, Rudy Demotte, proposed in March 2010 to discuss what should compose the Walloon identity.

4 The Walloon identity and the pitfalls of political exclusivism

If one looks at what constitutes the Walloon political identity, despite its civic element, we must admit – a bit like in the case of contemporary Quebec nationalism – that the French language is a cultural vehicle central to identi-fication among its members. As mentioned earlier, it still remains a civic identity.[20] However, the linguistic dimension itself does not differentiate the Walloon identity from the French identity.[21] Thus, in order to thicken its identity, Wallonia needs additional political references. Some have therefore stressed that the practice of democracy was a feature of the Walloon identity, just as its respect for equality between men and women as well as its openness to "the other" (Thayse 2010). If we confine ourselves to these few aspects, it is clear that the Walloons are no different from other Western nations. For example, in early 1990, the Citizens' Forum on Canada's future had identified a set of substantial political values, which were, according to the authors of the report, at the heart of Canada's collective identity. It referred to a commitment to equality and fairness, consultation and dialogue, the importance of recognition of others and tolerance, appreciation of diversity and pluralism, compassion and generosity, commitment to a quality environment and, finally, a commitment to peace, freedom and non-violent options (Kymlicka 2001: 264). In both cases, it is far too broad as rhetoric that does not distinguish effectively between members and non-community members. Further elements need, therefore, to be searched for in our understanding of the Walloon identity.

The political element that seems to come up most often in the Walloon identity discourse is probably the fact that Walloon society and its collective imagination are marked by ideological values of the left. We largely owe this to André Renard, the founder of the "renardiste" current, and his movement, the *Mouvement populaire wallon* (Walloon people's movement), which has combined trade-union struggles and Walloon militancy (Moreau 1984: 119). In political terms, this congruence seems to have been a strong foundation, since the *Parti socialiste* (Socialist Party) has spent 37 of the last 40 years in power – alone or in coalition – in Wallonia. The advantage of such a construction appears to be similar to the anti-American English-Canadian identity. It operates and takes advantage of otherness to better highlight the peculiarities of the Walloon people. In this case, the "other" is obviously the Flemish, as it is typically presented as being conservative and to the right economically.[22] In political terms, it is clear that this reality has been proved, unlike in Quebec where the social-democratic ideological reality is, as I have indicated earlier, rather exaggerated. In fact, the majority of Walloons vote for parties on the left and centre-left, while the majority of Flemings vote for parties on the right or centre-right.

The fact remains that the pitfalls of identity essentialism is the same in Wallonia as in Quebec. Defining an identity around Walloon political drivers may cause a risk of exclusion for some members of the community who define themselves in terms of an ideology associated with the political right – which is not a crime in itself. It would be paradoxical in the context of a civic project that is based around a free membership and rational individuals and that presupposes no "insurmountable barrier nor the inclusion or accession" (Karmis 2003: 91). Some might see in this type of discourse a form of social perfectionism and identity able to transform individuals and forge them into a mould that is superior to the others. I think we should be wary of all projects associated with the idea of a "New Man" who tends to bully the individuality of people and cast a thick veil of ideological diversity that crosses democratic societies.

4 Conclusion

Québécois and Walloon societies have much in common and are symptomatic of the dangers associated with essentialist civic identities: a danger similar to those of ethnic nationalism. The psychological dimension that determines the perceived affiliation of individuals to their community's policies requires a relatively thick substrate and meaningful dialogue so that individuals are able to receive their rewards from other people. In the case of political identities, political values came to play the role of ersatz references to ethnic nationalism that goes back to Herder. But to be able to play a significant role, these values should not be too general. In such cases, community members would not be able to stand out from other people who are animated by similar values. To do so requires that they have a limited size and are presented as truly exclusive to the people in question. As I have tried to show in this chapter, the risk of identity exclusion is high in this case. Québécois clearly demonstrate this and the Walloon identity also shows problematic elements in this vein. This leads me to doubt that a balance can be struck between self-perceived and effective representation of the people around political values without a form of exclusive identity. But unfortunately this discussion goes beyond the scope of this chapter.

Notes

1 This term should be used only in Quebec's case, insofar as intellectuals and Walloon politicians do not seem to favour multiple belongings. Genevieve Warland states that

"The nation remains a problematic concept for historians of the Walloon movement" (2008: 68).

2 In the case of Wallonia, we might even talk about another layer of identity due to the institutional level of the European Union.

3 Several empirical studies have attempted to grasp this complex identity. Between 1991 and 1999, the number of Walloons who felt Belgian first has fluctuated between 66% and 73%, whereas the French-speaking community showed between 5% to 11%, and the Walloon region just above 10% (van Haute *et al.* 2007: 37–53). In a more recent contribution, Kris Deschouwer and Dave Sinardet have shown that the identities of the Walloons in Belgium remained at a similar level during the 2000s to that observed during the previous decade; more specifically, 9% claimed to feel first and foremost Walloons and 24% ranked it their second identity importance (2010: 65).

4 I am aware that the level of city/town is generally considered in the analyses. However, it will not be considered in this analysis, since its premises are not within the variables associated with "national identity". I shall not consider the provincial level either because the sense of belonging that goes with it is far too marginal.

5 For their part, independence and *rattachisme* to France – i.e. the unification of Wallonia with France – remain two other options but with much less support: the former was polled at about 12% among the Walloon population in 2007, and the result for the party *Rassemblement Wallonie France* that advocates the unification of Wallonia with France was only a few per cent.

6 It is to this congress that we owe the adoption of the flag in 1913 and the choice of Namur as the capital of Wallonia.

7 This status was granted in 1932.

8 Most of the problems associated with the electoral and judicial districts Brussels-Hal/Halle-Vilvorde/Vilvoorde, which were contentious issues, refer to these special rights (Deschouwer and Reuchamps 2013).

9 The full text of this manifesto is available from: www.larevuetoudi.org/fr/story/manifeste-pour-la-culture-wallonne-1983 (accessed 1 March 2014).

10 A similar appeal was launched again in 2003 with the publication of a new manifesto: www.larevuetoudi.org/fr/story/manifeste-pour-une-wallonie-ma%C3%AEtresse-de-sa-culture-de-son-%C3%A9ducation-et-de-sa-recherche-2003 (accessed 1 March 2014).

11 "It is time to say that the population of Brussels cannot be reduced to two groups, Flemings on one side, francophones on the other" (our translation). The manifesto is available from: www.larevuetoudi.org/fr/story/lappel-bruxellois-nous-existons-2006 (accessed 1 March 2014).

12 "It is time to leave behind us for good a Belgium where two communities are facing, to allow the three regions of the country to flourish side by side, each with its own identity and effective institutions. We, the inhabitants of Brussels, are likely to be born outside Belgium. We speak mostly more than one language and, even within our families, languages often coexist. As Europe settles more, Brussels is a city ever more international and more complex, a city region increasingly different from Wallonia and Flanders. This complexity is a challenge. But it would be absurd to try to lock it into the bi-communitarian straitjacket" (our translation).

13 One can mention here the signatories of the 2006 manifesto for francophone unity that supported the cultural unity of francophones in Belgium and, according to them, it is unthinkable that Brussels is separated from Wallonia. It should be emphasised that the manifesto established a semantic distinction between the Walloons and Brussels. It can be concluded that even for the signatories of the document it was clear that the imagined identity of these two communities is not the same (Demoulin and Kuper 2004: 339; de Bruycker 1998: 60; Dauw 2003).

14 In the Tremblay Commission (1953–56), Quebec's national citizenship was defined in this way: "The French Canadians are nearly all of the Catholic faith … . French

Canadians are of French origin and culture. ... French Canadians are the only group whose cultural and religious particularities coincide almost exactly. Only the French Canada, as a homogeneous group, has the double differentiator of religion and culture" (Keating 1997: 90).

15 See, for instance, the theoretical attempts by Bouchard seeking to redevelop the great symbolic legacy of French Canadians so that the new Quebeckers are able to identify with Québécois identity (2001: 314–16).

16 In his books, English-Canadian political scientist Philip Resnick shows clearly that the ideological sphere of English Canada is composed of three ideologies: liberal, conservative and social democratic (1994, 2005). It would therefore be wrong to claim that all Canadians can agree on the same political values.

17 The European example is conclusive in this regard. Citizenship, which became a legal concept in 1992 with the Maastricht Treaty, has not been able to develop among Europeans a sense of common identity in 20 years. Today, only 4% of the inhabitants of the European Union and only 2% of the citizens of countries that joined in 2004 feel primarily European (Jeanbart 2004: 18). This is why some scholars contend that the European identity could be thought about strictly in terms of political values inherent in its space, namely the value placed on human life, solidarity associated with the state office and membership in a supranational system of protection of human rights (Stephanou 1999: 256–57).

18 We know that 62% of Canadians and 69% of Quebeckers are in favour of the death penalty. See for instance: www.ledevoir.com/societe/actualites-en-societe/ 281709/62-des-canadiens-diraient-oui-a-la-peine-de-mort (accessed 17 January 2012). We also know that it is among Quebeckers that we find the most people who want to reopen the debate about abortion (38%). The "very conservative" Alberta is second with 33% of citizens who want to reopen this debate: www.cyberpresse. ca/actualites/quebec-canada/national/201008/02/01-4303308-les-canadiens-sont-divi ses-sur-lavortement.php (accessed 17 January 2012). The polling firm Angus Reid conducted in 2007 an extensive survey on the values of Canadians. It reveals many similarities between Quebeckers and English Canadians: www.angus-reid.com/polls/ 29842/canadians_review_what_is_morally_acceptable/ (accessed 28 February 2012).

19 One can, for instance, think of the member of parliament Justin Trudeau, son of the former prime minister Pierre Elliot Trudeau, who said he "would think of wanting to make Quebec a country" if he had the conviction that "[i]t was really like Stephen Harper's Canada".

20 For example, the Jules Destrée Institute launched a debate on a draft constitution in 1997 where Article 5 stated "Wallonia defines as Walloons all her inhabitants, whatever their origin": www.wallonie-en-ligne.net/Wallonie_Citoyennete/1997_ Constitution-wallonne_Preambule.htm (accessed 1 March 2014).

21 This also explains the presence of the *rattachiste* current in the Walloon movement.

22 This impression is even clearly assumed by the Flemish nationalists, including Bart De Wever, the president of the *Nieuw-Vlaamse Alliantie* (N-VA), the main political party in Flanders; see, for instance, www.dhnet.be/infos/belgique/article/333949/ reynders-apres-six-mois-on-a-enfin-le-point-de-vue-d-un-negociateur.html (accessed 21 January 2012).

References

Balthazar, Louis (1986). *Bilan du nationalisme au Québec*, Montreal: L'Hexagone.

Baum, Gregory (1998). *Le nationalisme, perspectives religieuses, éthiques et religieuses*, Montreal: Bellarmin.

Bashevkin, Sylvia (1991). *True Patriotic Love. The Politics of Canadian Nationalism*, Toronto: Oxford University Press.

Béland, Daniel and André Lecours (2011). "Le nationalisme et la gauche au Québec", *Globe. Revue internationale d'études québécoises*, 14(1): 37–52.

Bouchard, Gérard (2001). "Ouvrir le cercle de la nation. Activer la cohésion sociale. Réflexion sur le Québec et la diversité". In *Les nationalismes au Québec du XIXè au XXIè siècle*, ed. Michel Sarra-Bournet and Jocelyn Saint-Pierre, 307–28. Quebec: Les Presses de l'Université Laval.

Brown, Robert Craig and Sydney F. Wise (1967). *Canada Views the United States: Nineteenth-Century Political Attitudes*, Toronto: Macmillan.

Caron, Jean-François (2008). "Le dogmatisme de Duceppe". Available from: www. vigile.net/Le-dogmatisme-de-Duceppe (accessed 1 March 2014).

Caron, Jean-François (2013). "The Exclusive Nature of Quebec's Contemporary Nationalism: the Pitfalls of Civic Nationalism", *International Journal of Canadian Studies*, 47: 221–38.

Centre d'études wallonnes et de République (1983). "Manifesto for Walloon culture (1983)". Available from: www.larevuetoudi.org/en/story/manifesto-walloon-culture-1983 (accessed 21 August 2014).

Courtois, Jean-Luc and Jean Pirotte (1994). "Introduction à la recherche du dessin sous-jacent". In *L'imaginaire wallon: jalons pour une identité qui se construit*, ed. Jean-Luc Courtois and Jean Pirotte, 13–18. Louvain-la-Neuve: Publications de la Fondation wallonne P.-M. et J.-F. Humblet.

Deschouwer, Kris and Dave Sinardet (2010). "Langue, identité et comportement électoral". In *Les voix du peuple. Le comportement électoral au scrutin du 10 juin 2009*, ed. Kris Deschouwer, Pascal Delwit, Marc Hooghe and Stefaan Walgrave, 61–81. Brussels: Les Éditions de l'Université de Bruxelles.

Deschouwer, Kris and Min Reuchamps (2013). "The Belgian Federation at a Crossroad", *Regional and Federal Studies*, 23(3): 261–70.

Destatte, Philippe (1997). *L'identité wallonne*, Charleroi: Institut Jules Destrée.

Dauw, Annie (2003). "Le tournant de l'identité wallonne", *Toudi mensuel*, 56–57. Available from: www.larevuetoudi.org/fr/story/le-tournant-de-l'identité-wallonne-1 (accessed 1 March 2014).

de Bruycker, Philippe (1998). "La problématique de l'État-nation en Belgique". In *Les mutations de l'État-nation en Europe à l'aube du XXIème siècle*, Actes de colloque: Commission européenne pour la démocratie et le droit, Conseil de l'Europe, 6–8 November 1997, 53–66. Strasbourg: Council of Europe.

Demoulin, Bruno and Jean-Louis Kupper (2004). *Histoire de la Wallonie: de la préhistoire au 21ème siècle*, Toulouse: Éditions Privat.

Granatstein, Jack (1996). *Yankee Go Home? Canadians and anti-Americanism*, Toronto: Harper Collins.

Gwyn, Richard (1985). *The 49th Paradox. Canada in North America*, Toronto: Totem Books.

Jeanbart, Bruno (2004). "L'appartenance à l'Europe, un sentiment largement partagé mais très évolutif". In *Le nouvel état de l'Europe*, ed. Mario Dehove, 18–20. Paris: La Découverte.

Jongen, François (1989). "Communauté française et Région wallonne. Wallonie-Bruxelles, même combat ?", *La Revue de l'Université de Bruxelles*, 3–4: 95–103.

Joris, Freddy (1999). "Les projets fédéralistes wallons: 1898–1970". In *L'idée fédéraliste dans les États-nations. Regards croisés entre la Wallonie et le monde*, ed. Philippe Destatte, 253–59. Brussels: Presses interuniversitaires européennes.

Karmis, Dimitrios (2003). "Pluralisme et identité(s) nationale(s) dans le Québec contemporain: clarifications conceptuelles, typologie et analyse du discours". In *Québec: État et Société*, ed. Alain-G. Gagnon, 85–116. Montreal: Québec Amérique.

Keating, Michael (1997). *Les défis du nationalisme moderne. Québec, Catalogne, Écosse*, Montreal: Les Presses de l'Université de Montréal.

Kesteloot, Chantal (1997). "Etre ou vouloir être. Le cheminement difficile de l'identité wallonne", *Cahiers d'histoire du temps présent*, 3: 181–201.

Kymlicka, Will (2001). *La citoyenneté multiculturelle. Une théorie libérale du droit des minorités*, Montreal: Boréal.

Langlois, Simon (2003). "Briser les solitudes entre francophones". In *Briser les solitudes. Les francophonies canadiennes et québécoise*, ed. Simon Langlois and Jean-Louis Roy, 173–83. Quebec: Éditions Nota Bene.

Lothe, Jeannine (1976). "Les débuts du Mouvement wallon". In *La Wallonie, Le Pays et les Hommes*, vol. 2, ed. Hervé Hasquin, 191–210. Brussels: Renaissance du livre.

McRoberts, Kenneth (1999). *Un pays à refaire. L'échec des politiques constitutionnelles canadiennes*, Montreal: Boréal.

Moreau, Robert (1984). *Combat syndical et conscience wallonne: du syndicalisme clandestin au mouvement populaire wallon, 1943–1963*, Liège-Brussels-Charleroi: Fondation A. Renard-Vie ouvrière-Institut J. Destrée.

Resnick, Philip (1994). *Thinking English Canada*, Toronto: Stoddard.

Resnick, Philip (2005). *The European Roots of Canadian Identity*, Toronto: University of Toronto Press.

Reuchamps, Min (2008). "Les Belges francophones et le fédéralisme. À la découverte de leurs perceptions et de leurs préférences fédérales", *Fédéralisme Régionalisme*, 8(2). http://popups.ulg.ac.be/1374-3864/index.php?id=731 (accessed 21 August 2014).

Russell, Peter (1966). *Nationalism in Canada*, 3rd edn, Toronto: McGraw-Hill.

Schreiber, Jean-Philippe (1995). "Jules Destrée, entre séparatisme et nationalisme". In *Les Grands Mythes de l'histoire de Belgique – De Flandre et de Wallonie*, ed. Anne Morelli, 243–54. Brussels: Vie Ouvrière.

Stairs, Denis and Gilbert R. Winham (1985). *The Politics of Canada's Economic Relationship with the United States*, Toronto: University of Toronto Press.

Stephanou, Constantin (1999). "L'identité européenne et les identités nationales". In *Les racines de l'identité européenne*, ed. Gérard-François Dumont, 252–59. Paris: Economica.

Thayse, Claude (2010). "Un débat sur l'identité wallonne, mais quelle excellente chose". Available from: www.claude-thayse.net/article-un-debat-sur-l-identite-wallonne-mais-quelle-excellente-chose-45904219.html (accessed 1 March 2014).

van Haute, Émilie, Régis Dandoy, Nicolas de Decker and Pascal Delwit (2007). "Complexes identitaires ou identités complexes en Belgique fédérale". In *L'espace Wallonie-Bruxelles: voyage au bout de la Belgique*, ed. Benoît Bayenet, Henri Capron and Philippe Liégeois, 37–53. Brussels: De Boeck.

Warland, Geneviève (2008). "Nationalismes: le débat des historiens belges", *La Revue nouvelle*, 1: 60–69.

Part II
Politics in Quebec and Wallonia

3   Constructing Quebec and Wallonia

How political parties speak about their region

Heidi Mercenier, Julien Perrez and
Min Reuchamps

Political parties are key political actors in both Quebec and Wallonia. As their foremost ambition is to govern their region, these parties clearly contribute to shaping its identity and image. This chapter aims at exploring how political parties in Quebec and in Wallonia speak about their region by focusing on an analysis of their electoral manifestos for the period 1994–2014. Using a quantitative and qualitative approach combining insights from lexicometry, cognitive linguistics and political science, the aims of this contribution are (i) to unravel how the parties perceive their region and its future development, (ii) to identify relevant evolutions in their perception of their respective region, and (iii) to assess to what extent parallels can be drawn between the two regions.

Accordingly, this chapter is structured as follows: section 1 is devoted to a brief introduction to linguistic approaches to the study of political discourses. In section 2 we present the political parties in Quebec and Wallonia, before turning, in section 3, to a description of our data and methods. In sections 4 and 5, we present the respective results of our analyses for Quebec and Wallonia, before discussing, in section 6, the main issues raised by the study.

1 Linguistic approaches to the study of political discourses

Political discourse plays a central role in the construction of political meaning and can be regarded as the meeting point par excellence between language and society (Mayaffre 2005). This particular use of language to create political meaning may explain why political discourse has frequently been an object of linguistic analysis (Perrez and Reuchamps 2012). There are two well-established traditions that offer – complementary – linguistic approaches to the study of political discourses. Both rely on the performative nature of words, which have the ability to create conceptual categories; in other words, both approaches focus on the analysis of specific forms conveying political meaning.

On the one hand, lexicometric approaches build on tools that automatically analyse large corpora in order to capture the frequency and collocational patterns of words in a given discourse. Such a perspective enables the researcher to identify the word forms framing particular political issues at a given point in time, thereby extracting the political essence of the discourses under study (Mayaffre 2007). In this approach, the analyst's task is to integrate the discourses under study within their broader epistemic and ideological contexts, after a thorough lexicometric analysis, in order to understand which words frame a given political debate.

On the other hand, with the development of cognitive linguistics, and more specifically of conceptual metaphor theory (Lakoff and Johnson 1980), the linguistic analysis of political discourse has been enhanced by the insight that metaphors play a major role in our perception of abstract entities and our understanding of complex processes. There is currently a widespread scientific endeavour to use conceptual metaphors as analytic tools to explore political discourse from a new perspective (Chilton 1996). As Semino puts it (2008: 90): "it is often claimed that the use of metaphor is particularly necessary in politics, since politics is an abstract and complex domain of experience, and metaphors can provide ways of simplifying complexities and making abstractions accessible". The importance of metaphors in politics has also been stressed by Charteris-Black, who highlights their contribution to the construction of more accessible "mental representations of political issues" and suggests their power resides in their ability to "activate unconscious emotional associations", which "contributes to myth creation" (Charteris-Black 2011: 28). Wilson and Hay have also stressed the importance of conceptual metaphors in the discursive construction of collective identities:

> [A] focus on the use of conceptual metaphors within discourses of ethnicity provides a valuable insight into ethnic self-understanding at a given point in time, and that, consequently, this approach is a valuable addition to the analytic repertoire for researchers concerned with issues of emergent ethnicity and the construction of ethnic identities in general.
>
> (Wilson and Hay 2013: 49)

The aim of the present study is to examine the political discourse in general, and political-party manifestos in particular for Quebec and Wallonia, from the combined perspective of lexicology and metaphor analysis. This approach will help us understand how the political parties concerned try to frame the electoral debate. At a more detailed level, this approach should also reveal specific political visions for the two regions under study. This perspective is an original way of looking at these data, departing from more traditional content analyses of political manifestos as used in the Comparative Manifestos Project, which attempts to classify the content of manifestos into different categories in order to measure the political stance of each party (for examples on Quebec political parties and on Walloon political parties, see, respectively, Pétry 2006; Collette and Pétry 2012; Dandoy 2012a).

2 Political parties in Quebec and Wallonia

Over the last 20 years in Quebec, three main opponents have competed for seats in the provincial parliament: the liberal PLQ (*Parti libéral du Québec*) and the sovereignist PQ (*Parti Québécois*), as well as, more recently, the autonomist and conservative ADQ (*Action démocratique du Québec*).[1] In 2012, the ADQ merged with the CAQ (*Coalition Avenir Québec*). In Wallonia, four political parties have been continuously represented in the Walloon parliament since its first direct elections in 1995. The first of these is the Christian democratic cdH (*Centre démocrate humaniste* – known until 2002 as the PSC, *Parti social chrétien*). The second party is the ecologist Ecolo (*Écologistes confédérés pour l'organisation de luttes originales*). The third is the liberal MR (*Mouvement réformateur*). This party initially consisted of an alliance beginning in 1993 between the liberal PRL (*Parti réformateur libéral*) and the francophone regionalist FDF (*Front démocratique des Francophones* – known since 2010 as the *Fédéralistes démocrates francophones*), which was joined in 1998 by the MCC (*Mouvement citoyen pour le changement*). In 2002, the PRL, FDF and MCC together became known as the current MR, but the FDF left the party in 2011. Last but not least, the fourth political party represented in the Walloon parliament is the socialist PS (*Parti socialiste*).

Historically, since the party's creation in 1968, the ongoing opposition between the federalists (PLQ) and the sovereignists (PQ) has shaped the political dynamics in Quebec. Since then, these two parties have alternatingly led the provincial government. As suggested by Table 3.1, this competition between the two main political parties has continued over the last two decades: the PQ being in power from 1994 until 2003, the PLQ between 2003 and 2012 (although with a minority government between 2007 and 2008 for the first time since 1878) and the PQ returning to power in 2012 for only two years before ceding victory to the PLQ in the 2014 elections. This government–opposition dynamic, fostered by the majoritarian electoral system, is key to understanding Quebec politics, as it has been shown that holding the reins of government influences the form and content of a party's political manifesto (Pétry 2006; Collette and Pétry 2012).

Alongside these strong bipartisan dynamics, however, third-party dynamics are not to be ignored in the recent history of Quebec politics. The ADQ was created in 1994 and fielded candidates at the elections immediately after its creation. What is more, in 2007, the ADQ became, for the first time, the

Table 3.1 Election results in Quebec and the party in government (1989–2014)

	1989	1994	1998	2003	2007	2008	2012	2014
ADQ	–	6.46	11.81	18.18	30.84	16.37	–	–
CAQ	–	–	–	–	–	–	27.05	23.06
PLQ	49.95	44.4	43.55	45.99	33.08	42.08	31.20	41.50
PQ	40.16	44.75	42.87	33.24	28.35	35.17	31.95	25.38

Note: Percentage of vote by party.

official opposition, leaving the PQ as a second opposition party in such a way that some authors have argued that the traditional bipartisan politics was disappearing (Bélanger and Nadeau, 2008). However, the emerging third-party dynamics evolved quickly with the swift rise of the ADQ in the 2008 elections (where it gained 16.37% of the vote) and, finally, with its merger in February 2012 with the CAQ (the merged party gained 27.05% of the vote in the 2012 elections). In 2014, the PQ chose to trigger an election in an attempt to secure the chance to form a majority government. The PLQ ultimately won the election (with 41.5% of the vote), while the PQ clearly lost support (their share of the vote was down from 31.95% to 25.38%). Third-party dynamics seemed to be back at the forefront of Quebec politics with the results of the CAQ (23.06%) coming close to those of the PQ.

In Wallonia, by contrast, one party – the PS – has been the dominant political actor in the region for the whole of the twentieth century and into the twenty-first century (Table 3.2), gaining for each – national – election a handful of seats, even within a proportional system (Bouhon and Reuchamps 2012). The creation of the regions in the 1980s and more specifically the direct election of the Walloon parliament have not changed these dynamics. Since 1995, the socialists have uninterruptedly held power, but, given the proportional system, this has always been within a coalition. In 1995, the PS governed with the Christian democrats and then in a rainbow coalition made up of socialists, liberals and greens from 1999 until 2004. That year, the PS and the MR retained power but left the Ecolo in opposition. Then, in 2009, the Ecolo was brought back into the coalition along with the Christian democrats, this time leaving the liberals in opposition.

In these two polities, two main cleavages have shaped between the parties. On the one hand, the *identity cleavage* is a key driver of both Quebec and Wallonia (Reuchamps 2011). In Quebec, the question of the future of the province has shaped the political debate since the Quiet Revolution in the 1960s. The so-called sovereignism–federalism cleavage places the federalists who want a strong Quebec inside Canada against the sovereignists who want a strong Quebec outside Canada (Pelletier 2008). This basic opposition led to two referendums on the sovereignty of Quebec in 1980 and in 1995. Nonetheless, the choice taken to remain within the Canadian federation has not pacified the tensions, and the debate about the future of Quebec is still ongoing today (see the chapters by Turgeon and by Caron in this book).

Table 3.2 Election results in Wallonia and the parties in government (1995–2014)

	1995	1999	2004	2009	2014
cdH (PSC)	21.56	17.07	17.62	16.14	15.17
ECOLO	10.42	18.22	8.52	18.54	8.62
MR	23.67	24.69	24.29	23.41	26.69
PS	35.22	29.44	36.91	32.77	30.90

Note: At the time of print, the parties in government for the period 2014–2019 were not known yet.

In Wallonia, too, the identity cleavage goes to the core of Belgian federalism and to the organisation of lines of solidarity. One difficult question relates to the nature of the link between the French speakers of Wallonia and the French speakers of Brussels. That is the question of the existence of the so-called French-speaking Community, in addition to the Walloon Region and the Brussels-Capital Region (Deschouwer and Reuchamps 2013). On this specific question, there are different competing views both between and within the political parties: one view favours the existence of two regions only, another remains in favour of the current encompassing community, while a third view combines both visions with the proposed renaming of the French-speaking Community as the Federation Wallonia-Brussels (Reuchamps, Kavadias and Deschouwer 2014). So, in Wallonia, too, the debate about the future is still ongoing.

On the other hand, the *socioeconomic cleavage* is far from being unimportant. In Quebec, while the sovereignism–federalism cleavage has overshadowed the socioeconomic cleavage, and this was particularly the case in the 1980s and 1990s (Pelletier 2012), a left–right opposition has also shaped the competition between parties, as was especially evident in the 2000s. Indeed, an expert survey carried out in 2007 showed the ADQ to be on the right, the PLQ in the centre-right and the PQ in the centre-left (Collette and Pétry 2012: 115–16), with the PQ being more in favour of welfare-state-oriented policies and the PLQ more prone to neoliberal policies. In Wallonia, the socioeconomic cleavage is also important, even more so than the identity cleavage. In favour of large-scale state intervention, the main political actor – the PS – is a social-democratic party, positioned on the left of the political Walloon landscape, along with smaller extreme-left parties such as the PTB (*Parti des travailleurs de Belgique*). The liberal MR is located on the right, with a programme in favour of entrepreneurs and business and, above all, less state intervention. Between these two main parties, the cdH and Ecolo are usually seen to be in the centre – centre-right for the Christian democrats and centre-left for the ecologists. On the far right, there are several parties such as the FN (*Front national*) and the FNB (*Front nouveau de Belgique*) with an anti-immigration and anti-system platform.

Above all, both in Quebec and in Wallonia, it can be observed that these two cleavages interact with each other and are in fact quite intertwined, especially on the question at the core of this chapter: the future of their region. It is for this reason that the position of each party regarding these two important cleavages needs to be understood – because each party engenders a specific vision of their region. Moreover, the potential prominence of one cleavage over the other also asserts a particular perception of each region. It is for this reason that attention needs to be paid to how political parties view their region, as demonstrated through their political manifestos.

3 Data and methods

Political parties have a chief role in structuring politics because they hold a quasi-monopoly of representation in parliament. In fact, in Quebec and in

Wallonia, there are very few independents, except for those who leave their party during a legislative session (Pelletier 2012). A political party's manifesto is the masterpiece of the party's structuring role. In this study, we focus on political-party manifestos for several reasons. First, the manifesto is the document par excellence that states the official position of any party at each election. It has therefore both an external function – to inform the electorate as well as the other political actors of the position of a given party – and an internal function – to ensure that the candidates and also the rank and file of a given party rally around the same position. Indeed, it is quite usual for the majority of party members to be required to formally approve the political manifesto of their party (Dandoy 2012b: 12). Electoral programmes are often considered as a valid indicator of a political party's position at a given moment (Volkens 2002) and, above all, as the most comprehensive expression of salience, policy preference and reasoning of a party (Budge *et al.* 2001; Morsink and Sinardet 2011: 3).

Of course, one should be aware that political manifestos do not reflect the entire nature of a given political party and its members, not even at election time, considering that political campaigning demands a constant adaptation to events and thus to interactions with other political actors. This might thus force a political party to adapt or to adopt a stance different from the one stated in its political manifesto. Furthermore, as Morsink and Sinardet state:

> [I]t wouldn't come as a surprise to see parties or candidates take more extreme positions in electoral propaganda or televised debates than those written in their electoral manifesto, as these [the political manifestos] are compromises of different factions within a party.
>
> (Morsink and Sinardet 2011: 3)

Nonetheless, this "mean" position of a party, given by its political manifesto, is of interest for our study, which seeks to compare the position of political parties regarding their region. In fact, when one aims at comparing the views of political parties, it is rather difficult to do so using "hot" political discourses; for instance, on the political discourses given in political debates or in the media because the issues may be addressed in a very different linguistic manner (timing and/or framing) by the actors to be comparable. By contrast, political manifestos, which are "cold" political discourses, are more easily comparable because each political party undertakes the same exercise (they may well do it differently, but then it is also possible and interesting to study these differences). What is more, in Quebec, studies have demonstrated that political parties in government tend to keep their electoral promises: 75% for the PQ and 70% for the PLQ (Pétry 2002; Pétry and Collette 2006). This is much more difficult to verify in Wallonia where the presence of coalitions in government blurs the responsibilities of each partner.

In this study, we analyse the political manifestos of the main parties in Quebec and in Wallonia, namely the ADQ, the PLQ, the PQ and the CAQ for

Quebec, and the cdH, the Ecolo, the MR and the PS for Wallonia. We analyse the manifestos of these parties for each election since 1994 in Quebec and
since 1995 in Wallonia, which amounts to an overall corpus of more than two
million words. In this chapter, we focus mainly on the first and last elections in
both regions. The manifestos were all initially written in French, which makes
the comparison easier; some of them also exist in another language such as
English. These manifestos are compared synchronically and diachronically.
All analyses are performed with the software Wordsmith tools version 6.0,
which allows quantitative and qualitative analysis. This software helps to
systematise and control the identification of representations in the texts through
wordlists and analysis of concordance. It therefore enables a more systematic
and transparent reading of the texts, instead of a mere interpretation. The
analysis is performed in three steps.

First, the most employed lemmas – that is the canonical form or dictionary
form of various forms of the same word – are identified and counted in absolute
terms (i.e. their frequency) and in relative terms (i.e. their percentage within
the manifesto, so as to enable the comparison between manifestos). In this
initial step, lemmas relating to the identity cleavage are highlighted. From this
preliminary analysis, both the nature of the words and their frequency can
already provide insights into a political party's stance. The second step builds
on this analysis and looks for the concordance between the most frequently
used terms, especially those that characterise the vision of the region, in order
to identify the domains used to conceptualise Quebec and Wallonia. The third
and final step takes a qualitative approach to these conceptualisations – what
we refer to as conceptual metaphors – in order to offer a comprehensive
appraisal of how each political party views its own region and its future.

4 Analysis of political manifestos in Quebec

Table 3.3 and Table 3.4 present the top 20 most frequently used lemmas in the
manifestos of the ADQ, PLQ and PQ in 1994 and of the CAQ, PLQ and PQ
in 2014, respectively.[2] A first look at the political manifestos in Quebec reveals
that "*Québec/Québécois**" are the most frequently used lemmas across parties
and across elections. These occur in various forms, such as a place of power ("*le
gouvernement québécois*", "*le Québec*"), a location ("*au Québec*"), a proper
noun or an adjective ("*Université du Québec*", "*Hydro-Québec*") or as part of
the name of a party (*Action démocratique du Québec, Parti libéral du Québec,
Parti Québécois, Coalition Avenir Québec*).[3]

Three main findings come out of our analysis of the political manifestos in
Quebec. First, there is confirmation of the shift from the identity cleavage to
the socioeconomic cleavage. Second, the identity cleavage is shown not to have
disappeared from the political debate, but to have evolved in several ways.
Third, competing political metaphors concerning Quebec politics can be seen
to derive from the political manifestos depending on the party's position, i.e.
whether in government or in opposition.

Table 3.3 Most frequently used lemmas in political manifestos in Quebec (1994)

#	ADQ 1994 Lemma	Freq.	%	PLQ 1994 Lemma	Freq.	%	PQ 1994 Lemma	Freq.	%
1	QUÉBEC	156	0.84	QUÉBEC	169	0.71	QUÉBEC	238	1.17
2	DÉVELOPPEMENT	112	0.61	QUÉBÉCOIS*	131	0.55	QUÉBÉCOIS*	158	0.78
3	ENTREPRISE*	80	0.44	GOUVERNEMENT*	127	0.54	GOUVERNEMENT*	144	0.71
4	PROPOSITION	66	0.36	DÉVELOPPEMENT	90	0.38	PARTI	101	0.50
5	QUÉBÉCOIS*	65	0.35	LIBÉRAL	90	0.38	DÉVELOPPEMENT	94	0.47
6	ETAT	63	0.34	EMPLOI*	89	0.37	ÉCONOMIQUE*	67	0.33
7	GOUVERNEMENT	60	0.33	ENTREPRISE*	88	0.37	SOCIAL*-AUX	66	0.33
8	CITOYEN*	58	0.26	SOCIÉTÉ*	81	0.34	POLITIQUE	61	0.29
9	PUBLIC*-QUE*	58	0.31	ÉCONOMIQUE*	80	0.34	SOCIÉTÉ*	60	0.29
10	ÉCONOMIQUE	55	0.29	SERVICE*	80	0.34	ENTREPRISE*	56	0.28
11	POLITIQUE*	55	0.30	FORMATION	70	0.30	SERVICE*	56	0.28
12	RÉGION*	45	0.24	POLITIQUE*	62	0.26	EMPLOI	46	0.22
13	SERVICE*	43	0.23	ETAT	58	0.25	DROIT*	44	0.22
14	ACTION	39	0.21	SYSTÈME*	58	0.25	PROGRAMME	41	0.20
15	DÉMOCRATIQUE	37	0.20	TRAVAIL	54	0.23	SOUVERAINETÉ	39	0.19
16	ŒUVRE	34	0.18	SANTÉ	50	0.21	PUBLIC*-QUE*	39	0.19
17	POPULATION	33	0.18	PLQ	49	0.21	FORMATION	36	0.18
18	SOCIÉTÉ	31	0.17	ÉDUCATION	43	0.18	LIBÉRAL	35	0.17
19	QUALITÉ	29	0.16	PUBLIC*-QUE*	43	0.18	ACTION*	34	0.17
20	ANNÉE*	28	0.15	JEUNE*	42	0.18	ÉDUCATION	34	0.17
19	STRATÉGIE*	28	0.15	OBJECTIF*	41	0.18	SANTÉ	34	0,17
20	PARTI	24	0.13	PARTI	39	0.17	LANGUE	31	0.15
	SOUVERAINETÉ	6	0.03	SOUVERAINETÉ	1	<0.01	SOUVERAINETÉ	39	0.19
	SOUVERAIN*	1	<0.01	SOUVERAIN*	2	<0.01	SOUVERAIN*	8	0.03
	AUTONOMIE	1	<0.01	AUTONOMIE	8	0.03	AUTONOMIE	9	0.04
	AUTONOM*	1	<0.01	AUTONOM*	5	0.02	AUTONOM*	6	0.29
	NATION	6	0.03	NATION	0	0	NATION	3	0.01
	NATIONAL*-AUX	18	0.09	NATIONAL*-AUX	9	0.03	NATIONAL*-AUX	22	0.10

Table 3.4 Most frequently used lemmas in political manifestos in Quebec (2014)

	CAQ 2014			PLQ 2014			PQ 2014		
	Lemma	Freq.	%	Lemma	Freq.	%	Lemma	Freq.	%
1	QUÉBEC	178	1.60	QUÉBEC	236	1.12	QUÉBÉCOIS*	69	0.96
2	GOUVERNEMENT*	69	0.62	LIBÉRAL	197	0.93	QUÉBEC	66	0.92
3	AVENIR	61	0.55	GOUVERNEMENT	160	0.76	DÉTERMINÉ*	40	0.55
4	COALITION	60	0.54	PARTI	115	0.55	PARTI	36	0.50
5	QUÉBÉCOIS*	50	0.46	PLAN	78	0.37	DÉVELOPPEMENT	33	0.46
6	SANTÉ	47	0.42	ENTREPRISE	77	0.36	POLITIQUE*	32	0.43
7	CONTRIBUABLE*	44	0.40	QUÉBÉCOIS	75	0.35	RÉGION*	31	0.43
8	QUALITÉ	37	0.33	DÉVELOPPEMENT	72	0.34	NOUVEAU*/NOUVEL*	30	0.42
9	SERVICE*	36	0.33	ÉCONOMIQUE	67	0.32	SERVICE*	28	0.39
10	SAINT-LAURENT	34	0.31	PROJET	66	0.31	ACCÈS	26	0.36
11	FAMILLE*	32	0.28	SERVICE	61	0.29	LOI	24	0.33
12	SCOLAIRE*	26	0.24	ÉCONOMIE	59	0.28	PERSONNE*	24	0.34
13	SOINS	25	0.22	SANTÉ	59	0.28	ENTREPRISES	22	0.31
14	PROJET*	24	0.22	MONTRÉAL	50	0.24	ÉCONOMIQUE*	19	0.27
15	INNOVATION	22	0.20	INVESTISSEMENT	50	0.24	EMPLOI*	19	0.27
16	RESSOURCES	21	0.19	INFRASTRUCTURE	49	0.24	ACTION*	17	0.24
17	FISCAL	20	0.18	PROGRAMME	49	0.23	NATIONAL*	17	0.24
18	RÉSEAU	18	0.16	FAMILLE	40	0.19	PLACE	16	0.22
19	ENFANTS	18	0.16	EMPLOI	39	0.19	GOUVERNEMENT	15	0.21
20	ENTREPRISES	17	0.15	MESURE	38	0.18	PLAN	15	0.21
	SOUVERAINETÉ	0	0	SOUVERAINETÉ	0	0	SOUVERAINETÉ	6	0.08
	SOUVERAIN*	0	0	SOUVERAIN	0	0	SOUVERAIN*	1	0.01
	AUTONOMIE	3	0.03	AUTONOMIE	7	0.03	AUTONOMIE	5	0.07
	AUTONOM*	1	<0.01	AUTONOM*	1	<0.01	AUTONOM*	0	0
	NATION	2	0.02	NATION	0	0	NATION	5	0.07
	NATIONAL*-AUX	1	<0.01	NATIONAL*-AUX	4	0.02	NATIONAL*-AUX	17	0.24

4.1 The socioeconomic shift

As already mentioned, two main cleavages have shaped politics in Quebec: the identity cleavage (federalism versus sovereignty) and the socioeconomic cleavage (support for welfare state policies versus neoliberal policies). Over the last 20 years, the political dynamics have experienced a socioeconomic shift. In 1994, in the wake of the failure of the Lake Meech and Charlottetown accords, the debate over the sovereignty of Quebec was very heated. The prominence of the lemmas "*souveraineté/souverain**" (sovereignty/sovereign*) in the PQ manifesto (1994) clearly demonstrates the party's position in favour of independence, a stance that would lead to the organisation of the 1995 referendum. In contrast, these word forms appear only once in the PLQ 1994 manifesto, and here they have a negative sense. One can observe that the liberals were adopting a strategy of *évitement* (avoidance) rather than direct confrontation. Furthermore, the occurrence of "*langue*" (language) in the top 20 lemmas used in the PQ 1994 manifesto reveals the importance of this issue. The analysis of the political manifestos clearly shows that this cleavage discriminates the positions of the three main political parties at the time.

Yet, by the 2000s, the socioeconomic cleavage has increasingly gained in importance and has become the most significant concern of the political agenda (Bélanger and Nadeau 2008). The identity cleavage, meanwhile, has not disappeared but rather has evolved, as we discuss below. What is striking is the links that can be found between the two cleavages. As Changfoot and Cullen (2011) have shown, the neoliberal orientation of the federation has forced parties to strengthen their position on the socioeconomic axis. It is for this reason that Quebec separatism, as it is often called in English Canada, is now off the agenda. Moreover, the elections of 2003 and above all of 2007 marked a socioeconomic shift (Dufour 2007; Changfoot and Cullen 2011), with the liberal PLQ regaining power and, in 2007, the rightist ADQ becoming the official opposition, i.e. the second largest party, at the national assembly in Quebec city. As in 1994, the PLQ in 2012 promoted a policy of continuity by using words relating to specific policies that it implemented as the "*Plan Nord*". In the PQ 2012 manifesto, the Quebec question is still mentioned, but it is framed from a different perspective, as we discuss below. The question of whether the election of the PQ in 2012 reflected a collective will to bring the sovereignty debate back onto the agenda (Bélanger and Chhim 2012) was answered in 2014 with the victory of the PLQ. In the CAQ and the PLQ manifestos, the sovereignty debate is clearly off the agenda and socioeconomic topics come first; yet the Quebec question still remains.

4.2 The Quebec question

Even though the socioeconomic cleavage has become more predominant nowadays, the identity cleavage, or in other words, the Quebec question, has historically been central to Quebec politics and it is therefore key to understanding the evolution of the representations of Quebec in the political-party manifestos. As a result, we chose to analyse in more detail the uses over time of the lemmas "*nation/national-aux**" (nation/national*), "*autonomie/ autonom**" (autonomy/autonomous) and "*souveraineté/souverain**" (sovereignty/ sovereign*).

A general overview reveals that in the PQ manifestos the lemmas "*souveraineté/souverain**" are significantly present in 1994 (0.22%), while their number decreases in the 2000s. "*Nation/national-aux**" becomes more frequent in 2008 (0.20%). In the ADQ manifestos, the lemmas "*autonomie/ autonomy*" are almost never employed in 1994 (0.01%), but with the so-called autonomist shift of the party in 2007 and 2008 (Boily 2012), these become the third most used lemmas in their manifestos (0.26% in 2008). In 2012, a new shift occurs: the CAQ officially declared that the constitutional debate should be put aside. This trend is confirmed in 2014. The PLQ has always been reluctant to engage directly in this word fight; these lemmas rarely appear in their manifestos. But the absence of words can also reveal a specific political vision. In 2014, the PLQ clearly implies that the PQ's referendum proposal is totally impractical, while emphasising that the PLQ itself focuses on "*vraies affaires*" ("real concerns"). In order to explore this complex political and linguistic reality, the concordance of these lemmas with other linguistic expressions may uncover the broader picture behind these words.

4.2.1 Sovereignty and nation(hood)

In 1994, the qualification of Quebec as a "*nation*" is relatively scarce in the three manifestos; rather, it is used in the plural form to refer to the autochthonous nations. By contrast, the words "*souveraineté/souverain**" occur significantly frequently, especially in the PQ manifesto. As we discuss below, the conceptual metaphors used to frame this debate underline its strong position. As far as the PLQ is concerned, it makes only one reference to "sovereignty" and from a negative perspective (1, below). This is not a surprise as this party is clearly opposed to the idea of sovereignty partnership and is in favour of Canadian unity (Lemieux 2012: 251). The position of the ADQ (1994) regarding sovereignty is ambiguous; it does not really define what kind of relationship it proposes with the Canadian federation (2). On the one hand, like the PQ, the ADQ promises to hold a referendum on sovereignty, but, on the other hand, it proposes a new (undefined) union with the rest of Canada. Indeed, it is only after the elections that the ADQ really clarifies its position and its desire to create a confederation between Quebec and the rest of Canada (Boily 2012).

> (1) *Dans ce nouveau contexte, le projet de* souveraineté, *qui entraîne le démantèlement de l'union économique canadienne, va à* contre-courant *de notre époque.*
> In this new context, the *sovereignty* project, which leads to the dismantling of the Canadian economic union, goes *against the tide* of our time.[4]
>
> (PLQ 1994: 4)

(2) *Un gouvernement de l'Action démocratique tiendra un référendum sur la* souveraineté, *en proposant* une nouvelle union au reste du Canada, *dans un esprit d'ouverture et de cooperation.*

An ADQ government will hold a referendum on the *sovereignty* issue and propose *a new union with the rest of Canada*, in a spirit of openness and cooperation.

(ADQ 1994: 3)

By the 2000s, the situation has evolved: use of the word *"nation"* in relation to Quebec becomes more common than *"souveraineté/souverain*"*, especially in the PQ 2008 manifesto and to a certain extent in the ADQ manifesto (2008). This prominence seems to reflect the adoption two years earlier by the Canadian House of Commons of the motion recognising that "[t]he Québécois form a nation within a united Canada", in the wake of the *"fédéralisme d'ouverture"* promised by the conservative prime minister Stephen Harper (Montpetit 2007). The position of the PQ in relation to the Quebec question is especially worth investigating over time.

In 2008, the PQ modifies its strategy: it focuses on the defence of the interests of the *nation* of Quebec rather than on *sovereignty*. It has learned from the events of 2007, and it has adapted its discourse to the expectations of its electorate (Bélanger 2008, 2009). Thus, the electoral resurgence of the PQ in 2008 (and then again in 2012) does not reflect the party's renewed support of sovereignty, as the PQ moderates its position on this very topic (Boily 2012: 307). What is striking in both 2012 and 2014 is the overall decrease in the use of the lemmas relating to the identity cleavage in the party's manifestos. At the same time, these lemmas also become associated with different topics. For instance, until that time, all occurrences of *"souveraineté/souverain*"* are associated with the Quebec question, but in 2012 and 2014 they begin to be used to refer to other issues, especially regarding food sovereignty (three occurrences out of six in 2012 and three out of seven in 2014). As Pétry and Birch (2014) demonstrate, the part of the PQ manifestos relating to the question of identity cleavage has remained stable since 1976. However, as shown in Table 3.5, fewer words are used directly in relation to this question. Above all, in 2012 and with the use of the same words in 2014, the PQ has not abandoned the sovereignty question. More

Table 3.5 Use of the lemmas "nation" and "souveraineté/souverain" in the PQ political manifestos in Quebec (1994–2014)

	1994		1998		2003		2007		2008		2012		2014	
	Freq.	%	Freq.	%	Freq.	%	Freq.	%	Freq.	%	Freq.	%	Freq.	%
Nation	3	0.01	1	<0.01	9	0.03	6	0.06	19	0.20	5	0.09	5	0.07
Souveraineté	47	0.22	19	0.07	18	0.06	11	0.11	3	0.03	5	0.09	6	0.08
Souverain	8	0.03	14	0.04	32	0.12	7	0.07	5	0.08	1	0.02	1	0.01

than ever before, it is addressing sovereignty in an indirect way and with a long-term perspective (3).

(3) *Réaliser la* souveraineté *du Québec à la suite d'une consultation de la population par référendum tenu* au moment qu'il jugera approprié.

Realising the *sovereignty* of Quebec as the result of the consultation of the population by referendum, *at the time the party deems appropriate*.

(PQ 2012: 8, 2014: 6)

4.2.2 Autonomy

The lemmas *"autonomie/autonome*"* are also worth mentioning, especially for the 2007 and 2008 elections (Table 3.6). Indeed, they are largely absent from the manifestos in the 1990s. In 1994, there are very few occurrences in the PLQ manifestos relating to the autonomy of Quebec. In other cases, they are used to refer to the autonomy of First Nations or to public policy inside Quebec. By contrast, these lemmas occur more significantly ten years later, especially in the political manifestos of the ADQ (2008).

The topic of autonomy appears in 2007 when the ADQ proposed an alternative to the sovereignty project of the PQ. This trend is confirmed in 2008. A qualitative exploration shows that these lemmas refer not only to the identity cleavage but also – and even more so – to the socioeconomic cleavage (for instance, in relation to the autonomy of schools, municipalities, regions, hospitals, workers, etc.). In fact, the ADQ considers autonomy as the basis not only for managing its relationship with the federal state but also for organising all relationships inside Quebec itself (4). This is called *"le nouveau modèle autonomiste québécois"*, the new autonomist Quebec model.

(4) *Contrairement à l'option fédéraliste, qui consiste à accepter le statu quo, et à l'option souverainiste, qui prône l'indépendance du* Québec *à tout prix, l'ADQ suggère que le* Québec *adopte une vision* autonomiste.

Contrary to the federalist option, which consists of accepting the status quo, and to the sovereignist option, advocating the independence of *Quebec* at all costs, the ADQ proposes that *Quebec* should adopt an *autonomist* vision.

(ADQ 2008: 17)

Table 3.6 Use of the lemma "autonomie/autonome" in the ADQ/CAQ political manifestos (1994–2014) in Quebec

	1994 (ADQ)		1998 (ADQ)		2003 (ADQ)		2007 (ADQ)		2008 (ADQ)		2012 (CAQ)		2014 (CAQ)	
	Freq.	%	Freq.	%	Freq.	%	Freq.	%	Freq.	%	Freq.	%	Freq.	%
Identity	0	0	1	0.02	3	0.01	25	0.24	49	0.11	0	0	0	0
Other topics	2	0.01	5	0.08	20	0.07	21	0.20	72	0.15	10	0.1	4	0.04
Total	2	0.01	6	0.10	23	0.08	46	0.44	121	0.26	10	0.1	4	0.04

In 2012, the socioeconomic shift has been clearly confirmed as the CAQ considers the debate on sovereignty to be a disease paralysing Quebec (5). In 2014, the party's constitutional position follows this statement by stating that Quebec should always come first (*"Le Québec d'abord"*).

> (5) *La division entre fédéralistes et souverainistes nous [les Québécois] paralyse. Pour que le Québec se remette véritablement à avancer, il nous faut mettre le débat constitutionnel de côté.*
>
>   The division between federalists and sovereignists is *paralysing* us [the Quebec people]. In order for Quebec to really move forward again, we have to *put the constitutional debate aside.*
>
> (CAQ 2012: 8)

In conclusion, our analyses of the use of the words relating to the identity cleavage have highlighted the evolution of perceptions of the status of Quebec. The PQ strongly defended sovereignty in 1994, while in 2008 it turned the focus of its discourse to the nation of Quebec. After an ambiguous position in the 1990s, the ADQ took its position in this debate with an alternative centred on autonomy as a way to defend the interest of Quebec's economy and identity. In the case of the PLQ, the quasi-absence or the negative use of these lemmas confirmed the party's stance on the Quebec question; that is, its support for a strong Quebec within a united Canada. More recently, the 2012 elections showed that the Quebec question has clearly been reshaped. The PLQ has continued to avoid this issue in its manifestos, stating that this debate would represent a pathway to division; the CAQ has officially excluded the issue from its manifesto, while the PQ has framed it in a more indirect way. This trend was confirmed in 2014. The lexicometric approach taken here has enabled us to detect relevant shifts in the position of the political parties vis-à-vis their region.

4.3 Quebec in metaphors

The final step of our analysis is to go beyond the words and try to capture the conceptual representations that they bring about. In other words, we seek to capture Quebec – the target domain – through the dominant source domains of the conceptual metaphors. The most prominent domain in the political manifestos is the conceptual metaphor: *Quebec is a building*. The instantiation of this conceptual metaphor can be identified through the presence of specific words, for instance *"bâtir"* (to build). Different aspects of the Quebec *building* – its strength, its foundations and its design – also emerge. In 1994, the PLQ – in power since 1985 – states that *Quebec is a solid building* on which one can continue to build. Such a conceptual metaphor conveys two political meanings: on the one hand, it emphasises the achievements of the liberal governments since 1985 (6) and, on the other hand, it stresses the decisive role of the Canadian federation for Quebec and of Quebec for the Canadian federation (7). This conceptual metaphor is used by the PLQ to convey an optimistic scenario of the lasting and well-structured foundations of Quebec *building*.

(6) *Le Parti libéral du Québec s'engage à* bâtir *sur ces* acquis.
The Quebec Liberal Party promises to *build* on these *achievements*.
(PLQ 1994: 52)

(7) *Notre conviction profonde est que l'orientation libérale sur la place du Québec au sein de l'ensemble canadien, inspirée d'une philosophie d'ouverture et de coopération, constitue* une assise.
Our profound conviction is that the liberal orientation on the question of Quebec's place within the Canadian whole, inspired by a philosophy of openness and cooperation, constitutes a *foundation*.
(PLQ 1994: 11)

For the same elections, the ADQ (1994) also employs this source domain but from a negative perspective; it states that *Quebec is not yet a solid building*. Quebec is rather seen as a *problematic building*; the *foundations* that should support the entire *structure* do not yet exist (8). The ADQ proposes to *build* them.

(8) [R]edonner *un nouvel élan* au Québec sur *des bases solides, qui soient nécessaires de redonner le goût de* bâtir *à la population.*
[T]o give Quebec a fresh impetus *based on a solid foundation*, which is necessary to restore the population's taste for *building*.
(ADQ 1994: 4)

By comparison, the PQ (1994) – the official opposition at that time – describes the Quebec situation in terms of *war* rather than in terms of *building*. As we have already noted, the issue of sovereignty is fundamental in the PQ manifesto. The manifesto frames change in this domain by referring to "*l'acte de naissance du Québec*" ("birth certificate of Quebec") (9), while the existing status quo is seen as representing "*reddition*" ("surrender") (10). The use of this assertive metaphor is a way to give a valid justification for the PQ's strong opposition to the current situation. This metaphor contributes to the creation of the cognitive foundations necessary to legitimate the party's position regarding the Quebec question.

(9) *Le Parti Québécois entend procéder à la réalisation de la* souveraineté *de la façon suivante: le référendum sera* l'acte de naissance du Québec souverain.
The Quebec Party intends to proceed towards the achievement of *sovereignty* in the following way: the referendum will be the *birth certificate* of *sovereign Quebec*.
(PQ 1994: 17)

(10) Le statu quo *est non seulement dénoncé par l'ensemble du* Québec, *mais c'est aussi une illusion qui cache des* reculs *qui consacreraient* une reddition *totale et sans condition du* Québec.

The status quo has not only been denounced by the whole of *Quebec*, but it is also an illusion hiding a *step backwards*, which would sanction the total and conditionless *surrender* of *Quebec*.

(PQ 1994: 14)

In the early 2000s, the political context seems less conflict ridden than in the 1990s around the question of Quebec's future. However, political manifestos, and thus political competition, return to politics as usual where the majority–opposition dynamic shapes policy. The PLQ, which governed Quebec between 2003 and 2012, has a discourse of continuity, while the PQ and the ADQ – harshly – criticise the record of the incumbent government in relation to the Quebec question. In 2014, the PQ has been governing Quebec for two years, while the PLQ and CAQ have been in opposition. The conceptual metaphor *Quebec is a building* is still frequently being used by the political parties. As in 1994, the PLQ (2007) is using the metaphor to defend its results and its political project (11). Similarly, in the PLQ manifesto of 2012, Quebec's future is framed as a *path/journey* (12). Through this metaphor, progress is seen as a movement forward. The PLQ states its ability to remove all the obstacles on the path to full employment, i.e. the final *destination* of the *journey* it proposes. It should also be mentioned that metaphors are less numerous in the manifestos of the incumbent government than in those of the other parties. In 2014, the PLQ forms the official opposition. It uses metaphorical expressions only when it refers to the target domain of Quebec's economy. It frames the economy as *a means of transport* that has *broken down* (13). The use of this source domain contributes to the creation of the cognitive foundations necessary for placing emphasis on the significance of the economic situation and on the ability of the PLQ to "*redémarrer*" ("restart") the economy.

(11) *Avec ces mesures, nous continuerons à* bâtir *un Québec pour tous.*
    With these measures, we shall continue to *building* a Quebec for everyone.

(PLQ 2007: 39)

(12) *[N]otre formation politique a toujours su ouvrir de* nouvelles voies *d'avenir pour incarner l'ambition des Québécois et assurer le développement économique de notre nation.*
    [O]ur political party has always been able to open up *new avenues* for the future in order to embody the ambition of the Quebec people and to ensure the economic development of our nation.

(PLQ 2012: 2)

(13) L'économie du Québec est *maintenant en panne.*
    Quebec's economy has *broken down.*

(PLQ 2014: 1–2)

Meanwhile, the ADQ and then the CAQ use similar metaphors but in order to stress the need for change. The Quebec *building* is still considered as being *fragile* and in need of reconstruction (14). In 2012 and also in 2014, the CAQ frames Quebec *as a means of transport* that has almost *broken down* (15). The party therefore offers major modifications to its *journey map* (16). In addition, it frequently uses verbs relating to the domain of *war*, such as *"abolir"* (to abolish)/ *"attaquer"* (to attack)/*"éliminer"* (to eliminate) to frame the importance and the necessity of these changes. Through all these conceptual metaphors, the CAQ frames the situation of Quebec in such a way as to justify the need for deep changes. It attempts to demonstrate that other parties are not able to play such a role; the CAQ is the only party that is able to embody change in Quebec.

(14) Reconstruire *[le Québec], c'est la mission même de la voix autonomiste.*
    Rebuilding [Quebec], this is the very mission of the autonomist voice.

(ADQ 2008: 3)

(15) Plusieurs voyants rouges sont allumés sur le tableau de bord *[du Québec]: manque d'investissements privés, décrochage élevé.*
    Several [of Quebec's] dashboard warning lights are on: lack of private investment, high levels of disengagement.

(CAQ 2012: 67)

(16) *Un* coup de barre *s'impose.*
    A *change of direction* is absolutely necessary.

(CAQ 2014: 3)

The PQ frames Quebec in terms of change but the *building* domain is hardly ever used, except once in 2014 when the party is the incumbent government (17). Thus, as we can see, the conceptual metaphor *Quebec is a building* has recently been used more by governing parties, while the *journey* metaphor can be traced back to the parties in opposition. In 2008, the PQ has been in opposition for five years. For them, Quebec is in a *turbulent maritime journey*, Quebec is a *boat in a storm* and a change of direction is needed (18). In 2012, in the same way as the CAQ, the PQ states that the *journey* towards a better destination has been blocked by the actions of the PLQ government during the last nine years (19). It is also the metaphor of a *journey* that is used to frame the issue of sovereignty. As already mentioned, while this question was initially framed in terms of war, the issue is now mostly addressed indirectly, even though the PQ's position in favour of sovereignty is still strong. The sovereignty project remains the *final destination* of the *journey* proposed by the PQ, but it appears to be a *distant destination*, as illustrated in (3) above.

(17) *Nous mettons tout en place pour* bâtir *un Québec plus fort.*
    We are putting everything in place to *build* a stronger Quebec.

(PQ 2014: 5)

(18) Il faut protéger l'équipage et le navire [le Québec] durant la tempête. ... *Il faut comprendre que le temps est venu de* donner un coup de barre.
The crew and the ship [Quebec] must be protected during the storm. ... It has to be understood that the time has come to *change course.*

(PQ 2008: 4)

(19) Le Québec fait du surplace *depuis neuf ans.*
Quebec has been *stuck* for nine years.

(PQ 2012: 3)

Political parties speak about Quebec in several different ways. Yet our empirical analysis confirms insights gained from other studies that *states* are generally conceptualised through four main source domains: *building, machines, plants* and *the human body* (Kovecses 2010). Secondly, conceptual metaphors are present in all the Quebec manifestos. As stated by Charteris-Black: "[m]etaphors are very effective in the communication of policy because they provide cognitively accessible ways of communicating political policy" (2009: 109). Nonetheless, the political situation of each party, especially according to whether it is in government or in opposition, clearly induces the presence of particular conceptual metaphors in their manifestos. While the *building* and the *path/journey* domains are used by both sides in a positive or a negative way, the *war/machine/means of transport* domains are mainly identified in the manifestos of the opposition from 1994 to 2012 (ADQ/CAQ and PQ) and in 2014 (PLQ and CAQ). Overall, it is worth mentioning that metaphors are less numerous in the manifestos of the incumbent government than in those of the other parties. The incumbent party relies more on its own achievements, whereas the opposition parties feel the need to capture the attention of the voters with metaphors that negatively depict the actions of the government.

5 Analysis of political manifestos in Wallonia

A first look at the political manifestos of Wallonia for the period 1995–2009 shows an interesting contrast with the ones of Quebec (Tables 3.7 and 3.8 give the top 20 most frequently used lemmas in the Walloon manifestos for the 1995 elections and the 2014 elections, respectively). Whereas in the 2014 elections in Quebec, the lemma "*Québec**" is the one most frequently used across parties and across time, in the Walloon 1995 elections, the lemma "*Wallon**" scores very differently across parties and across time. One of the reasons for this relates to the names of the parties in competition: in Quebec, all the parties use Quebec in their name, whereas in Wallonia, the parties never use the word *Wallon* in this way. But besides this linguistic difference, there is a political difference in the representation of their respective region by the political parties. This is what we aim to examine in this section on Wallonia.

Table 3.7 Most frequently used lemmas in political manifestos in Wallonia (1995)

	PSC 1995 (becomes cdH)			ECOLO 1995			PRL-FDF 1995 (becomes MR)			PS 1995		
	Lemma	Freq.	%	Lemma	Freq.	%	Lemma	Freq.	%	Lemma	Freq.	%
1	PSC	145	0.72	SOCIAL	37	0.53	WALLON/IE	49	1.68	POLITIQUE	282	0.58
2	SOCIAL	107	0.53	POLITIQUE	24	0.35	REGION	23	0.79	SOCIAL	270	0.55
3	POLITIQUE	86	0.43	QUALITÉ	23	0.33	EMPLOI	15	0.51	SERVICE	203	0.41
4	ENSEIGNEMENT	66	0.33	LOGEMENT	22	0.32	FDF	13	0.44	PUBLIC	155	0.32
5	SERVICE	60	0.3	ECOLO	19	0.27	PRL	13	0.44	SOCIALISTE	155	0.32
6	DEVELOPPEMENT	52	0.26	TRAVAIL	18	0.26	AIDE	12	0.41	EMPLOI	151	0.31
7	SOCIETE	47	0.23	VIE	18	0.26	SOCIAL	12	0.41	BRUXELLOIS/ES	138	0.28
8	EUROP*	47	0.23	ÉNERGIE	17	0.25	ENTREPRISE	11	0.38	DEVELOPPEMENT	135	0.28
9	ETAT	44	0.22	ENVIRONNEMENT	17	0.25	POLITIQUE	11	0.38	WALLON/IE	129	0.26
10	CITOYEN	40	0.2	MOYEN	16	0.23	LOGEMENT	10	0.34	REGION	121	0.25
11	FORMATION	35	0.17	BESOIN	14	0.2	DÉVELOPPER	9	0.31	MATIERE	113	0.23
12	PERSONNES	34	0.17	SANTÉ	13	0.19	PERSONNES	9	0.31	MOYEN	97	0.2
13	RENFORCER	34	0.17	DÉCHETS	12	0.17	RECHERCHE	9	0.31	FORMATION	88	0.18
14	SECURITE	33	0.16	NUCLÉAIRE	12	0.17	PUBLIC	8	0.27	SOLIDARITE	86	0.18
15	FAMILLE	33	0.16	OBJECTIF	12	0.17	EUROPÉEN/E	7	0.24	PERSONNES	84	0.17
16	REGION	32	0.16	PROPOSITION	12	0.17	INVESTISSEMENT	7	0.24	SOCIAL	84	0.17
17	TRAVAIL	30	0.15	SOCIÉTÉ	12	0.17	PLACE	7	0.24	EUROPÉEN/E	81	0.17
18	BELG*	30	0.15	BIEN	11	0.16	RENFORCER	7	0.24	PS	81	0.17
19	FINANCEMENT	28	0.14	CHÔMAGE	11	0.16	ANNÉE	6	0.21	SANTE	79	0.16
20	JUSTICE	28	0.14	EFFET	11	0.16	SECTEUR	6	0.21	SECURITE	74	0.15
	BELG*	30	0.15	BELG*	2	0.03	BELG*	4	0.14	BELG*	26	0.03
	BRUXELL*	16	0.08	BRUXELL*	0	0	BRUXELL*	1	0.03	BRUXELL*	138	0.28
	COMMUNAUTE	18	0.09	COMMUNAUTE/	5	0.07	COMMUNAUTE/	3	0.1	COMMUNAUTE/	40	0.08
	EUROP*	47	0.23	EUROP*	5	0.07	EUROP*	7	0.24	EUROP*	81	0.17
	FEDERA*	13	0.06	FEDERA*	5	0.07	FEDERA*	2	0.07	FEDERA*	43	0.06
	FLANDRE/FLAMAND*	2	0.01	FLANDRE/FLAMAND*	1	0.01	FLANDRE/FLAMAND*	5	0.17	FLANDRE/FLAMAND*	6	0.01
	FRANCOPHONE*	12	0.06	FRANCOPHONE*	0	0	FRANCOPHONE*	3	0.1	FRANCOPHONE*	33	0.05
	GERMANOPHONE*	0	0	GERMANOPHONE*	0	0	GERMANOPHONE*	0	0	GERMANOPHONE*	2	0
	WALLON*	27	0.13	WALLON*	0	0	WALLON*	49	1.68	WALLON*	129	0.26

Table 3.8 Most frequently used lemmas in political manifestos in Wallonia (2014)

	cdH 2014			ECOLO 2014			MR 2014			PS 2014		
	Lemma	Freq.	%	Lemma	Freq.	%	Lemma	Freq.	%	Lemma	Freq.	%
1	cdH	986	0.57	ECOLO	3214	0.78	WALLON*	493	0.47	PS	1215	0.66
2	PROPOSITION	767	0.45	DEVOIR (VERB)	2021	0.49	DEVOIR (VERB)	437	0.42	SOCIALE	754	0.41
3	DEVOIR	664	0.39	PROPOSITION	1445	0.35	PUBLIC	286	0.27	DEVOIR (VERB)	672	0.36
4	EUROP*	609	0.35	PUBLIC	1384	0.34	POUVOIR (VERB)	255	0.24	PUBLIC	661	0.36
5	SERVICE	506	0.29	SOCIAL	1304	0.32	FAIRE	231	0.22	PROPOSER	600	0.33
6	PROPOSER	493	0.29	POLITIQUE	1202	0.29	SECTEUR	206	0.20	SERVICE	578	0.31
7	RENFORCER	438	0.25	EUROP*	1064	0.26	SOCIAL	204	0.20	ENTREPRISE	524	0.28
8	PUBLIC	411	0.24	CHAPITRE	1029	0.25	PERMETTRE	203	0.19	EUROP*	504	0.27
9	EMPLOI	405	0.23	PERMETTRE	1028	0.25	MR	200	0.19	EMPLOI	498	0.27
10	FORMATION	368	0.21	SERVICES	947	0.23	EMPLOI	195	0.19	FORMATION	482	0.26
11	ENTREPRISE	362	0.21	PROPOSER	882	0.22	LOGEMENT	194	0.19	PERMETTRE	462	0.25
12	ENSEIGNEMENT	331	0.19	FAIRE	861	0.21	PENSION	187	0.18	RENFORCER	455	0.25
13	ENFANT	324	0.19	DROIT	859	0.21	SERVICE	183	0.18	DÉVELOPPEMENT	430	0.23
14	PERSONNES	321	0.19	PROGRAMME	856	0.21	POLITIQUE	182	0.17	POLITIQUE	422	0.23
15	ÉCOLE	588	0.34	LIVRE	747	0.18	ENTREPRISES	180	0.17	ENSEIGNEMENT	355	0.19
16	VIE	306	0.18	PERSONNES	722	0.18	EUROP*	174	0.17	WALLON*	352	0.19
17	DÉVELOPPEMENT	301	0.17	BELG*	713	0.17	RÉGION	173	0.17	NIVEAU	349	0.19
18	TRAVAIL	292	0.17	TRAVAIL	695	0.17	FALLOIR	172	0.16	DÉVELOPPER	335	0.18
19	BRUXELL*	283	0.16	EMPLOI	683	0.17	NIVEAU	170	0.16	SECTEUR	331	0.18
20	FAIRE	279	0.16	MATIÈRE	668	0.16	ÉCONOMIQUE	169	0.16	QUALITÉ	309	0.17
	BELG*	246	0.14	BELG*	713	0.17	BELG*	141	0.17	BELG*	196	0.11
	BRUXELL*	283	0.16	BRUXELL*	602	0.15	BRUXELL*	114	0.15	BRUXELL*	157	0.09
	COMMUNAUTE	76	0.04	COMMUNAUTE	134	0.03	COMMUNAUTE	32	0.03	COMMUNAUTE	44	0.02
	EUROP*	609	0.35	EUROP*	1064	0.26	EUROP*	174	0.17	EUROP*	504	0.27
	FEDERA*	108	0.06	FEDERA*	382	0.09	FEDERA*	90	0.09	FEDERA*	147	0.08
	FLANDRE/FLAMAND*	21	0.01	FLANDRE/FLAMAND*	72	0.02	FLANDRE/FLAMAND*	55	0.05	FLANDRE/FLAMAND*	8	0.00
	FRANCOPHONE*	20	0.01	FRANCOPHONE*	37	0.01	FRANCOPHONE*	24	0.02	FRANCOPHONE*	18	0.01
	GERMANOPHONE*	17	0.01	GERMANOPHONE*	31	0.01	GERMANOPHONE*	26	0.02	GERMANOPHONE*	15	0.01
	WALLON*	255	0.15	WALLON*	601	0.15	WALLON*	493	0.47	WALLON*	352	0.19

How do Walloon political parties perceive Wallonia? In order to disentangle this key question, we first searched for the lemma "*Wallon**" within the political-party manifestos. We then analysed the manifestos in order to capture the political dynamics before attempting to outline the conceptual metaphors used to describe Wallonia.

5.1 In search of Wallonia

In 1995, at the time of the first direct elections of the Walloon parliament, the lemma "*Wallon**" can scarcely be found in the manifestos of the political parties in Wallonia. Only the liberal MR uses the word, and in fact uses it often, as it is the most frequently used lemma (1.68%) in its political manifesto. The other three main parties show a different use of the lemma "*Wallon**". The socialist PS mentions it 129 times. However, as a percentage of the total, this frequency of usage by the PS amounts to only 0.26%, which is much less than its use of the lemmas "*politique**", "*social**", "*socialist**", "*service**", "*public**" or "*emploi**". The Christian democrat cdH uses the lemma "*Wallon**" 27 times (0.13%), which is less than its use of the lemma "*Belg**" (0.15%) and even less than the lemma "*Europ**" (0.23%). The green party Ecolo, on the other hand, simply never refers to the lemma "*Wallon**".

However, this widespread absence of the lemma "*Wallon**" in the political manifestos is not so surprising given the recent history of Wallonia. The Walloon Region, as it is officially known, was created in the 1970s but came into existence in 1980 (Reuchamps and Onclin 2009). In this initial stage, the Walloon parliament – which at the time was known as the Walloon Regional Council – was composed of French-speaking representatives elected to the national parliament, so no elections were held at the regional level until the first direct elections in 1995. Thus, the political manifestos of 1995 herald a new political era, and the relative absence of references to Wallonia may find an explanation within this new political context. In fact, 20 years later, in the elections of 2014, the lemma "*Wallon**" is much more frequently used by the political parties.

It comes in first place in the manifesto of the MR (0.47%) and in the top 20 in the manifesto of the PS (0.19%). In the manifestos of the cdH and of the Ecolo it reaches 0.15%, with several hundred occurrences. The use of lemma "*Wallon**" has thus definitely increased across the political manifestos.

The lemma "*Wallon**" is often – but not exclusively – associated with the word "*region*" so as to form the "*Région wallonne*" (Walloon Region). This term has taken a significant place in the political manifestos of the Walloon parties. This reflects an increased interest in and attention to Wallonia as a region in its own right, different from Belgium and from the other Belgian regions (Brussels-Capital and Flanders). There is now a real intra-Walloon political competition to govern the Walloon Region, with accordingly different views on Wallonia and its future. By contrast with the political dynamics in Quebec, in Wallonia the socioeconomic cleavage rather than the identity cleavage seems to shape the dynamics of the political debate. It would thus seem appropriate to examine the nature of the political manifestos of the Walloon parties where the notion of change plays a major role.

5.2 Wallonia: to change or not to change?

What is striking from the Walloon 1995 manifestos is the chief opposition between two projects for Wallonia. On the one hand, there is a discourse of continuity, especially by the socialists, who were in power at the time, along with the Christian democrats. On the other hand, there is a discourse of change, especially from the liberals, who were then in opposition. As the leading incumbent party, the PS defends its results and stresses its desire to continue its work within the Walloon government. Its project for Wallonia is based on continuity. The verbs used to emphasise this continuity are unambiguous: "*conserver*" ("keep"), "*poursuivre*" ("continue") (20) and "*consolider*" ("consolidate") (21).

> (20) *[Q]ue peut présenter le PS pour inviter* les Wallons à *lui conserver leur confiance afin de* poursuivre les politiques différentes *qui préparent la Wallonie du 3eme millénaire.*
> [T]hat the PS can put forward to invite the *Walloon people* to *maintain their confidence in it* [the party] in order to *pursue the different policies* that will prepare Wallonia for the third millennium.
>
> (PS 1995: 53)

> (21) *Socialistes* wallons *entendent* consolider *les acquis substantiels.*
> The *Walloon* socialists intend to *consolidate* their significant achievements.
>
> (PS 1995: 68)

This is in sharp contrast with the liberals' view of Wallonia: they call for a deep political change there. They claim to offer a "true Walloon project", stating their aim to change most of what has been done in the past. This critical stance regarding the actions of previous governments explains why the liberals use the lemma "*Wallon**" much more frequently than the other parties: they want to highlight the fact that Wallonia is not destined to follow the political direction set by the socialists. From this perspective, the liberals do not so much use verbs to emphasise their goal, but instead use adjectives such as "*nouveau*" ("new") (22) and "*vrai*" ("true", "real") (23).

> (22) *[U]n* nouveau souffle *pour l'Assemblée* wallonne.
> *[B]reathing new life* into the *Walloon* assembly.
>
> (PRL-FDF 1995: 11)

> (23) *[P]ropositions pour un* vrai *projet wallon.*
> [P]ropositions for a *true* Walloon project.
>
> (PRL-FDF 1995: 5)

It should be no great surprise that the dynamics of government opposition are directly reflected in the manifestos of the two main political parties, in a similar way as was observed in the mainly bipartisan Quebec. Yet, in Wallonia, this raises the question of the position of the smaller political parties within such dynamics. In this hot debate between socialists and liberals, it is rather difficult for the smaller political parties to find their way. On the one hand, the Christian democrats were previously part of the governing coalition so they are obliged, at least to some extent, to defend the results of the government. However they also need to maintain some distance, since the leading governing party during their time in office was the PS. Therefore, unsurprisingly, the cdH defends a fairly neutral discourse that favours continuity over change and which is focused on the core values of Christian democracy – family, religion and education – as can be seen in Table 3.7. On the other hand, the ecologists seem reluctant to enter into the continuity–change debate, preferring instead to defend its traditional position. Indeed, the analysis of its manifesto shows that words relating to topics such as the environment, development, waste and nuclear energy are very often used. By contrast, the larger debate about the identity cleavage is not part of its discourse. Almost no identity-loaded terms can be found in the Ecolo manifesto (Table 3.7).

Above all, the features of this first series of manifestos can also be found in the manifestos that follow (1999 and 2004). The main dynamics remain the opposition between continuity and change. And, again, given the fact that the PS has been in power during this whole period, but with different partners, these political dynamics look very much like a game of table tennis between the governing parties, on the one hand, and the opposition parties, on the other. In 2009, the liberal MR had been in opposition for five years but the political context had changed. Following the 2007 federal elections, the liberals became, for the first time ever, the leading political party in Wallonia, with 31.2% of the vote versus 29.5% for the PS. Nonetheless, the strategy of the liberals has remained the same but with an even greater emphasis: a very negative vision of Wallonia and therefore a discourse of change. Their manifesto focuses on the very bad results of the incumbent PS–cdH government, especially on economic grounds but also on political grounds. The incumbent government is described in negative terms such as *"incroyable lourdeur"* ("incredible complexity") (24) and, as a consequence, the general image of Wallonia as depicted by the MR is negative. Against this background, the only solution is a deep change, a *"revolution en profondeur"* ("a profound revolution"), in numerous sectors in order to rescue Wallonia (25). In 2014, after five years in opposition, the discourse of the MR keeps the same negative tone but with an emphasis on possible change: there is no such thing as destiny (26).

(24) Le *Gouvernement actuel est devenu un outil d'une* incroyable lourdeur.
Today's government has become an *incredibly complex* instrument.

(MR 2009: 127)

(25) *Il faut* une *révolution en profondeur dans quantité de secteurs.*
A profound revolution is needed *in a huge number of areas.*

(MR 2009: 7)

(26) *Nous ne pouvons plus nous contenter de* végéter en queue de peloton ... .
La fatalité n'existe pas.
We cannot content ourselves with *languishing at the back of the pack.* ... There is no such thing as destiny.

(MR 2014: 4)

By contrast, both in 2009 and in 2014, the discourse of the PS is much more positive and calls for a continuation of the development of the region. The party wants to build on the strengths of Wallonia, whose further development it claims to have assisted. However, in this discourse emphasising continuity, there is also room for change. And these changes should build on what has been done previously, with an emphasis on existing achievements, as suggested by the frequent use of keywords such as *"poursuivre"* ("continue") and *"approfondir"* ("deepen"), and by references to what has been achieved to date (27) (28). The cdH, the junior partner of the coalition, is also advocating change from a stance of continuity. It wants to build on the past in order to improve the future (29).

(27) *Le PS prône* une poursuite *et* un approfondissement ... *par la recherche de partenariats à* gains réciproques *et par* l'approfondissement des synergies actuelles.
The PS is advocating *a pursuit* and *a deepening* ... by seeking *"win-win"* partnerships and by *improving current synergies.*

(PS 2009 139)

(28) *Le PS entend par ailleurs* poursuivre *les efforts entrepris* ces dernières années.
The PS also intends to *pursue* the efforts already undertaken during *recent years.*

(PS 2014: 23)

(29) *Le cdH propose de* changer *l'image de la Wallonie* en poursuivant *les investissements.*
The cdH proposes to *change* the image of Wallonia *by continuing* the investments.

(cdH 2009: 300)

Ecolo, as in its previous manifestos, stands out to some extent in comparison with the other parties. It offers a fairly positive vision of Wallonia, but portrays it as a place where changes are still much needed. A lot of emphasis is still given to its traditional areas of interest: sustainable development (30), rural areas, mobility and participation, to name but a few. What can also be observed is the fact that Ecolo is no longer the sole party to defend an environmental agenda, as was the case 20 years ago. These topics are also directly addressed in the manifestos of all the other three parties. In 2014, as an incumbent government partner, Ecolo has also to defend the results of its actions while in government. As a consequence, there is a strong emphasis on the will to *"poursuivre"* ("continue") what has been achieved (31).

(30) *Nous pouvons aussi noter la création d'un nouveau cluster wallon orienté* développement durable.
We can also note the creation of a new Walloon cluster oriented towards *sustainable development*.

(Ecolo 2009: Livre/Book IV, 38)

(31) *Il est donc indispensable de* poursuivre *et amplifier les mesures prises.*
It is therefore essential to *continue* and to develop further the measures undertaken so far.

(Ecolo 2014: Livre J*ustice sociale*/Book *Social Justice*, 13)

In sum, one striking element of our analysis is that the image of Wallonia is not really a very positive one. Even for the main political party, the PS, which has been in power throughout the period of study (1994–2014), Wallonia is still in need of improvement, but this should be in line with actions that have been taken in the past. For the other three political parties, which have all been in government at one time or another, the image they portray of Wallonia is even worse, especially in the case of the MR, which criticises harshly the economic and political situation of the region. Furthermore, there is also a strong division between the socialists and the liberals, which is not so much in terms of an opposition between left and right, but rather in terms of the opposition between continuity and change.

5.3 Wallonia in metaphors

This polarisation between continuity and change has led to two main competing conceptual metaphors. On the one hand, the PS in particular uses the conceptual metaphor *Wallonia is a living environment* ("*cadre de vie*") that needs to be taken care of (32) (33). This vision is not as strong as the image of a *house*, which can often be found in political discourses (Kovecses 2010). But the flexibility of the concept of the living environment is interesting because it implies that something is already good but it could even be better. All policies aim at improving this comprehensive living environment. What is interesting is that the MR uses this image negatively, as a way to criticise the work of the incumbent government (34).

(32) *Des politiques d'amélioration durable du* cadre de vie des Wallons.
Policies aiming at the long-term improvement of the *Walloon people's living environment.*

(PS 1995: 53)

(33) *Et l'amélioration de l'attractivité et de la qualité du* cadre de vie wallon. *Des avancées importantes ont été enregistrées ces dernières années.*
And the improvement of the attractiveness and the quality of the *Walloon living environment.* Major advances have been made in recent years.

(PS 2009: 78)

(34) Le cadre de vie *des* Wallons *n'a pas été amélioré.*
The living environment of the *Walloon people* has not been improved.

(PRL-FDF 1995: 3)

Moreover, according to the socialists, this living environment should be based on solidarity. Indeed, the PS places great emphasis on the importance of solidarity both between individuals and between the substate entities; that is, between the Walloon Region and the French-speaking Community, but also between Wallonia and Brussels, and between the Walloon Region and the German-speaking Community, as well as within Europe. Of course, the PS does not have the monopoly on the promotion of solidarity. All the political parties argue for some form of solidarity, but they do so in different ways. For instance, in 2009, Ecolo also argues for solidarity between Brussels and its hinterland, but with both the Flemish and the Walloon Brabant, and thus not only with the French-speaking part of the country. This represents a different stance from the one adopted by the PS. Above all, it is clear from the manifestos that the socialists see themselves as the leading force in Wallonia. As such, it aims at *"piloter la Wallonie"* ("steering Wallonia"), a region understood as a living environment that should be shaped by their party.

On the other hand, the liberals, who over the last 20 years have been the main opponent to the socialists (they governed together for only five years), use the conceptual metaphor of illness, namely *Wallonia is ill* (35) (36). This metaphor, which is deliberate and direct, is widely used in the liberal manifestos. It relies on a personification of Wallonia, following the basic conceptual metaphor: *the state is a person* (Lakoff and Johnson 1980). In this case, the metaphor is used to criticise the work of the governing parties, and in particular the PS.

(35) *[L]a Wallonie* va-t-elle mieux?
Is Wallonia *getting better*?

(PRL-FDF 1995: 2; MR 2014: 3)

(36) *La Wallonie* pâtit structurellement.
Wallonia is *suffering structurally.*

(MR 2009: 11)

Finally, while the identity dimension is not as present in Wallonia as it is in Quebec, it is interesting to observe that it is still being used, albeit indirectly; not so much in defining the characteristics of the in-group but rather in contrasting it to the Flemish. Research on political identity has shown that in the construction of a collective identity, the definition of the out-group matters as much as the definition of the in-group. Linguistically, this process of identity construction can be seen in deictic tools such as the references to the "them" in discourses (Sinardet 2012). This is not a metaphor per se, but it is interesting to observe the use of this linguistic tool in the construction of political discourses. More specifically, the liberals use this deictic comparison in order to criticise the work of the socialists; that is, to contend that, in comparison with Flanders, Wallonia is faring worse and that the governing parties are responsible for this poor state of affairs (37). By contrast, Ecolo avoids such a deictic posture and prefers to put the Walloons and the Flemings on an equal footing (38).

(37) *Par comparaison, la Flandre est* plus *active. Les réserves en Flandre froment* plus *du double des réserves wallonnes.*
By comparison, Flanders is *more* active. The reserves in Flanders account *for more than* double the Walloon reserves.
(MR 2009: 18)

(38) *Nous connaissons le dynamisme, l'enthousiasme et l'optimisme des entrepreneurs ou travailleurs(euses) wallon(ne)s, flamand(e)s et bruxellois (es), lorsque ils peuvent s'exprimer et nous voulons* libérer *cette expression.*
We witness he dynamism, the enthusiasm and optimism of the Walloon, Flemish and Brussels entrepreneurs and workers when they have the opportunity of expressing themselves, and we want to *liberate* this expression.
(Ecolo 2009: Livre/Book IV, 56)

The socialists also use this indirect comparison with Flanders, not to criticise Wallonia, but rather to show their collaboration with Flanders (39) and, above all, especially in the 1990s, to depict an identity that is more open than the Flemish identity (40). Indeed, the socialists imply that the Walloons seem to be afraid to develop their own identity because of the tensions between them and the Flemish people, which the party explains in terms of a strong identity-building process, i.e. nationalism, in Flanders. So while the socialists would like the Walloons to develop a stronger Walloon identity, they do not want this identity-building process to be nationalist, as that would be close-minded and exclusive. They want the Walloon identity to be open-minded and based on a strong cooperation with Brussels.

(39) *Avec la Flandre, via une mobilisation des entreprises flamandes, la sensibilisation de 50 000 demandeurs d'emploi wallons, la constitution d'équipes mixtes FOREM-VDAB (son équivalent flamand).*

With Flanders, through a mobilisation of Flemish firms, the consciousness raising of 50,000 Walloon job-seekers, the creation of combined teams from the FOREM-VDAB (the public service for employment and formation and its Flemish equivalent).

(PS 2009: 35)

(40) *Une Wallonie plus affirmée mais* toujours ouverte.
A more assertive but *still open-minded* Wallonia"

(PS 1995: 54)

The Walloon political parties offer quite different visions of their region. There is no consensus on what Wallonia currently is and even less so on what Wallonia should be. Yet all the parties agree that there is still work to be done in order to improve the *living environment* in Wallonia. To this end, the main dynamics in the political manifestos revolve around the change versus continuity debate. These dynamics can be explained by the political system of the region, which is built on coalition government. Therefore, each of the four main political parties has been part of the governing coalition for at least a few of the last 20 years. The MR is the Walloon political party that has been in power the least during this period and its political manifestos feature a stronger emphasis on change than on continuity. By contrast, the discourse of the PS, the political party that has been continually in power, frames change from the perspective of continuity, as a means to emphasise both its past and future achievements.

6 Discussion: how political parties speak about their region

Party politics in Quebec and in Wallonia are quite different. In Quebec, a bipartisan situation with a majority government has often been the norm but with a rotation of the party in power. In Wallonia, four main parties have shaped the political dynamics, but with one dominant actor, the PS, that has been in power uninterruptedly since 1988, albeit as part of successive coalition governments. Nonetheless, both the identity question (between sovereignty and federalism in Quebec, and regarding the nature of Walloon identity in Wallonia) and the socioeconomic dimension evidently shape the nature of politics in these two regions. And these dual dynamics are reflected in the political manifestos the parties have drafted for recent elections.

Our quantitative and qualitative analysis of these electoral manifestos demonstrates the predominance of the identity dynamics in Quebec in the 1990s, while socioeconomic issues can be seen to return to the forefront there in the 2000s. In Wallonia, throughout the last 20 years, the political dynamics have been built around the change versus continuity discourses that are fed by both the identity and socioeconomic issues. In these political discourses, conceptual metaphors are very present and offer a more concrete grasp of abstract and complex issues. In Quebec, two types of metaphor predominate: on the one hand, Quebec as a *building*, a *means of transport* or a *machine*, and, on the other hand, the political process in Quebec as a *war* or a *path/journey*. In Wallonia, we find a fairly negative image of the region, with the metaphor of the *living environment* and an even more negative image with the metaphor of *disease*. What remains to be studied, however, and thus to be understood, is whether such metaphors have an impact or not on the representations and the preferences of the citizens of Quebec and of Wallonia.

As the length of political manifestos keeps on growing, especially in Wallonia where their size has grown from a few dozen pages to the current minimum of a couple of hundred pages, it is more crucial than ever for a party to get its main message across to the voters. To this end, metaphors can be useful shortcuts as they have the potential to deliver an argument within a complex domain through a more familiar domain. What is more, our study shows that the choice of this domain is not random but rather is led by strategic choices. Yet the choice to use metaphors should not be over-emphasised as political competition is not only made of party politics, which we have tried to unravel in this chapter, but also of the individual men and women in politics, a subject to which we turn in the next chapter.

Notes

1 Another left-wing party, namely *Québec Solidaire* (QS), was created in 2006, but, given its marginal role in Quebec politics, we do not analyse its manifestos as part of the present study.
2 Tables 3.3 and 3.4 take into account nouns and adjectives, while prepositions, verbs and pronouns have been left out. The * at the end of a word means that its various inflectional forms have been taken into account (for instance, plural/singular and/or maculine/feminine gender).
3 It should be noted that even when the party name is excluded, these lemmas are still the ones most frequently used in the manifestos.
4 All extract translations are the authors'.

References

Bélanger, Éric (2008). "The 2007 provincial election in Quebec", *Canadian Political Science Review*, 2(1): 72–73.

Bélanger, Éric (2009). "The 2008 provincial election in Quebec", *Canadian Political Science Review*, 3(1): 93–99.

Bélanger, Éric (2012). "Les partis tiennent-ils leurs promesses?" In *Les partis politiques québécois dans la tourmente. Mieux comprendre et évaluer leur rôle*, ed. Réjean Pelletier, 195–223. Québec: Presses de l'Université Laval.

Bélanger, Éric and Chris Chhim (2012). "Is the Independence Issue back on the Agenda in Quebec?", *e-International Relations* October 2012. Available from: www.e-ir.info/2012/10/21/is-the-independence-issue-back-on-the-agenda-in-quebec/ (accessed 19 August 2014).

Bélanger, Eric and Richard Nadeau (2008). "La montée des tiers partis au Québec à l'élection de 2007: conjoncture ou tendance?", *Choix IRPP*, 14(17).

Boily, Frédéric (2012). "L'action démocratique du Québec: si près, si loin du pouvoir". In *Les partis politiques québécois dans la tourmente. Mieux comprendre et évaluer leur rôle*, ed. Réjean Pelletier, 301–32. Québec: Presses de l'Université Laval.

Bouhon, Frédéric and Min Reuchamps (2012). *Les systèmes électoraux de la Belgique*, Bruxelles: Bruylant.

Budge, Ian, Hans-Dieter Klingemann, Andrea Volkens, Judith Bara and Eric Tanenbaum (2001). *Mapping Policy Preferences: Estimates for Parties, Electors, and Governments 1945–1998*, Oxford: Oxford University Press.

Changfoot, Nadine and Blair Cullen (2011). "Why is Quebec Separatism off the Agenda? Reducing National Unity Crisis in the Neoliberal Era", *Canadian Journal of Political Science/Revue canadienne de science politique*, 44(4): 769–87.

Charteris-Black, Jonathan (2009). "Metaphor and political communication". In *Metaphor and Discourse*, ed. Andreas Musolff and Jorg Zinken, 99–115. Houndmills: Palgrave Macmillan.

Charteris-Black, Jonathan (2011). *Politicians and Rhetoric: The Persuasive Power of Metaphor*, 2nd edn, Houndsmills: Palgrave Macmillan.

Chilton, Paul (1996). *Security Metaphors: Cold War Discourse from Containment to Common European Home*, Berne and New York: Peter Lang.

Collette, Benoît and François Pétry (2012). "Le positionnement des partis sur l'échiquier politique québécois". In *Les partis politiques québécois dans la tourmente. Mieux comprendre et évaluer leur rôle*, ed. Réjean Pelletier, 111–30. Québec: Presses de l'Université Laval.

Dandoy, Régis (2012a). *Determinants of Party Preferences. Evidence from Party Manifestos in Belgium*, Université libre de Bruxelles: Brussels.

Dandoy, Régis (2012b). Explaining Party Preferences on Decentralisation in Belgium, Paper presented at the *ECPR Joint Sessions*, Universiteit Antwerpen, Antwerp [not published].

Deschouwer, Kris and Min Reuchamps (2013). "The Belgian Federation at a Crossroad", *Regional and Federal Studies*, 23(3): 261–70.

Dufour, Pascale (2007). "Globalization as a new political space: the end of the Quebec-Quebec debate?" In *Canada: The State of the Federation 2005. Quebec and Canada in the New Century: New Dynamics, New Opportunities*, ed. Michael Murphy, 131–52. Montreal and Kingston: McGill-Queen's University Press.

Kovecses, Zoltan (2010). *Metaphor: A Practical Introduction*, 2nd edn, Oxford: Oxford University Press.

Lakoff, George and Mark Johnson (1980). *Metaphors we live by*, Chicago, IL: University of Chicago Press.

Lemieux, Vincent (2012). "Le Parti libéral du Québec et la formulation des politiques". In *Les partis politiques québécois dans la tourmente. Mieux comprendre et évaluer leur rôle*, ed. Réjean Pelletier, 249–71. Québec: Presses de l'Université Laval.

Mayaffre, Damon (2005). Les corpus politiques: objet, méthode et contenu. Introduction, *Corpus*, 4. http://corpus.revues.org/index292.html (accessed 19 August 2014).

Mayaffre, Damon (2007). "L'analyse de données textuelles aujourd'hui: du corpus comme une urne, au corpus comme un plan. Bilan sur les travaux actuels de topo graphie/topologie textuelle", *Lexicométrica*, (9). Available from: http://lexicometrica.univ-paris3.fr/numspeciaux/special9/mayaffre.pdf (accessed 21 August 2014).

Montpetit, Éric (2007). *Le fédéralisme d'ouverture: La recherche d'une légitimité canadienne au Québec*, Sillery: Septentrion.

Morsink, Niels and Dave Sinardet (2011). Contamination or containment? Sub state nationalism in electoral pograms of Belgian political parties (1965–2010), Paper presented at the *6th ECPR General Conference*, University of Iceland, Reykjavik [not published].

Pelletier, Réjean (2008). *Le Québec et le fédéralisme canadien. Un regard critique*, Québec: Presses de l'Université Laval.

Pelletier, Réjean (2012). *Les partis politiques québécois dans la tourmente. Mieux comprendre et évaluer leur rôle*, Québec: Presses de l'Université Laval.

Perrez, Julien and Min Reuchamps (2012). "Quand lingusitique et science politique se rencontrent". In *Les relations communautaires en Belgique: Approches politiques et linguistiques*, ed. Julien Perrez and Min Reuchamps, 17–30. Louvain-la-Neuve: Academia-L'harmattan.

Pétry, François (2006). "Comparaison chiffrée des plateformes électorales". In *Le Parti libéral: enquête sur les réalisations du gouvernement Charest*, ed. François Pétry, Éric Bélanger and Louis M. Imbeau, 67–82. Québec: Les presses de l'Université Laval.

Pétry, François (2002). "La réalisation des engagements du Parti québécois: analyse d'ensemble". In *Le Parti québécois. Bilan des engagements électoraux, 1994–2000*, ed. François Pétry, 161–90. Québec: Les Presses de l'Université Laval.

Pétry, François and Lisa Birch (2014). "Continuité et changement dans le positionnement idéologique des partis dans l'espace politique québécois", *Le Devoir*, 2 April.

Pétry, François and Benoît Collette (2006). "Le gouvernement Charest a-t-il respecté ses promesses?" In *Le Parti libéral: enquête sur les réalisations du gouvernement Charest*, ed. François Pétry, Éric Bélanger and Louis M. Imbeau, 83–102. Québec: Les presses de l'Université Laval.

Reuchamps, Min (2011). *L'avenir du fédéralisme en Belgique et au Canada. Quand les citoyens en parlent*, Bruxelles: P.I.E.-Peter Lang.

Reuchamps, Min, Dimokritos Kavadias and Kris Deschouwer (2014). "Drawing Belgium: using mental maps to measure territorial conflict", *Territory, Politics, Governance*, 2(1): 30–51.

Reuchamps, Min and François Onclin (2009). "La fédération belge". In *Le fédéralisme en Belgique et au Canada. Comparaison sociopolitique*, ed. Bernard Fournier and Min Reuchamps, 21–40. Bruxelles: De Boeck Université.

Semino, Elena (2008). *Metaphor in Discourse*, Cambridge: Cambridge University Press.

Sinardet, Dave (2012). "Le rôle des médias dans le conflit communautaire belge: Le traitement du dossier 'Bruxelles-Hal-Vilvorde' lors des débats politiques télévisés francophones et neéerlandophones en Belgique". In *Les relations communautaires en Belgique: Approches politiques et linguistiques*, ed. Julien Perrez and Min Reuchamps, 105–31. Louvain-la-Neuve: Academia-L'harmattan.

Volkens, Andrea (2002). "Manifesto coding instructions". In *WZB Discussion papers FS*. Berlin: Wissenschaftzentrum Berlin für Sozialforschung. Available from: https://manifestoproject.wzb.eu (accessed 21 August 2014).

Wilson, John and Martin Hay (2013). "Internal media, conceptual metaphors and minority cultural identities", *Ethnicities*, 13(1): 49–67.

Political manifestos in Quebec

ADQ (*Action démocratique du Québec*) (1994). *Un Québec responsable*, 31pp.

ADQ (*Action démocratique du Québec*) (1998). *Des idées. Des convictions. Du vrai!*, 8pp.

ADQ (*Action démocratique du Québec*) (2003). *Pour un gouvernement responsable: Plan d'action pour un premier mandat de l'Action démocratique du Québec*, 72pp.

ADQ (*Action démocratique du Québec*) (2007). *Une vision. Un plan. Une parole. Un Plan A pour le Québec*, 27pp.

ADQ (*Action démocratique du Québec*) (2008). *Le nouveau modèle québécois autonomiste, un plan pour défendre le pouvoir d'achat*, 171pp.

CAQ (*Coalition Avenir Québec*) (2012). *C'est assez, faut que ça change!* 114pp.

CAQ (*Coalition Avenir Québec*) (2014). *Un parti pris pour les contribuables*, 28pp.

PLQ (*Parti libéral du Québec*) (1994). *Agir pour le Québec: Document d'orientation politique*, 80pp.

PLQ (*Parti libéral du Québec*) (1998). *Le Plan pour un Québec plus fort: Le résumé*, 28pp.

PLQ (*Parti libéral du Québec*) (2003). *Un gouvernement au service des Québécois: Ensemble, réinventons le Québec: Le Plan d'action du prochain gouvernement libéral*, 47pp.

PLQ (*Parti libéral du Québec*) (2007). *S'unir pour réussir le Québec de demain: Plateforme électorale*, 80pp.

PLQ (*Parti libéral du Québec*) (2008). *Programme électoral du Parti libéral québécois. L'économie d'abord, oui.* 16pp.

PLQ (*Parti libéral du Québec*) (2012). *Pour le Québec*, 28pp.

PLQ (*Parti libéral du Québec*) (2014): *Ensemble, On s'occupe des vraies affaires.* 56pp.

PQ (*Parti québécois*) (1994). *Programme électoral du Parti québécois*, 70pp.

PQ (*Parti québécois*) (1998). *J'ai confiance, je vote Parti québécois, Les orientations du programme électoral du Parti québécois*, 69pp.

PQ (*Parti québécois*) (2003). *Restons forts. Plateforme électorale 2003*, 102pp.

PQ (*Parti québécois*) (2007). *Reconstruisons notre Québec: Feuille de route du Parti québécois: Élections 2007*, 42pp.

PQ (*Parti québécois*) (2008). *Le plan Marois*, 32pp.

PQ (*Parti québécois*) (2012). *L'avenir du Québec est entre vos mains. Agir honnêtement, s'affirmer, s'enrichir et s'entraider. A nous de choisir*, 25pp.

PQ (*Parti québécois*) (2014). *Plus prospère. Plus fort. Plus indépendant. Plus accueillant. Déterminée*, 13pp.

Political manifestos in Wallonia

cdH (*Centre démocrate Humaniste*) (2004). *Votez pour moi: programme électoral – Résumé/ Wallonie 2004*, 130pp.

cdH (*Centre démocrate Humaniste*) (2009). *Programme électoral 2009 – Wallonie*, 351pp.

Ecolo (*Écologistes confédérés pour l'organisation de luttes originales*) (1995). *L'avenir est ouvert*, 41pp.

Ecolo (*Écologistes confédérés pour l'organisation de luttes originales*) (1999). *Le programme d'Ecolo*, 1554pp.

Ecolo (*Écologistes confédérés pour l'organisation de luttes originales*) (2004). *Priorités de champagne 2004: projet pour la Région wallonne*, 27pp.

Ecolo (*Écologistes confédérés pour l'organisation de luttes originales*) (2009). *Programme Élections 2009*, 109pp., 116pp., 130pp., 77pp., 65pp., 80pp.

Ecolo (*Écologistes confédérés pour l'organisation de luttes originales*) (2014). *Programme 2014*, 808pp.

MR (*Mouvement réformateur*) (2004). *Programme électoral Wallonie*, 37pp.

MR (*Mouvement réformateur*) (2009). *Le programme complet du mouvement réformateur: élections 2009 – Pour la Région wallonne*, 136pp.

MR (*Mouvement réformateur*) (2014). *Programme wallon*, 262pp.

PRL-FDF (*Parti réformateur libéral-Front démocratique des Francophones*) (1995). *Changer de politique: Programme pour la Région wallonne*, 11pp.

PRL-FDF-MCC (*Parti réformateur libéral-Front démocratique des Francophones-Mouvement citoyen pour le changement*) (1999). *Le programme de la Fédération PRL FDF MCC*, 96pp.

PSC (*Parti social chrétien*) (1995). *Programme électoral 1995*, 37pp.

PSC (*Parti social chrétien*) (1999). *Programme électoral 1999*, 27pp.

PS (*Parti socialiste*) (1995). *Programme électoral 1995*, 94pp.

PS (*Parti socialiste*) (1999). *Programme électoral 1999*, 67pp.

PS (*Parti socialiste*) (2004). *Garantie de l'avenir à chacun – Programme PS pour la Région wallonne pour les élections du 13 juin 2004*, 201pp.

PS (*Parti socialiste*) (2009). *Programme Région wallonne 2009: nos valeurs ne sont pas cotées en bourse, nos actions profitent à tous*, 139pp.

PS (*Parti socialiste*) (2014). *Plus forts ensemble: pour un avenir plus juste – Programme 2014 Elections européennes, fédérales et régionales*, 498pp.

4 Career patterns in multilevel Quebec and Wallonia

Towards a substate and federal political class?

Jérémy Dodeigne

In representative democracies, where parliaments are at the centre of political life, the study of elected politicians has always fascinated political scientists. In the literature on legislative recruitment, the core research questions are threefold (Moncrief 1999: 175; Norris 1997): "*who* are the MPs entering parliament?"; "*how* are they recruited?" and "*why* did they choose to enter politics?" Because there is a limited number of offices in competition, the question of "who goes to parliament" has produced a vast debate in the literature. It is an unmistakable trend that "opportunities to serve in legislatures are quite unevenly distributed in all societies" (Matthews 1984: 548). A second extensive area of research relates to the conditions of candidates' election and selection. The influence of legal dispositions and electoral systems has been particularly explored, as well as the key role of political parties as "gatekeepers". Although political parties have increasingly democratised and opened the process of candidates' selection (Bille 2001), candidate selection remains largely the "secret garden of politics" (Gallagher and Marsh 1988).

The third line of research investigates circulation of politicians through analysis of candidates' ambition. This is the perspective adopted in this chapter. In the Belgian and Canadian federal systems, elite circulation requires a multilevel approach. The process of regionalisation in Western Europe has renewed the interest in political careers, not only for newly regionalised unitary states but also for established federations (Stolz 2003). Recently, Docherty (2011: 186) rightly stated that "there has been little analytical work on the Canadian political career". And, arguably, even less on political careers in Quebec. Though, since the end of the 1990s, Walloon political careers have received greater attention (Fiers 2001a, 2001b; Pilet, Fiers and Steyvers 2007; Vanlangenakker, Maddens and Put 2010). Based on an original dataset, this chapter proposes a comprehensive analyses of federal and regional careers since the 1990s in Quebec and in Wallonia. More specifically, it presents and explains the circulation of members of parliament (MPs) in the two federations, with a specific focus on career maintenance at a single level of government (professional political careers) and career advancement (level-hopping movements between political arenas).

This chapter starts with a brief review of the existing studies on the two case studies. In terms of political careers, the Canadian and Québécois political arenas are hermetic to each other, whilst Belgium presents an integrated institutional structure between the regional and federal levels. Despite those strong differences, I demonstrate that the development of the substate and federal political class is not that dissimilar. To do so, I introduce a specific analytical framework as well as the concept of political class in section 2. Based on career patterns identified in data presented in section 3, I show in section 4 how Quebec and Wallonia share important elements in terms of territorial structure of the substate and federal political class.

1 Comparing political careers in Quebec and Wallonia

At first sight, Quebec and Wallonia have little in common regarding career patterns. First and foremost, the two countries are very different in terms of age. Contrary to the established Canadian federation founded in 1867, Belgium presents a relatively young federal political system that emerged through the regionalisation of a formerly unitary state since the 1970s. Regional parliaments are thus relatively new institutions with merely four legislative terms of experience, the first direct regional elections taking place in 1995 while the recent elections of May 2014 opened the fifth legislature.[1] In this context, Belgian political actors are still adapting their strategies to the structure of opportunity, especially where new rules of the game are constantly being modified (e.g. the new electoral reforms for the federal and regional elections of May 2014). In contrast, career patterns are much more stabilised in Canada, reflecting decades of electoral behaviour even though important discrepancies are found over time and across provinces.

Another striking difference between Quebec and Wallonia is the structure of political careers regarding movements of politicians between the federal and substate political arenas. A quick overview of the literature on political careers indicates that movements are frequently observed between the federal and regional levels in Belgium (especially in Wallonia), whereas there are almost no transfers of politicians between the provincial legislative assemblies and the federal parliament in Ottawa (especially in Quebec). Contrary to their close US neighbours where most Congressmen first experienced politics in state legislatures before entering national politics, few Canadian MPs at "Parliament Hill" have primarily served in provincial legislative assemblies. And this reflects a historical tend. In a research note published in the late 1980s, Barrie and Gibbins (1989) analysed a comprehensive dataset of 3,803 parliamentary careers from 1867 to 1984 inclusive on the members of the Canadian House of Commons and/or the appointed senators. At that time, they concluded that "career mobility from provincial to national office is the exception rather than the rule" (Barrie and Gibbins 1989: 138). They observed that only 534 federal MPs (14.25%) had acquired a former provincial experience, a ratio that is even lower than MPs and senators who previously held a municipal office (973 or 25.6%). Furthermore, half of all federal MPs with a previous provincial office originate from the 1867–1917 period (Docherty 1997: 41) – at a time when the federal House of Commons presented even fewer offices and when there were fewer provinces. Therefore, in the 1960s and the 1970s, the percentage of federal MPs who had served in legislative assemblies at provincial level was as little as around 7% (Barrie and Gibbins 1989: 142). Canadian politics is undoubtedly not familiar with cross-level-hoppers as federal MPs are rarely recruited among provincial ranks.

This conclusion has been reaffirmed recently by Docherty (2011: 188) who scrutinised the composition of the 35th parliament (1993–97) and 39th parliament (2008–11). The percentages of federal MPs with previous provincial experience remained very low, respectively 10.1 and 11.6%. Quebec is no exception and, quite the opposite, it is an extreme case study as well as in Ontario. During the period 1954–84, Barrie and Gibbins (1989: 144) found that only 2.9% Quebec MPs had a former provincial experience in the National Assembly of Quebec and/or in the Executive Council of Quebec, in comparison to the average 15.4% for other Atlantic MPs. The recurring absence of movement in the Canadian political system is also valid from the provincial viewpoint, namely the presence of members of provincial legislative assemblies who first served at federal level. Based on movements from the federal to the provincial level, it can be concluded that Canadian MPs rarely stand down from Parliament Hill to run for provincial elections (Barrie and Gibbins 1989: 141). The authors established that only 3% of the federal MPs successfully developed a provincial political career after leaving the federal parliament,[2] apart from the 44 individuals who became lieutenant governors. "As a result, we see a unidirectional path in some areas (namely the east), an integrated career in the west, where members may move back and forth, and a mixture of the two in Ontario and Quebec" (Docherty 2011: 201).

Career patterns in Canada strongly contrast with what has been observed in Belgium. Whereas a general lack of movement best describes the political context in Canada/Quebec, the magnitude of movements is certainly one of the distinguishing features of the Belgian political system. The first studies were published by Fiers (2001a, 2001b), following just after the first two regional and two federal elections that had taken place in 1995 and in 1999.[3] After the first 1995 regional elections, I observe, based on my own data, that 84 former Flemish federal MPs and 55 Walloon federal MPs decided to continue their careers at the regional instead of the national level.[4] Because first regional elections in newly federal systems very often integrate former national MPs running for regional offices,[5] it is not surprising to observe so many transfers after the Belgian 1995 regional elections. An important number of movements were nonetheless also found during the second regional legislature, although they were less prominent: 17 Flemish and 12 Walloon MPs/federal ministers conducted level-hopping movements from the federal to the regional parliaments. At the 1999 federal elections, I observe that several regional MPs also conducted level-hopping movements but in the opposite direction: 10 Flemish and 10 Walloon regional MPs or regional ministers moved to the federal parliament to become either members of the Chamber of Representatives or senators.

According to Vanlangenakker, Maddens and Put (2010), the vertical concurrence of regional and federal elections in the 1990s might have enhanced the incentive for politicians to switch levels. Nevertheless, level-hopping movements were also observed when regional elections (2004 and 2009) and federal elections (2003, 2007 and 2010) were organised separately. In the 2000s, I find that the total number of transfers from the federal to the regional political arena (at the Flemish and Walloon parliaments) accounts for 82 level-hopping movements, while a similar number of movements has been observed in the opposite direction with 54 regional politicians moving to the federal parliament. In conclusion, at the early stage of its federal era in the 1990s, Belgium presented a substantial amount of level-hopping movements in both directions (regional to federal and federal to national) when elections were organised jointly. A characteristic that was also detected in the 2000s, even though there was non-vertical simultaneity. Because of all these transfers between political arenas, it is not surprising that Belgium is often presented as "a textbook example" of a highly integrated political arena (Vanlangenakker, Maddens and Put 2010).

From a comparative point of view, Quebec and Wallonia have not developed *sui generis* patterns. In order to locate the two regions in the universe of cases, let us briefly review the conceptual distinctions of career patterns in multilevel systems. In the literature on political careers in multilevel systems, the ladder pattern conceptualised by Schlesinger (1966) in the US political systems has been very influential. In his framework, the most successful and ambitious politicians start at the local level to progressively reach the state level and ultimately the national political arena. This model assumes therefore a hierarchic division between levels of government as well as a progressive ambition from the lowest to the highest positions in multilevel polities. In this context, national positions – ranked before substate positions, that are ranked before local offices – are the genuine object of covetousness and where the competition is the highest. The model of progressive ambition has often constituted the starting assumption for many students of political careers in multilevel systems. Methodological nationalism in electoral studies – where empirical and conceptual research mainly focuses on national institutions – is probably part of the explanation (Jeffery and Schakel 2013). Nevertheless, in newly regionalised and federalised Western democracies, with strong demands from regionalist and nationalist parties to reorganise the territorial structure of the state, it can be assumed that "regionalism matters for professional careers" (Stolz 2011: 224).

Recent comparative research has challenged the classic assumption of politicians being driven mostly by progressive national ambition. Stolz (2003) proposed an analytical framework that aimed at disentangling territorial dynamics between political arenas. His classification is based on the magnitude

	High centripetal ratios	Low centripetal ratios
Low centrifugal ratios	(1) Unidirectional from region to centre	(2) Alternative Careers
High Centrifugal ratios	(3) Nondirectionally integrated	(4) Unidirectional from centre to region

Figure 4.1 Stolz's matrix of career patterns in multilevel systems
Source: Stolz 2003, 2010.

and direction of movements between levels of government. The direction of movements is twofold. The "centripetal" dynamic reflects politicians starting at the substate level who seek to obtain positions at federal level, while the "centrifugal" dynamic reveals politicians taking the opposite path, moving from the federal level towards the substate level. The magnitude of movements takes into account the importance of the centripetal and centrifugal forces, be it low or high degree of transfers between political institutions. Overall, his framework presents a double matrix as described in Figure 4.1.

Cell (1) of Figure 4.1 represents the "classic springboard" that best describes the trajectory of Congressmen in the US political system as theorised by Schlesinger. In political systems where regionalism is stronger, the dominant pattern shapes in the reversed direction – "inverse springboard model" – toward the substate legislative assemblies that have the most attractive offices (cell (4)). In models 1 and 4, the highest ratio of centripetal and centrifugal movements shows that level-hopping movements are mainly driven in a single direction, be it the federal or the substate political arena. An intermediary situation is found in countries where both the federal and substate parliaments present attractive positions whilst movements between federal and substate political arenas are almost inexistent ("alternative careers pattern" in cell (2), i.e. low centrifugal and low centripetal transfers). In that context, distinct kinds of ambition (substate or federal) lead to distinct positions: there are nationally oriented and regionally oriented politicians. Contrary to all other patterns, in the integrated pattern the federal and substate levels are very connected to each other. Careers are defined as "integrated" because of the high ratio of movements towards the federal and towards the substate levels (cell (3)).

Based on this conceptual framework, it can be concluded that Quebec best fits the alternative career pattern, likewise Scotland in the UK for instance. However, Wallonia is described as a typical region with integrated career pattern which presents many similarities with a region such as Catalonia in

Spain. This brief and general overview tends also to confirm that Quebec and Wallonia share little in terms of career patterns. Despite important differences in career patterns, I nonetheless argue that the two polities are not that dissimilar in terms of the structure of the political class. This requires adopting a specific analytical framework – which does not take level-hopping movements but individual trajectories as the unit of analysis – to assess how and why the structure of the political class in Quebec and Wallonia share more than it appears at first sight. The analytical framework developed in section 3 is introduced for that purpose.

2 Political class and career patterns in multilevel systems: analytical framework

Initially developed by Italian scholars at the end of the nineteenth century (see the review of Von Beyme 1996), the concept of political class is best known thanks to Weber (1946)'s seminal distinction of politicians who live "off politics" and those who live "for politics". Political offices have become jobs that provide a regular source of income, job security (career maintenance) and prospects for further promotion (career advancement on the political ladder). The concept of political class reflects therefore the historical process of democratisation and professionalisation of politics. Following Borchert and Golsch (1995) (translated by Stolz 2001: 82), it is "this collective interest of a regular income and the maintenance of the chosen professional career, that constitutes the political class". The concept of political class in multilevel systems is defined on two dimensions. First, there is a *social distinctiveness* between "career politicians" who have long-term political positions, distinct from "citizens politicians" who briefly experience politics before returning to "civil life" (Stolz 2001). Secondly, in multilevel systems, there is a *territorial distinctiveness* of the political class that corresponds to the "homogeneity and autonomy of regional politicians in relation to their national counterparts and to national institutions" (Stolz 2001: 84). In regions where politicians mostly aim at being elected in national institutions, politicians are considered as being part of the national political class. In contrast, when ambitions candidates deliberately try to obtain and maintain positions in substate institutions, a regional political class emerges in its own right and independently from its national counterpart.

As I developed in a recent article (Dodeigne 2014), current classification of career patterns (with a focus on level-hopping movements) is not the best entry point to assess the structure of political class in multilevel systems. The study of movements provides limited knowledge of intra-territorial dynamics and their impact on the development of a regional and/or a national political class. For instance, political systems that present an alternative career pattern (i.e. a quasi-absence of level-hopping movements between levels of government) arguably tend to favour the development of a regional political class distinct from the national political class. However, this remains a hypothesis that has to be proved through the analysis of intra-territorial dynamics. Let me take the example of Scotland and Quebec. In these two regions, level-hopping movements are exceptional. Yet, the electoral turnover is generally low in Scotland, while Canada has one of the largest turnovers observed in advanced democracies (Matland and Studlar 2004). Consequently, the development of a regional political class is more likely to take place in Scotland, whereas in many Canadian provinces the high percentage of regional "citizen politicians" casts doubt on the emergence of a regional political class. In order to bypass this problem, some studies might combine the analysis of level-hopping movements with an analysis of turnover. It is nonetheless risky to draw conclusions on individual political trajectories based on aggregated indicators such as turnover because of the well-known problems of ecological fallacy.

Firstly, most definitions of turnover – and thus most data available – do not integrate changes between elections, which potentially create empirical bias (Moncrief 1998: 363). While it is not a serious problem in political systems where changes are marginal, it becomes highly problematic in integrated systems such as Belgium where changes are frequently observed due to level-hopping movements. In that case, turnover at regional elections mixes newly elected politicians with no political experience and newly elected regional politicians with a professional experience at the national level. Secondly, it is necessary to adopt a peculiar definition of turnover because most data is on winning candidates instead of candidates who effectively hold an office. In constitutional systems where the accumulation of parliamentary and government offices is prohibited (such as Belgium), the composition of parliaments is strongly affected after government formation. A quick comparison of the turnover at election time and at the end of the legislature proves how serious this issue is. The ratio of newly elected Walloon federal representatives is, on average, almost 6.8% higher (from 28.2 to 35.0%) at the end of the legislature for the period 1992–2010. Even though it is lower at the Walloon parliament, there is also an average difference of 4.3% (from 36.0 to 40.3%) for the period 1995–2014. Thirdly, it is crucial to take into account the number of individuals who conduct movements. Are level-hopping movements conducted by as many individuals? Or rather, is it a limited number of politicians conducting all movements? This is a crucial difference to analyse in order to assess the structure of the political class because level-hoppers are often the trees hiding the forest, i.e. they constitute a minor proportion of all political careers studied.

For those reasons, I argue that individual political careers (instead of level-hopping movements) must be used as the unit of analysis. Adopting this micro-approach allows a comprehensive longitudinal analysis of the sequence and maintenance of offices for every political career. Although this approach is not new, it has rarely been applied to the analysis of political careers in multilevel systems (see, however, Herzog 1975; Real-Dato, Rodríguez-Teruel and Jerez-Mir 2011; Kjaer 2011; Borchert and Stolz 2011). Based on the duration of political careers at the federal level and the duration of political careers at the substate level, I distinguish four ideal types of career pattern in multilevel systems: the federal career pattern (professionalised career at the federal level only), the substate career pattern (professionalised career at the substate level only), the multilevel career pattern (experience at both levels) and the discrete career pattern (very short career) (for more details on the conceptual distinction, see Dodeigne 2014). A minimum of two complete legislative terms is used to distinguish individuals with discrete careers ("citizen politicians") and professionalized politicians ("career politicians") at the regional level and the federal level.

3 Data

The data gathers 647 individual careers in Quebec and 535 careers in Wallonia. In the latter, the dataset covers all parliamentarians and all members of government in office at the federal level since 1992 – the most recent national elections before the first direct Walloon elections – and all regional politicians who were in office since 1995. Although data collection starts with the 1992 federal elections, I recorded the whole political career for those who were in office before and after the 1992 (some of them being elected since 1968). For Quebec, the data includes all elected politicians who were in office at the federal and provincial levels. For the sake of comparability with Wallonia, I limited the coding to the 1993 federal elections and the 1994 provincial elections. One the one hand, it permits an analysis of a time-scope similar to Wallonia (about 20 years); on the other hand, the beginning of the 1990s marked a rupture in political life in Canada and in Quebec most particularly. At the 1993 federal election, the newly founded *Bloc Québécois* sent 54 MPs to the Canadian House of Commons and became the official opposition, while the progressive conservatives suffered a dramatic reduction of their majority (minus 167 seats in comparison to the 1988 elections) leaving it with only two MPs in Ottawa (Young and Archer 2002).

Regarding the types of office, I am interested only in directly elected offices. The analysis is thus on the members of the Canadian House of Commons (MPs), excluding appointed senators in Canada. In Wallonia, it concerns regional careers at the Walloon parliament and/or at government, and federal careers at the Chamber of Representatives and the Senate.[6] With the 2012 electoral reforms coming into effect at the 2014 federal elections, the Senate is no longer composed of directly elected senators but of 50 members of regional and community senators as well as ten co-opted senators (*sénateurs cooptés*) (Dodeigne and Vandeleene 2013). Besides, I take into account the experience at the European parliament, even though my analysis is primarily on political careers at the regional and federal levels in Wallonia. A final methodological issue concerns the distinction between parliamentary and ministerial offices. Contrary to the Canadian political system, not only is it common to see non-elected Belgian politicians appointed as regional and federal ministers, but it has also been forbidden since 1995 to accumulate parliamentary and government offices (see above). For that reason, I use in this chapter the more general term of "politicians" which includes all parliamentarians and members of governments.

The data collection is based on my own compilation of parliamentary reports and official electoral results. It includes the provincial elections of April 2014 in Quebec and the regional and federal elections of May 2014 (data collected until June 2014).

4 Career patterns in Quebec and Wallonia

4.1 Mutlilevel careers

Politicians with multilevel careers are self-explicitly politicians who present experience at both the substate and federal political arenas. In Quebec, the situation is clear and simple: it concerns federal candidates who used the provincial legislative assemblies as a stepping stone towards Parliament Hill as well as provincial candidates who first served in the House of Commons before entering the National Assembly of Quebec. In Wallonia, the situation is slightly more diversified. In addition to parliamentarians moving from one level to another, it also concerns candidates elected at the regional or national parliament, but called to serve in the government at another level. Furthermore, politicians with multilevel careers are also members of the regional and national parliaments/governments with experience at the European level. As already presented above, Wallonia and Quebec strongly diverge in terms of the magnitude of level-hopping movements. This section goes one step further by analysing when, why and how politicians move between the different layers of the institutional multilevel structure in Quebec and in Wallonia.

In Wallonia, 107 level-hopping movements have been observed since 1995 (Table 4.1), 43 are centripetal transfers (regional → federal), whilst 63 are centrifugal transfers (federal → regional). For the sake of clarity, European careers are not illustrated in Table 4.1 but there are 13 level-hopping movements from and towards the European parliament. In Quebec, there are 16 former provincial members who entered the House of Commons and eight former federal parliamentarians became members of the National Assembly of Quebec (Table 4.1). Yet, only seven Quebec politicians decided to resign from their office to run at another level, whereas the remaining 17 ran for elections after not being re-elected to their incumbent office.

All level-hopping movements in Quebec are conducted by as many distinct individuals, whereas the 107 level-hopping movements in Wallonia are the result of solely 72 individuals. In other words, some politicians move back and forth more than once. In fact, 24 individuals conducted 65.5% of all the movements observed. In other words, even though level-hopping movements

Table 4.1 Level-hopping movements in Wallonia and Quebec

Wallonia		Federal level		Regional level	Quebec		Federal level		Provincial level
1995–1999	Reg. Leg.	1	↔	55	1994–1997	Fed. Leg.	3	↔	0
1995–1999	Fed. Leg.	0	↔	1	1994–1998	Prov. Leg.	1	↔	1
1999–2003	Fed. Leg.	10	↔	5	1997–2000	Fed. Leg.	2	↔	0
1999–2004	Reg. Leg.	2	↔	7	1998–2003	Prov. Leg.	0	↔	2
2003–2007	Fed. Leg.	3	↔	5	2001–2004	Fed. Leg.	3	↔	0
2004–2009	Reg. Leg.	4	↔	8	2003–2007	Prov. Leg.	0	↔	2
2007–2010	Fed. Leg.	10	↔	6	2004–2005	Fed. Leg.	3	↔	0
2009–2014	Reg. Leg.	1	↔	14	2006–2008	Fed. Leg.	2	↔	0
2010–2014	Fed. Leg.	6	↔	3	2007–2008	Prov. Leg.	0	↔	1
2014–2019	Reg. Leg.	0	↔	14	2008–2011	Fed. Leg.	1	↔	0
2014–2019	Fed. Leg.	6	↔	0	2009–2012	Prov. Leg.	0	↔	0
					2011– …	Fed. Leg.	1	↔	0
					2012–2014	Prov. Leg.	0	↔	2
Total		43	↔	118	Total		16	↔	8
Total but 1995		43	↔	63					

Source: Author's own compilation of parliamentary reports and official electoral results until April 2014 (Quebec) and June 2014 (Wallonia).

appear far more frequently in Wallonia, the number of level-hoppers involved is very similar to level-hoppers in Quebec. In percentage, Quebec politicians with a multilevel experience represent 4.6% of all the careers examined, while they account for 18.8% of all the Walloon careers. Yet, the percentage drops to 6.2 once the analysis is limited to the 24 politicians who accounted most of it. Unsurprisingly, the latter are the major figures of Walloon politics and they were all federal and regional members of governments (except four parliamentarians who moved back and forth between federal and regional parliaments three times). In Belgium, the formation of the regional and federal governments implies frequent 'multilevel reshuffles' and ministers are called to another level according to the political context of the moment (Dandoy and Dumont 2012). Furthermore, members of government often became ministers at a level of government to which they were not primarily elected (e.g. a federal minister but elected to the Walloon parliament). The Belgian political system is often labelled as a "partitocracy" that reserves a predominant role to political parties for all delegation of power (including ministerial appointments and the composition of electoral lists) (De Winter, Della Porta and Deschouwer 1996). Because of the Belgian semi-open list system – electors vote for a party list and/or express a preferential vote for certain candidates (Bräuninger, Brunner and Däubler 2012), political parties position these ministerial figures on electoral lists in order to attract voters' ballots, even though ministers do not plan to stay in the office to which they are elected. As a result, a genuine game of "musical chairs" takes place in the days following elections with many ministers declining their elected positions – and being temporarily replaced by their successors – in order to stay in office at another level.

The formal electoral rules and the nature of the party system explain on the one hand, why there are more level-hopping movements in Wallonia and, on the other hand, why Walloon politicians tend to move back and forth between elections, whereas a transfer is somehow 'definitive' in Quebec. The first reason is electoral legislation. In Canada, members of the provincial legislative assemblies have to resign from their provincial position in order to run as candidates at the federal elections (Docherty 2011: 192). Because there are few "safe seats" at Canadian elections (Franks 1987), the risk of retiring from politics prematurely is high, which tends to discourage candidates from running for another level of government. The incentive for MPs in the House of Commons to become candidates at provincial elections is, however, slightly enhanced because federal legislation does not require MPs to resign from their office. In addition, even though there are no safe seats at provincial elections either, electoral constituencies are smaller and, therefore, "[the] smaller number of voters allows the federal member to select the most appropriate provincial district that both overlaps with his/her federal seat, but has a solid party support base" (Docherty 2011: 193). Yet, those differences seem to have little impact in practice because there are even more movements from the provincial to the federal arena despite the greater costs.

In Belgium the electoral legislation is much less "constraining", reducing the risk and costs of switching levels. Indeed, the electoral laws do not prohibit regional or federal MPs from becoming candidates at another level of government while holding their office. In fact, it is very common to observe (almost all) federal MPs on regional electoral lists and vice versa for regional MPs (Vanlangenakker, Maddens and Put 2010). When regional and federal elections were organised on the same day (1995 and 1999), some candidates were simultaneously candidates at both elections (e.g. based on my own data, I found 96 candidates in that situation in 1999 in Flanders, Brussels and Wallonia).[7] The new electoral reforms adopted for the 2014 regional, federal and European elections have, nonetheless, deeply transformed the Belgian structure of opportunity. First, it is now prohibited to be simultaneously a candidate at distinct elections. Secondly, candidates elected at regional elections are automatically declared as resigning from their national office, and it is the same for and similarly for regional MPs elected at federal elections. In other words, candidates must now "sit where they get elected" (Dodeigne and Vandeleene 2013). This is expected to enhance the territorial division of regional and federal arenas in the future.

Another reason explaining differences of level-hopping movements in Quebec and Wallonia is the nature of the party system. In Belgium, former national parties disaggregated at the end of the 1960s/1970s and political parties are now divided along community lines. Consequently, Wallonia has a regionalised party system (Brack and Pilet 2010). Nonetheless, all the major political parties – the socialists (*Parti socialiste* (PS)), the liberals (*Mouvement réformateur* (MR)), the Christian democrats (*Centre démocrate Humaniste* (cdH)), the greens (*Écologistes confédérés pour l'organisation de luttes originales*

(Ecolo)) and, since the last elections of May 2014, the radical right (*Parti populaire* (PP)) and the radical left (*Parti des travailleurs de Belgique* (PTB-GO!)) parties – present list of candidates at regional and federal elections.

In contrast, there is a clear-cut division in Quebec, with distinct parties competing at the provincial and the federal elections. With the shock of the 1993 federal elections, "[n]ational parties, national politics, and national electoral competition no longer existed in a Canada that was deeply divided and regionally fragmented" (Carty, Cross and Young 2000). On the one hand, the pro-sovereignty *Parti Québécois* (PQ), the *Parti libéral du Québec* (PLQ) (Quebec Liberal Party) and the *Action démocratique du Québec* (ADQ) that merged with the *Coalition Avenir Quebec* (CAQ) present candidates at provincial elections. On the other hand, the federal elections in Quebec are organised between the *Parti libéral du Canada* (PLC) (Liberal Party of Canada), the *Bloc Québécois* (BQ), the *Parti conservateur du Canada* (PCC) (Conservative Party of Canada) and the *Nouveau parti démocrate* (NPD) (New Democratic Party).

In terms of level-hopping movements, it is thus clearly "easier" for Walloon candidates to move between levels within the same party. More importantly, this structure of the party system enhances the political parties' coordination in terms of electoral strategy. Party strategy indeed explains why a minority of level-hoppers – mainly members of government – conducted most of the movements observed.

In Quebec, where parties do not match at the federal and provincial levels, switching levels of government requires integrating other party organisations, especially when "no other provincial party system in Canada is as distinct from the federal system as Quebec's" (Rayside 1978: 500). Indeed, even the Liberal Party that presents candidates at Ottawa and Quebec has a loose integrated structure, with the PLQ enjoying great autonomy (Detterbeck 2011: 259). Changing levels often entails changing political party. For Docherty (2011), the aftermath of 1993 elections has produced the rise of "free agents": politicians move from the federal towards the provincial arena by "crossing the floor". Out of the 24 Quebec level-hoppers mentioned in Table 4.2, five changed their party affiliation (without considering changes for BQ/PQ as well as PLC/PLQ candidates).

In conclusion, the magnitude of level-hopping is significantly higher in Wallonia than in Quebec. Yet, most of these movements are conducted by the same individuals – mainly members of regional and federal governments – moving back and forth after each elections. Overall, the ratio of Walloon politicians with multilevel career is therefore rather limited (18.8%, but only 6.2% when restricted to politicians responsible for two thirds of the movements) and in proportion much more comparable with Quebec (4.6%). This was the first step of the demonstration proving that the structure of political class in both regions is not that dissimilar in the two polities. Let us now turn to politicians who constitute the core of the regional and federal political, namely politicians with professionalised substate and federal careers.

4.2 Substate and federal class

Table 4.2 gives the proportion of political careers according to the four career patterns: the multilevel careers (describe in the above section), the substate and federal careers that regroup politicians who served (at least) two complete legislative terms in substate and Federal parliaments, and the discrete careers pattern for individuals who experienced less than two legislatures. At the present time, newly elected MPs cannot be classified into one of these patterns and are grouped in the 'others' category.

In Wallonia, the "others" category furthermore regroups all federal MPs elected in the 1992–95 legislature (who were integrated in the dataset in order to assess level-hopping movements at the first Walloon regional elections), but who were not subsequently elected at the federal or regional elections. Finally, European careers that were taken into consideration – to guarantee that all substate and federal careers present experience at a single level of government – are not presented in Table 4.2 for the sake of clarity and to facilitate the comparison with Quebec.

In Quebec, the development of a substate and federal political class is more striking for two reasons. First, the percentage of politicians with professional careers at the National Assembly of Quebec or at the Canadian House of Commons form the most important contingent of all Quebec MPs (56.2% of all careers analysed). Secondly, the separation between the two political classes is enhanced by the division of the party system at the provincial and federal levels. In Quebec the composition of the federal political class is primarily constituted around BQ MPs ($n = 62$) as well as PLC MPs ($n = 34$) and, more marginally, of PCC MPs ($n = 7$). On average, members of the federal political class served 11.8 years at the House of Commons. This is a pretty robust parliamentary experience considering that anticipated elections were very frequent in Canadian political life over the past two decades – the average duration of a legislative term being 2.92 years at Ottawa since 1993. At the provincial level, careers at the National Assembly of Quebec are almost equally composed of PQ MPs ($n = 89$) and PLQ MPs ($n = 92$) who formed the core of the provincial political class. Since their first participation at provincial elections, several deputies of the ADQ and the CAQ have also managed to pursue professional provincial careers. Overall, with an average experience of 12.05 years at the National Assembly of Quebec, there is thus a pretty robust pattern of professionalised substate careers allowing the development of a provincial political class.

In Wallonia, there is also a trend towards a territorial distinction between a federal and a regional political class. Federal and regional careers account for, respectively, 20.6 and 16.2% of all careers analysed, percentages that are distributed in comparable proportions among the four main political parties with the notorious exception of Ecolo (because of its ratio of unprofessionalised careers, see explanation below). The examination of career maintenance demonstrates a clear degree of professionalisation: federal MPs are on average

Table 4.2 Political careers patterns in Wallonia and Quebec

	Discrete career	Federal career	Regional career	Multilevel career	All patterns	Others	Total
Wallonia							
cdH	31	12	12	17	72	24	96
Ecolo	40	8	5	7	60	24	84
MR	39	26	19	17	101	40	141
PS	52	34	27	32	145	52	197
Others	10		1		11	7	18
Total	172	80	63	73	388	147	535
Quebec							
ADQ/C.A.Q.-É.F.L.	47	0	9	1	57	0	57
BQ/PQ	95	62	92	11	260	9	269
NPD	1	0	0	1	2	0	2
LP/LPQ	53	34	89	8	184	36	220
Progressive Conservative	6	7	0	3	16	0	16
Others	5	0	3	0	8	2	10
Total	207	103	193	24	527	119	646

Source: Author's own calculations.
Note: In case of party changes, careers are classified according to politicians' last affiliation.

in office for 13.02 years and regional MPs serve 11.64 years, whereas the theoretical regional duration is a maximum of 19 years since 1995. The territorial division of the political class is nevertheless not as clear as in Quebec because of the notorious percentage of politicians with multilevel careers (18.8% of all careers). Yet, a detailed analysis of MPs switching level of government only once during their career – Walloon politicians moving back and forth between political arenas being the extreme case of ministers – proves that a large majority of those level-hoppers have served most of their time at a single level of government (Dodeigne 2014). In other words, most of these level-hoppers also belong to either the federal or the regional political class, they simply used substate and federal offices as a stepping stone. In the Walloon inter-party and intra-party competitive environment, where the highest and safest places on the list have to be seized when the opportunity arises, it is crucial for candidates to start their parliamentary life where they can enter first, but not always where they aim to stay. As long as these candidates are in favour with their party leaders, it is always possible to move to the desired position at the next elections.

While the provincial National Assembly of Quebec is as old as the Canadian federation, the Walloon parliament is a relatively young institution (about to start its fifth legislature at the time of this writing). It is thus not that surprising to observe substate careers in greater proportion in Quebec than in Wallonia. The provincial arena has long been conceived as a professional political arena providing attractive positions not only in terms of policy scope (Docherty 2011: 192), but also in terms of status and salaries (Moncrief 1994). Furthermore, "an ambitious politician who places cabinet ahead of any other considerations, an elected life in the provinces is far better than Parliament Hill in Ottawa" (Docherty 2011: 191). In contrast, the process of regionalisation in the formerly unitary Belgium has incrementally transferred federal powers to regional institutions. For that reason, the regional arena was not always perceived as an attractive arena until recently, particularly after the 6th state reform. Regional institutions have received a large range of new powers (e.g. employment policy, health care, family benefits, etc.) associated with a significantly greater fiscal autonomy. All in all, it is expected to enhance the attractiveness of the Walloon arena and, therefore, the territorial distinction between a regional and federal political class.

4.3 Discrete careers

A striking observation in Table 4.2 is the large proportion of discrete careers. The latter form the most important pattern in Wallonia (44.3%), while it constitutes the second largest group of careers observed in Quebec (39.3%). The first explanation for short-term careers is electoral volatility. In democratic elections, the larger the electoral volatility, the larger the turnover (Rosenthal 1974: 613). The Pedersen (1979) index is a good proxy to measure the extent of electoral volatility: it assesses the "net change within the electoral party

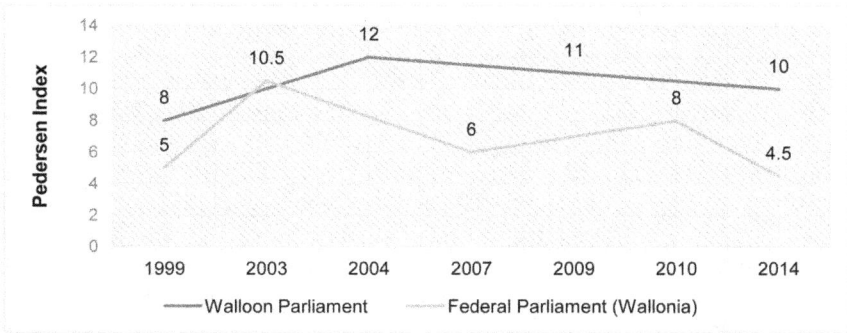

Figure 4.2 Electoral volatility in Wallonia

system resulting from individual vote transfers" (Ascher and Tarrow 1975). The index divides by two the sum of absolute values of the differences in seats or vote shares of all parties between two elections; it is here calculated on seats – instead of votes – because I am interested in the direct impact on career maintenance (Figure 4.2). The 0 value in the index entails the total absence of seat swing, while the 100 value indicates a complete reallocation of seats between two elections. In Wallonia, the average seat volatility index is 10.25 (at the federal parliament) and 7.25 (at the Walloon parliament) for the period 1995–2014.

Based on past studies on turnover, the volatility index is expected to be higher in Quebec (Atkinson and Docherty 1992; Moncrief 1998, 1994; Matland and Studlar 2004; Kerby and Blidook 2011). And it is, indeed, particularly high at the National Assembly of Quebec (index score of 28.0, including the elections of April 2014), while there is an average index score of 24.14 at the House of Commons for the period under examination (Figure 4.3).[8]

Although electoral volatility affects all political parties, it particularly affects the so called "third" or "protest" party (Lipset 1990) that directly challenges established parties. Consequently discrete careers are over-represented for

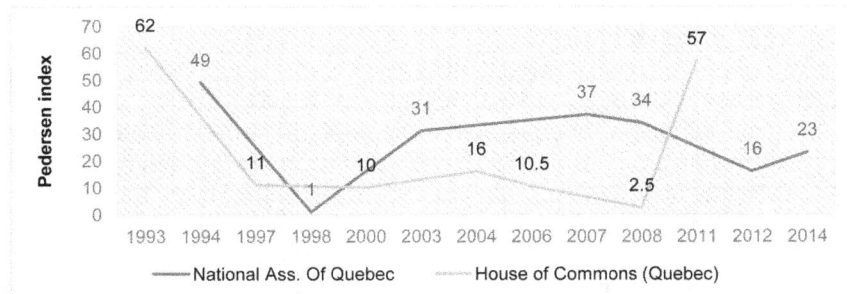

Figure 4.3 Electoral volatility in Quebec

those "third" or "protest" parties. Short-term careers account for 71.1% of the greens' careers (Ecolo) in Wallonia and 83.0% for the ADQ/CAQ in Quebec. The greens' electoral support often collapses after governmental participation. It was the case at the 2003 federal and 2004 regional elections (Buelens and Deschouwer 2002), a pattern that was recently repeated at the 2014 regional and federal elections. Furthermore, the greens' internal party rules preventing career maintenance (Bouhon, Reuchamps and Dodeigne 2012) contribute to explain Ecolo's unbalanced proportion of discrete careers. Likewise there was an exceptional electoral success of the ADQ in 2007 when the party became the official opposition in the National Assembly of Quebec (41 seats). Their success was so paramount that, for the first time since 1879, a minority government was formed in Quebec led by the liberal Jean Charest (Bélanger and Nadeau 2007). At the following provincial election of 2009, the ADQ performed poorly and the party managed to maintain only seven seats (Bélanger 2009).

The relatively high electoral volatility reduces the possibilities for career maintenance and enhances the proportion of discrete careers. Nonetheless, not all departures depend on the electors' choice: a significant proportion of careers are ended "voluntarily". To assess voluntary and involuntary departures, I distinguish between careers ending because of electoral defeat and those ending due to a decision to retire and not to run as candidate at the end of the legislative term.[9] According to Kerby and Blidook (2011: 636)'s recent findings, Quebec MPs in the Canadian House of Commons are, indeed, more likely to voluntarily exit compared to MPs from other provinces. Despite recent positive evolutions (Blidook 2010), the poor incentives of the assembly, along with party discipline that severely constraints MPs' freedom of speech and legislative behaviour, usually explain frustration, disillusion and disengagement (especially for those who are ultimately never called into the Cabinet). Overall, "[u]nlike Jimmy Stewart in Washington, the majority of the men and women who go to Ottawa end up accepting a limited policy role" (Docherty 1997). This is, however, at the National Assembly of Quebec where the ratio of voluntary turnover is the highest: 55.4% of the provincial careers end due to an absence of candidacy, whereas it accounts for only 31.8% at the provincial level. At the House of Commons, most careers in Quebec end therefore by electoral defeats (68.2%).

In Wallonia, there is a comparable percentage of discrete careers even though the volatility is generally lower than in Quebec. One of the reason is the fact that not all Walloon politicians are primarily driven by parliamentary ambition. Following Jones (2002)'s formulation, they are "amateur legislators" but "professional politicians". A large proportion of MPs with a discrete profile has indeed a local executive office – with often strong grassroots – *prior* to their election in the Walloon and Federal parliaments. This local position was held *during* their parliamentary mandate (simultaneity of offices), and most of them returned to these municipal offices *after* their parliamentary experience. In a recent study (Dodeigne 2014), I found that 54.96% of the MPs with discrete careers effectively return to an executive local office after their parliamentary experience. Executive local offices provide a relatively well-professionalised status in terms of income, local popularity, and personal as well as political rewards. Thus local politicians benefit from the prestige and resources available at the Walloon and Federal parliaments, but their primarily loyalty and ambition remain located at the municipality level.

5 Conclusion

This chapter has sought to offer a portrait of political trajectories in multi-level Quebec and Wallonia as well as the consequences of career patterns on the structure of the political class. There are notable differences observed between the two democracies, the most important one being the magnitude of level-hopping movements between substate and federal political arenas. In Wallonia, it is quite common to see Walloon politicians resigning from their federal office to run for regional elections, and vice versa at federal elections. In contrast, level-hopping movements between Ottawa and the National Assembly of Quebec are clearly the exception, likewise in most Canadian provinces.

Nonetheless, a detailed analysis of individuals conducting movements shows that the political class in the two political systems is not that dissimilar. In Wallonia, it has been demonstrated that the magnitude of movements has to be put into perspective, considering that about two thirds of them are conducted by a very small number of politicians who move back and forth between the regional and the federal arenas (6.2% of the careers analysed). The latter are not random MPs: they are the regional and federal ministers. Strategic considerations lead political parties to place those popular figures in winnable positions on the regional and federal electoral lists, even though they do not seek to sit where they get elected. By contrast, most level-hoppers start their political career at the Walloon parliament or at the federal parliament and remain in office (for most than a decade on average) until the end of their parliamentary career. Furthermore, most Walloon level-hoppers use their regional or federal office – which they hold briefly – as a stepping stone before serving the largest time of their career at another level.

Therefore, Walloon political trajectories are not that dissimilar to the situation identified in Quebec: most political careers are professionalised careers at the House of Commons or at the National Assembly of Quebec. In Quebec and Wallonia, there is thus a territorial differentiation between a substate and a federal political class, although it is clearly a process under construction in the case of Wallonia, considering the relatively young age of regional institutions. In this respect, Belgium is certainly at a crossroad. The last state reform has deepened and extended significantly the authority of regional and community institutions. Associated with the new Walloon electoral rules prohibiting accumulation of parliamentary and municipal offices, the structure of opportunity has been profoundly transformed. Although it is likely to make the regional arena as much attractive as the federal arena, only future analysis of political careers will show how political behaviours adapt to the new institutional environment.

A final point of similarity is the relative high ratio of discrete careers in both polities. Although electoral volatility is one of its main causes, another part of the explanation is 'voluntary' turnover. In Quebec there is a greater percentage of MPs ending their careers – after having served briefly in parliament – not as a consequence of electors' choice, but because they decided not to run again. In Wallonia, there is a significant proportion of politicians who are not primarily fuelled by (substate or federal) parliamentary ambition, but by municipal ambition. All in all, we encounter in both democracies a notable number of candidates who do not consider parliamentary office at the sub-state nor at the federal level as the greatest political achievement, although the reasons are not identical in Quebec and Wallonia. If elite renewal is crucial in a democracy, high turnover is as much problematic (Matland and Studlar 2004) (e.g. it prevents the development of a strong legislature vis-à-vis the government and the bureaucracy). From the viewpoint of regional and federal studies, it raises new interesting research questions. Minority groups – and even nations – such as Quebec and Wallonia (but also elsewhere in multinational federal political systems) have claimed further devolution of power and even independence. At the same time, it appears that the substate arena – that could arguably be seen as the political centre of those minority nations – does not appear to be the finest achievement for political elites. In multinational federations, the study of career patterns – through analysis of political ambition – remains, therefore, a valuable entry point to understand the genuine territorial dynamics between federal and substate dynamics.

Notes

1 When regional and community parliaments were established in 1980, national MPs had dual office at regional institutions until 1995.
2 The authors also observed that 21 individuals ran for provincial elections but not successfully.
3 At the moment, few studies have been published – even though the number is increasing rapidly – for a very simple reason: analysing career patterns in multilevel systems requires a certain amount of time to assess the types of political trajectory over time. Because regional legislative terms have a fixed duration of five years, it requires (at least) ten years to observe movements between two elections.
4 In 1995 and 1999 all regional and federal elections took place on the same day. The first regional legislative term (1995–99) was exceptionally four years, whereas all other subsequent legislatures had a five years duration.
5 In formerly unitary countries, the composition of the first regional legislature is often characterised by a high proportion of MPs who previously served in the national parliament. For instance, this has been observed in Scotland and Catalonia (Dodeigne 2013).
6 I also include Walloon politicians called into the government of the French-speaking Community, also known as the Walloon-Brussels Federation.

7 In fact, the number of double or even triple candidacy increases to 151 when candidates at European elections are included. Source: author's own compilation of archives at Elections Canada/*Élections Canada*.

8 The critical swing of seats following the 1993 federal elections (the index score of 62.0) is not an exception but a general trend of federal elections in Quebec and elsewhere in Canada. Since 1994 there have been large swings of seats for the *Bloc Québécois* and the *Parti libéral du Québec*, while the success of the *Nouveau parti démocrate* (New Democratic Party) in 2011 confirms the extremely high seat volatility (index score of 57.0).

9 The absence of candidacy at elections is yet a mere proxy of voluntary decisions to retire from politics. In several cases, candidates failed to be reselected as candidates or decided not to present their candidacy due to the low likelihood of being reselected.

References

Ascher, William and Sidney Tarrow (1975). "The stability of communist electorates: evidence from a longitudinal analysis of French and Italian aggregate data", *American Journal of Political Science*, 19(3): 475–99.

Atkinson, Michael M. and David C. Docherty (1992). "Moving right along: the roots of amateurism in the Canadian House of Commons", *Canadian Journal of Political Science/Revue canadienne de science politique*, 25(2): 295–318.

Barrie, Doreen and Roger Gibbins (1989). "Parliamentary careers in the Canadian federal state", *Canadian Journal of Political Science/Revue canadienne de science politique*, 22(1): 137–45.

Bélanger, Éric (2009). "The 2008 provincial election in Quebec", *Canadian Political Science Review*, 3(1): 93–99.

Bélanger, Éric and Richard Nadeau (2007). "La montée des tiers partis au Québec à l'élection de 2007: conjoncture ou tendance?", *IRPP choices*, 14(17): 3–36.

Bille, Lars (2001). "Democratizing a democratic procedure: myth or reality?", *Party Politics*, 7(3): 363–80.

Blidook, Kelly (2010). "Exploring the role of 'legislators' in Canada: do members of parliament influence policy?", *The Journal of Legislative Studies*, 16(1): 32–56.

Borchert, Jens and Lutz Golsch (1995). "Die politische Klasse in westlichen Demokratien: Rekrutierung, Karriereinteressen und institutioneller Wandel", *Politische Vierteljahresschrift*, 36: 609–29.

Borchert, Jens and Klaus Stolz (2011). "Institutional order and career patterns: some comparative considerations", *Regional and Federal Studies*, 21(2): 271–282.

Bouhon, Frédéric, Min Reuchamps and Jérémy Dodeigne (2012). "La confection des listes: règles juridiques et pratiques politiques". In *Les systèmes électoraux de la Belgique*, ed. Frédéric Bouhon and Min Reuchamps, 189–207. Bruxelles: Bruylant.

Brack, Nathalie and Jean-Benoit Pilet (2010). "One country, two party systems? The 2009 Belgian regional elections", *Regional and Federal Studies*, 20(4): 549–59.

Bräuninger, Thomas, Martin Brunner and Thomas Däubler (2012). "Personal vote-seeking in flexible list systems: how electoral incentives shape Belgian MPs' bill initiation behaviour", *European Journal of Political Research*, 51(5): 607–45.

Buelens, Jo and Kris Deschouwer (2002). "Belgium", *Environmental Politics*, 11(1): 112–32.

Carty, R. Kenneth, William Cross and Lisa Young (2000). *Rebuilding Canadian Party Politics*, Vancouver: UBC Press.

Dandoy, Régis and Patrick Dumont (2012). "Selecting, moving and firing regional ministers in Belgium". Paper presented at the conference *The Selection and De-Selection of Political Elites: Multi-Level Systems in Comparative Perspective*, Concordia University, Montreal, Canada.

De Winter, Lieven, Donatella Della Porta and Kris Deschouwer (1996). "Comparing similar countries: Belgium and Italy", *Res Publica*, 38(2): 215–36.

Detterbeck, Klaus (2011). "Party careers in federal systems. Vertical linkages within Austrian, German, Canadian and Australian parties", *Regional and Federal Studies*, 21(2): 245–270.

Docherty, David (1997). *Mr. Smith Goes to Ottawa: Life in the House of Commons*, Vancouver: UBC Press.

Docherty, David (2011). "The Canadian political career structure: from stability to free agency", *Regional and Federal Studies*, 21(2): 185–203.

Dodeigne, Jérémy (2013). "Identifying and explaining career patterns in multi-level democracies. A comparative analysis of Catalonia, Quebec, Scotland an Wallonia". Paper presented at the 7th ECPR General Conference, Bordeaux, France.

Dodeigne, Jérémy (2014). "(Re-)Assessing career patterns in multi-level systems: insights from Wallonia in Belgium", *Regional and Federal Studies*, 24(2): 151–71.

Dodeigne, Jérémy and Audrey Vandeleene (2013). "New rules, new political class? Analysis of the impact of the electoral reforms in Belgium on the 2014 elections and aftermath". Paper presented at the Second edition of the conference 'Belgium: The State of the Federation', Louvain-La-Neuve, Belgium.

Fiers, Stefaan (2001a). "Carrièrepatronen van Belgische parlementsleden in een multi-level omgeving (1979–99)", *Res Publica*, 43(1): 171–92.

Fiers, Stefaan (2001b). "Level-hopping in a multi-level political landscape: political careers in Belgium and France". Paper presented at the *ECPR Joint Sessions of Workshops*, Grenoble, France.

Franks, C.E.S. (1987). *The Parliament of Canada*, Toronto: University of Toronto Press.

Gallagher, Michael and Michael Marsh (eds) (1988). *Candidate Selection in Comparative Perspective: The Secret Garden of Politics*, London: Sage Publications.

Herzog, Dietrich (1975). *Politische Karrieren*, Opladen: Westdeutscher Verlag.

Jeffery, Charlie and Arjan H. Schakel (2012). "Insights: Methods and data beyond methodological nationalism", *Regional Studies*, 47(3): 402–4.

Jones, Mark P. (2002). "Amateur legislators – professional politicians: the consequences of party centred electoral rules in a federal system", *American Journal of Political Science*, 46(3): 656–69.

Kerby, Matthew and Kelly Blidook (2011). "It's not you, it's me: determinants of voluntary legislative turnover in Canada", *Legislative Studies Quarterly*, 36(4): 621–43.

Kjaer, Ulrik (2011). "The depth of parliamentary elite circulation: long-term trends and critical elections in Denmark", *Comparative Sociology*, 10(6): 873–86.

Lipset, Seymour Martin (1990). *Continental Divide: The Values and Institutions of the United States and Canada*, London: Routledge.

Matland, Richard E. and Donley T. Studlar (2004). "Determinants of legislative turnover: a cross-national analysis", *British Journal of Political Science*, 34(1): 87–108.

Matthews, Donald R. (1984). "Legislative recruitment and legislative careers", *Legislative Studies Quarterly*, 9(4): 547–85.

Moncrief, Gary F. (1994). "Professionalization and careerism in Canadian provincial assemblies: comparison to U.S. state legislatures", *Legislative Studies Quarterly*, 19(1): 33–48.

Moncrief, Gary F. (1998). "Terminating the provincial career: retirement and electoral defeat in Canadian provincial legislatures, 1960–97", *Canadian Journal of Political Science/Revue canadienne de science politique*, 31(2): 359–72.

Moncrief, Gary F. (1999). "Recruitment and retention in U. S. legislatures", *Legislative Studies Quarterly*, 24(2): 173–208.

Norris, Pippa (1997). *Passages to Power. Legislative Recruitment in Advanced Democracies*, Cambridge: Cambridge University Press.

Pedersen, Mogens N (1979). "The Dynamics of European party systems: changing patterns of electoral volatility", *European Journal of Political Research*, 7(1): 1–26.

Pilet, Jean-Benoit, Stefaan Fiers and Kristof Steyvers (2007). "Carrière politique et recrutement des élites politiques en Belgique". In *Action publique et changements d'échelles: Les nouvelles focales du politique*, ed. Alain Faure, Jean-Philippe Leresche, Pierre Muller and Stéphane Nahrath, 309–20. Paris: L'Harmattan.

Rayside, David M. (1978). "Federalism and the party system: provincial and federal liberals in the province of Quebec", *Canadian Journal of Political Science/Revue canadienne de science politique*, 11(3): 499–528.

Real-Dato, Jos, Juan Rodríguez-Teruel and Miguel Jerez-Mir (2011). "In search of the 'ladder model': career paths of Spanish diputados (1977–2010)". Paper presented at the 6th *ECPR General Conference*, Reykjavik, Iceland.

Rosenthal, Alan (1974). "Turnover in state legislatures", *American Journal of Political Science*, 18(3): 609–16.

Schlesinger, Joseph A. (1966). *Ambition and Politics. Political Careers in the United States*, Chicago, IL: Rand McNally & Company.

Stolz, Klaus (2001). "The political class and regional institution-building: a conceptual framework", *Regional and Federal Studies*, 11(1): 80–100.

Stolz, Klaus (2003). "Moving up, moving down: political careers across territorial levels", *European Journal of Political Research*, 42(2): 223–48.

Stolz, Klaus (2010). *Towards a Regional Political Class? Professional Politicians and Regional Institutions in Catalonia and Scotland*, Manchester: Manchester University Press

Stolz, Klaus (2011). "The regionalization of political careers in Spain and the UK", *Regional and Federal Studies*, 21(2): 223–243.

Vanlangenakker, Ine, Bart Maddens and Gert-Jan Put (2010). "Political careers in Belgium: an example of the integrated career model", *Fédéralisme-Régionalisme*, 10. Available from: http://popups.ulg.ac.be/federalisme/document.php?id=939 (accessed 21 August 2014).

Von Beyme, Klaus (1996). "The concept of political class: A new dimension of research on elites?", *West European Politics*, 19(1): 68–87.

Weber, Max (1946). "Politics as a vocation". In *From Max Weber: Essays in Sociology*, ed. H.H. Gerth and C. Mills Wright, 77–128. New York: Oxford University Press.

Young, Lisa and Keith Archer (eds) (2002). *Regionalism and Party Politics in Canada*, Oxford: Oxford University Press.

5 Local politics in Quebec and Wallonia

Local political dynamics as seen through the mayoral career

Sandra Breux and Vincent Jacquet

In most Western democracies, the 2000s were marked by the restructuring of the local government systems (Saltzstein *et al.* 2008). In their various configurations, these reforms often contributed to a redefinition of the role of local elected officials, in particular that of the position of mayor (Schaap, Daemen and Ringelling 2009). In Wallonia as well as in Quebec, this redefinition of the roles of mayor manifested in the expansion of the electoral base. In Quebec, the municipal restructuring (2001–3) reduced the number of municipalities by merging some of them. The resulting fewer yet larger municipal entities then comprised an enlarged electoral base for the mayors, elected by direct universal suffrage since 1968. In the Walloon Region, the municipal reform of 2005 significantly changed the mode of designation of the *bourgmestre*, i.e. the mayor. Since then, to become *bourgmestre*, a candidate must obtain the most preferential votes on the list that receives the most votes among the political groups forming the *pacte de majorité*, i.e. the coalition agreement, adopted by the communal council (Matagne *et al.* 2011). While not a direct election, this mode of designation also expanded the electoral base of the mayor, who had been up to then designated by the King.

These restructurings of the local government were beneficial for some municipalities in that they strengthened the legitimacy of the local level of politics and the position of the mayor within that institutional architecture (Borraz and John 2004). However, the authority of the office of mayor tends to be questioned (Steyvers *et al.* 2008; Sweeting 2003). This context gives rise to research on the role of mayor and the resources at their disposal, the policies adopted on the basis of their party affiliation and their performance (Wouter and Schaap 2010). This research, in turn, sheds light on the overall local political dynamics at work (Becquart-Leclercq 1980; Flanagan 2004). However, while these studies identify the salient characteristics of the mayoral function, they generally restrict their analysis to the nature of the mayoral mandate exercised for a given term, only rarely investigating the broader question of the place that the mayoral function holds within a larger political career and what this place reveals about the local political dynamics. As such, Pilet, Fiers and Kristof state that "few studies have, for the time being, tried to apprehend the effects of this proliferation of political arenas ... on political competition, even though this has profoundly reshaped the career perspectives offered to legal agents" (2007: 309, our translation). In other words, in a contemporary context of multilevel governance, is the position of mayor a stepping stone to other spheres or a culminating point of the political career? Or, what is the importance of the municipal scale within a larger political career and what does this importance reveal to us about the local political dynamics at work?

This question is very pertinent in a comparison between Quebec and Wallonia, as these two territories present similarities with regard to their political architecture and, above all, the political challenges they face. However, as reminded in the Introduction and the first two chapters, they also have different political cultures and histories. The objective of this chapter is to engage in this comparison by examining the mayoral career. In that effort, we focus more on identifying and outlining trends than on explaining them, although some explanatory hypotheses will be advanced throughout.

We begin by examining the main characteristics of the career of mayor in both Quebec and Wallonia. Beyond the various meanings that can be attributed to the notion of "career", the mayoral career is the result of a convergence of variables, including the local institutional structure. It is this variable that is of particular interest when comparing two distinct multilevel contexts. We then specify the differences and similarities between Quebec and Wallonia with regard to their institutional architecture of local politics. Then, based on an exploratory analysis and survey that we conducted of all Quebec and Walloon mayors in office in 2005 and in 2006, we describe their socio-demographic profiles as well as the political functions they performed before accessing the position of mayor. The results of this survey show, unsurprisingly, significant differences in the construction of the mayoral career. However, similarities nevertheless exist with regard to the notion of local democracy. Moreover, the analysis of the mayoral career reveals a tendency to water down or even suppress ideological debate at the local scale, even if, especially in Wallonia, politicisation is far from disappearing completely.

1 The mayoral career: overview of some trends

Literature on the careers of local elected officials, in particular of mayors, is relatively limited and generally restricted to descriptive research. Most of the published studies concentrate on one type of municipality, are not longitudinal and are very little comparative.[1] Nevertheless, they do allow an identification of the main trends and topics in this field to the extent that they examine the questions of "who is the mayor?" and "who governs?" (Kjaer 2006). The first question addresses the definition and meaning of the word "career", while the second question seeks to reveal the socio-demographic variables likely to influence the election of a candidate for the position of mayor.

To begin, the socio-demographic profile of a local elected government official is designed to capture if such characteristics are likely to be indicative of his/her chances of being elected (Steyvers and Reynaert 2006), his/her political ambition or the nature of the policies adopted (Ferreira and Gyourko 2007; Gerber and Hopkins 2011). Gender, age and type of socio-professional activity emerge as the three main indicators. The findings of such studies tend to be relatively similar, despite the political and geographical differences of the regions covered. For example, gender remains a discriminatory factor (Alibegovic, Sliijepecevic and Sipic 2013; Johansson 2006), with women generally less represented than men in the office of mayor. As for age, the men holding these offices are often middle-aged. And, the representation of socio-professional categories tends to be imbalanced (Guérin-Lavignotte and Kerrouche 2006). In sum, Steyvers and Reynaert (2006) underline that, in the European context, elected officials are generally middle-aged men with a high professional status and an above-average level of education. For North America, a study conducted by McNitt on the mayors of big cities between 1820 and 1995 produced nearly identical findings, namely that the average age of mayors at their first election is 47 years. McNitt also states that "mayors are more likely to have college degrees or professional training and to be lawyers than the general public. Big city mayors are also more likely to be businessmen than the general public, and business is a more common prior profession than law" (2011: 437).

However, the literature on the careers of local elected officials differs in its understanding and use of the term "career". Some researchers use the term very broadly, others associate it with a higher level of professionalisation (Guérin-Lavignotte and Kerrouche 2006) and still others with a political specialisation (McNitt 2011). The angle from which the career of mayor is approached also diverges among authors. Some place more emphasis on the recruitment of mayors (Bäck 2006; Guérin-Lavignotte and Kerrouche 2006; Verhelst, Reynaert and Stevyers 2013), while others opt for a temporal perspective. For example, Kjaer (2006) considers the mayoral career to be defined primarily by its beginning and its end. According to him, the mayoral career is shaped by six main parameters: the duration of a prior mandate as a councillor (if any); the size of the municipality; partisanship; the institutional system; the entirety of all other functions realised before; seniority (age at which the mayor takes office); and higher political ambitions. Applying this analysis grid to 14 European countries, Kjaer identified the following trends. In general, the mayor had been a municipal councillor for six years before taking office, even though this was not a prerequisite (one third attain the position of mayor without having had political experience at the local level); only 5% had been upper-level elected officials before; and, at the time of the survey, the mayors had been in office for seven years.

Moreover, the evolution of the career of mayor was found to be based on a specific "opportunity structure" (Schlesinger 1966). For McNitt, in the US context, this opportunity structure is defined as the "age first elected, length of service, political career before becoming mayor, political career after becoming mayor, and partisanship" (2011: 438). The most determining factor of this opportunity structure is, according to McNitt, the function held as an elected official before becoming mayor. McKenzie for his part, also in the US context, arrived at a similar finding, stating that "previous political experience constitutes one of the more important factors shaping mayoral careers" (2009: 26). Still others point to the transformation of the mayoral career, arguing that today any elective office can be perceived as an end in itself. This stance undermines the conventional view of the local level as the ideal stepping stone for attaining higher elective office, and as a means for modifying partisan strategies. Without calling the traditional view of a career that develops in successive stages entirely into question, the study of Pilet *et al.* (2007) highlights the impact of the institutional context of contemporary governance. These researchers argue that although certain career models do seem to take shape, we should not forget that these profiles and careers exist within a specific institutional context that, itself, influences those same profiles and careers. And, "given that the proliferation of the levels of power modifies this 'opportunity structure', the framework within which candidates and mayors manage their political career can be expected to be affected" (Pilet *et al.* 2007: 310, our translation). That said, we shall first examine this institutional structure before going further.

2 Local institutional structures and the mayoral function

Numerous studies have analysed the local institutional structure, with many establishing typologies to enhance our understanding of this structure. Often, these typologies are built around indicators such as the degree of autonomy of the local government with regard to the other levels of government or their financial resources. This allows a better assessment of the impact of these institutional structures on the local political dynamics. As a result, there are also many writings that establish a link between the institutional architecture and the leadership of the mayor (Borraz and John 2004). Other studies, in the footsteps of Heinelt and Hlepas (2006), consider that local government systems are often perceived as variables that can affect, among other aspects, the mayoral career.

Two main categories of complementary typologies stand out. The first category, shaped in particular by the work of Hesse and Sharpe (1991), aims to capture the nature of the relations that the local government maintains with the other levels of government. Here, Heinelt and Hlepas, building on typologies already realised by other authors, establish three groups of countries. In the first, the local government represents distinct territorial communities and the mayor represents interests with respect to other levels of government. Among these countries are France, Italy, Belgium, Spain, Portugal and Greece. The second group includes countries where the local government has a low degree of autonomy while nevertheless playing a key role in the provision of public services. In such a system, the mayor is relatively powerless as a political leader, while the councillors and the "executive officers" are often strong. This group is comprised of the United Kingdom, Ireland, Canada, Australia, New Zealand and, "in some respects, the USA", (Heinelt and Hlepas 2006: 26). The third group is composed of the "North and Middle European group with the Scandinavian countries, Germany and the Netherlands (to which Austria and Switzerland can be added)" (Heinelt and Hlepas 2006: 26), which differ from those of the two other groups in that they have a strong constitutional status with a focus on the provision of public services. This third category, although leaving room for improvement, demonstrates the way in which institutions structure the role and power of the mayor at the local scale.

The second category of typologies generally revolves around the nature of the relationships that the mayor maintains with the municipal council or the head of the local administration. The typology of Wollmann (2004), for example, demonstrates how, at the local scale, the legislative function is separate from the executive function on the basis of three principal criteria: "1. 'Monistic' versus 'dualistic' types of local government; 2. Collective/collegiate body versus an individual exercising the executive function; 3. Indirect election/ appointment versus direct election of the executive" (2004: 151). With this typology, the author establishes a link between the institutional structure and the ways in which a mayor's leadership can develop. While the relevance and applicability of this specific type of typology has been criticised (Heinelt and Hlepas 2006), many other typologies have been developed in this category (Mourtizen and Svara 2002; Sellers and Lidström 2008). Overall, what the typologies of the second category have in common is that they show the influence of institutions on local political dynamics and on careers in local politics.

This brief excursion into the existing literature does not claim to be exhaustive. Rather, it aims to be illustrative of a number of recent studies that are likely to shed light on how the institutional structure of the local government can influence both the political career of the mayor and the local political dynamics. This is all the more relevant given that this same context has significantly changed over the past years, if only through the emergence of governance and the multiplication of the levels of power in certain contexts.

3 The local institutional contexts in Quebec and in Wallonia

The above description of the typologies showed that Quebec and Wallonia have very different institutional structures. Since its independence in 1830, Belgium has had a double local level that includes a communal level, comprising the *communes*, or municipalities, and a provincial level, comprising the initial ten provinces. With the transformation of Belgium from a unitary state to a federal state starting with the end of the 1960s, additional levels of power were added between the national level, which then became federal, and the local level: the regional level (the Flemish regions, the Walloon Region and the Brussels-Capital Region) and the communities (Flemish, French and

German-speaking communities). In Wallonia, the following levels of government have since existed: federal (the Belgian federal state), regional (the Walloon Region), community (the French-speaking Community), provincial (the five Walloon provinces) and communal – each with its own elected assembly and executive.

Belgium belongs to the type of country where municipalities have a great degree of autonomy, where the mayor represents the interests of the community, and where the regions oversee the municipalities and their organisation. In 1979, the number of Belgian municipalities was reduced from 2,359 to 589, the main objective being to create economies of scale. Yet, the political consequences of this reform were the professionalisation of mayors, the strengthening of the role of political parties and the diminishing role of grassroots activists. In addition, from then on candidates had to convince a larger number of people during elections (as the *communes* had become larger), which required greater resources, be it from the party apparatus or from experts in communication. In this way, a reform that may have appeared purely territorial and organisational in the beginning ended up modifying the political dynamics of the *communes* in Belgium. Wallonia is today composed of 262 municipalities, comprising some 3.5 million inhabitants on a territory of 16,844 km^2.

Three major actors compose the local government in Belgium: the council, directly elected by the inhabitants of the municipality; the executive, or "communal college", composed of the mayor and the aldermen; and the mayor him/herself. As for the regional and federal levels of government, the executive (the college) dominates the legislative (the council) in local politics (Wayenberg *et al.* 2011). However, the council has control over the executive, since it appoints the members of the college (chosen from among the members of the council) and has the right to dismiss them (individually or collectively) through votes of no confidence. The mayor has a dual status: he/she is the leader of the local political system, yet also the representative of the federal and regional governments on the territory of the municipality. This two-fold function reflects the two types of local political activity: those of "municipal interest" and carried out independently of the other political levels of government; and those directly assigned by the federal, regional or community government. The municipality then acts as a de-concentrated and decentralised authority (Bouvier 2012: 51–52). With these two types of activity, the municipality is a co-producer of public goods, the main ones being local public infrastructure, municipal schools, spatial planning, culture, tourism, housing, environment and health.

In Wallonia, citizens formally elect only the members of the council. This election is held every six years on the second Sunday of October, on the same day in the whole region (and, so far, in the entire country). The vote is compulsory and, given the proportional electoral system (the Imperiali method (Muylle 2012)), it is based on lists. Belgium no longer has any national parties; however, in contrast with Canada, its main parties are present in both the federal and the regional arenas. In Wallonia, the socialists, the liberals, the

Christian-democrats and the greens are the four major political forces competing in federal and regional elections. Generally, they also compete in local elections, through the intermediary of more or less autonomous local sections. This is especially the case in urban municipalities (Deschouwer 2009). Apart from the local lists pushed by the main parties, the Belgian political landscape also has several more or less independent lists that tend to run under nondescript labels such as "list of the mayor" or "municipal interests" (Reuchamps *et al.* 2013). Some of these lists claim to be independent while nevertheless maintaining unofficial links with a major political party, others are coalitions of different political parties, and still others are lists with no political ties (Dandoy *et al.* 2013).

As in the other levels of government in Belgium, the local executive is generally formed by a coalition of lists. The electoral law provides that the mandates of the mayor and aldermen begin with the signing of the *pacte de majorité*, which stipulates which political groups belong to the communal majority.[2] In practice, however, in some 65% of municipalities only one party holds the majority (Deschouwer 2009). In the other municipalities, political lists have to negotiate a coalition agreement in order to form a majority in the council and thus elect the college. According to Deschouwer, many coalitions are in fact pre-electoral coalitions, meaning that they are formed before the elections (2009: 166). The most important change in local elections occurred recently, albeit only in the Walloon Region, with the (quasi-)direct election of the mayor. As mentioned above, the *bourgmestre* was traditionally appointed by the King and, following the federalisation of the country, by the regional government, essentially comprised of the members of the local council. Today, the *bourgmestre* is the councillor who obtains the most preference votes on the list that received the most votes among the lists of the majority, which are the lists signed by the majority pact. This reform has a double logic. First, it gives more power to the citizens because the number of preferential votes is now taken into account in the designation of the mayor. But at the same time, the power of the lists, and thus of political parties, is also strengthened. The appointed mayor has to be the member of the strongest party in the majority; in other words, individual popularity alone is not enough. This favours the largest lists. In the Belgian reform, there is thus an ambiguity between the "democracy of the public" and the particracy, which is a general characteristic of Belgian politics (Matagne *et al.* 2011: 35–36; Valke 2009: 256).

In contrast with Belgium (and thus Wallonia), Canada belongs to the group of countries where the local government has a very low degree of autonomy. In the Canadian Constitution of 1867, Section 92 gives the jurisdiction of municipal affairs to the provinces. According to Dillon's Rule, municipalities have only the powers and responsibilities explicitly granted to them by the provinces, divided into mandatory and optional responsibilities (Collin, Léveillée, Rivard and Robertson 2003).[3] The province of Quebec is composed of 1,100 municipalities that, spanning over a territory of 1,667,441 km², is home to 7.9 million people.⁴ However, nearly half the province's population lives in the ten largest cities of Quebec, being those with more than 100,000 inhabitants. In Canada, debates emerged from the 1960s on about the reduction of the number of municipalities and the merging of public services in order to provide more efficient services across the large territory and create more fiscal equity. In Quebec, the number of municipalities dropped from 1,646 in 1978 to 1,106 in 2003.

The areas of intervention are partially similar to the Walloon case: public security, transportation, sanitation and environment, planning and urban planning recreation, and culture. However, one major difference with Europe is that in Quebec, and in Canada in general, municipalities have no responsibilities in the areas of health, social services and education (Collin, Léveillée, Rivard and Robertson 2003: 10–11). The main function of municipalities is the provision of local public goods.

Contrary to the Walloon case, Quebec municipalities only have one institution, the council, which is composed of the mayor and a varying number of municipal councillors. That council is both executive and legislative. Voters of the entire municipality elect the mayor, who then represents the entire population of the municipality. As in Wallonia, the number of councillors varies according to the size of the population. In a city with more than 20,000 inhabitants, councillors are elected by district. The mayor and the councillors are directly elected by majority rule on a single ballot. Quebec has been favourable to partisan organisation since the adoption, in 1978, of the Act Respecting Elections in Certain Municipalities, which modified the Cities and Towns Act. However, the local political parties are few in number and do not maintain ties with the federal and provincial political parties.

To summarise, municipalities in Quebec and in Wallonia are based on two distinct rationales that are reflected by and reflect their positions within their respective federal political system. In Quebec, the role of municipalities is to ensure the good administration of delegated competences, while in Wallonia municipalities seek to represent the central power while also constituting a political arena at the local level. These notions also entail different opportunity structures, each giving rise to distinct mayoral careers and profiles, and consequently different local political dynamics. Studying the mayor, as the central figure of local politics, can thus shed light on these dynamics.

We collected official data in both regions in order to explore the figure of mayor, including the political functions performed by most mayors before taking the office of mayor. For Quebec, our data on gender, age of mayor and partisan affiliation was derived from a database compiled by MAMROT (*Ministère des Affaires municipales, des Régions et de l'Occupation du territoire*) in all municipalities during the 2005 elections. We complemented this database with information obtained from email surveys sent to all municipalities, asking these to document the biography of the mayor in office in 2005. It should be mentioned that obtaining data for research purposes from Quebec municipalities is difficult, namely because many municipalities, being small (less than 5,000 inhabitants) and remote from the main urban centres, operate with a skeleton staff. This is why we sometimes had to resort to other information-gathering techniques. Among these were press reviews, which often offered exhaustive information about the biographies and actions of mayors. Telephone interviews were also held with municipalities (archive services, secretaries and in some cases the mayors themselves) when necessary. In addition, we verified whether the names of the elected mayors appeared in the archives of the provincial and federal Canadian parliament websites. In 2005, Quebec had a total of 1,099 positions of mayor that were either filled or were in the process of being filled. In Wallonia, the field work proved to be easier than in Quebec. To complement the official data, we sent an email questionnaire to the mayors themselves in order to obtain the same additional data as in Quebec. The response rate here was 63.7%.

We chose the years 2005 and 2006 as these were election years for which the most data was available. In Wallonia, the 2006 elections were also the first elections using the new modes of designating the *bourgmestre*, which modified the electoral framework at the local level.

4 From profile to career: comparisons of Quebec mayors and Walloon *bourgmestres*

Unsurprisingly, the socio-demographic characteristics of the mayors are somewhat different from those of the rest of the population. As pointed out by Manin, an election is always a process of discrimination, which usually leads to the selection of an individual perceived as superior rather than one who "represents" the voters in the sense of being similar to them (Manin 1996: 186–87, 299–300). Yet, the profile of the typical representative changes over space and time, generally in accordance with the political dynamics of a given society. As a result, at the local as well as the national level, the likelihood of a candidate being voted into an elected office can be seen to depend on the characteristics of the prevailing social climate.

In both Quebec and Wallonia, gender is the characteristic for which there is the largest bias, as 86.5% of mayors in Quebec and 90.5% in Wallonia are male. These figures speak for themselves and confirm our view of the slow and difficult feminisation of political life in the two regions at the local level. Age is another important variable. While most local leaders range between 45 and 64 years of age, over 40% are between 55 and 64 in both regions (Table 5.1).

Table 5.1 Age of mayors at the time of entry into office (2005/2006)

Age group of the mayor	18–34 yrs	35–44 yrs	45–54 yrs	55–64 yrs	65+
Quebec (all mayors)	2.0%	10.6%	29.8%	45.1%	12.5%
Wallonia (mayors who participated in the survey)	0.6%	13.9%	20.5%	42.2%	22.9%

Thus, regional differences are not particularly pronounced with regard to gender and age, suggesting that the other attributes of a winning candidate might be similar in both regions as well. Nevertheless, our analysis of the mayoral profiles reveals certain distinctions, in particular with regard to the number of women elected at the local scale.

In Quebec, the number of elected women in 2005 at the municipal scale was overall on the rise, with 27% of municipal councillors and 13% of mayors being women. In Quebec, MAMROT as well as various regions of the province implemented a number of initiatives promoting female candidacies across all offices at the municipal scale (e.g. the programme *À égalité pour décider*).[5] These initiatives responded also to an imbalance with regard to these two positions, identified by MAMROT as follows (our translation):

> Women are still more likely to, in absolute numbers and in proportion, occupy the office of councillor than the office of mayor. Of the 1,999 women elected in 2005, 1,855 were voted in as municipal councillor and 144 as mayor. This corresponds to 93% and 7%, respectively, compared to their male counterparts, of whom 84% are elected as councillor and 16% as mayor.[6]
>
> (MAMROT 2010, online, see Note 6)

The results of the 2009 municipal elections then pointed to the continual increase of women, who obtained 29.3% of the positions of councillor and 16% of the positions of mayor (Secrétariat à la condition féminine 2010). Quebec could thus be seen to distinguish itself from the main trends observed elsewhere. In Wallonia, by contrast, the measures taken to improve gender representation were more radical. There, a decree from 8 December 2005 imposed parity in the lists, with the obligation that the two front-runners of the lists *must* be of different genders (Matagne *et al.* 2011).

Lastly, concerning age, our results for Quebec and Wallonia are similar as well as consistent with the recognised trend that applies to both North America and Europe. In Europe, "on average the mayor is around the age of fifty" (Steyvers and Reynaert 2006: 51), whereas in Quebec, at the 2005 municipal elections, "the average age of the mayors was five years higher than that of the councillors" and on average 51 years, with women slightly younger than the men" (MAMROT 2005: 2, our translation).

The different roles of partisanship in the two regions can also be expected to lead to different career types in Quebec and in Wallonia. In Quebec, only 6.8% of mayors are members of authorised local political parties. In Wallonia, local politics relies more on a competition of political lists, which are, as discussed, often linked with a political party. For example, 41.6% of elected mayors come from independent local lists; yet the "independence" of these lists from political parties is ambiguous and their degree of autonomy is often difficult to determine (Steyvers *et al.* 2008). Two types of independent *bourgmestre* can be distinguished. Those who are truly independent and who have no national political background; and those who are members of a national political party yet who prefer to present themselves under the "independent" label, considering that local politics is of a different nature than the other levels of power. We shall return to this point in the final discussion.

Aside from the label of the list, the nature of the mayoral career helps to shed light on their real political profile. We distinguish here between the career at the local level (internal) and the political activity outside the municipality (external). On the internal side, we should underline an incumbency effect in both regions. Some 36% of the mayors in Quebec had held a local mandate before being elected. This percentage is even greater in the Walloon case, where 95.2% of the mayors who responded to our questionnaire had a prior local mandate. Thus, an internal path seems to exist in both regions. On the external side, there are differences in the opportunity structure between Quebec and Wallonia. In Quebec, only 4.5% of the mayors had been candidates or elected officials at another level of government prior to taking office. This confirms the relative independence of Quebec local politics from provincial and federal levels of government. Only very few mayors had political experience outside their municipality. On average they are younger than their Walloon counterparts and more often than not (62.5%) they come from cities with less than 5,000 inhabitants. Intuitively, one could have assumed that the larger the municipality, the more likely its mayor is to engage in provincial or federal politics. But, this is not the case in Quebec, quite the contrary.

Moreover, unsurprisingly, there is a link between partisanship at the local level and candidacy at another level of government. There are more members of authorised parties (18%) among the mayors who had prior extra-local experience. When looking at the political career of mayors who had served in other political functions (Table 5.2), there is a difference between the provincial level and the federal level. The provincial level is much more attractive than the federal level, and also has a slightly higher success rate (one out of three mayors who were candidates for provincial elections got elected, and one out of four mayors who were candidates for federal elections got elected). The number of mayors who had been candidates at both levels of government is extremely low.

Table 5.2 Political career of mayors in Quebec who had served in other political functions

Political function held before	Frequency
Municipal councillor	34%
Candidate for a federal election	38%
Federal MP	10%
Candidate for a provincial elections	60%
Provincial MP	26%
Candidate for both levels of government	2%

Note: n = 50 out of a total of 1,099

The general trends in Belgium show a reverse picture. Some 70.3% of our respondents had been or are involved in an activity at one other level in Belgium. (That percentage is approximately twice as high as that of Quebec respondents, which could possibly be attributed to the fact that Belgium has, in addition to the regional and federal levels, the provincial and the European levels of government). In terms of gender, there is no significant difference with Quebec. In terms of age, mid-life mayors (35–44 years and 45–54 years) are those who cumulate the most votes. As for the size of the municipality, we observed that mayors of municipalities with more than 10,000 inhabitants are more likely to have had prior experience at one other level of competency. So, in contrast with Quebec, the larger the municipality, the more likely a mayor is to compete at other levels of politics. This not only correlates with the size of the municipality but also with partisanship (on this issue Wallonia is similar to Quebec). Indeed, mayors elected on a list with the name of a political party are almost invariably candidates at other levels of power (Table 5.3). This does not mean that mayors from independent lists engage only in local politics (44.9% have experience at another level of government), but that they are proportionally less likely to do so.

From a multilevel perspective, the prior external careers of mayors are quite different. There is no one single path to becoming mayor. This diversity is reflected in both the large opportunity structure in Wallonia and in the political choices of the mayors seeking extra-local activities. More than one third of them are or have been members of the provincial assembly. In Belgium and in Wallonia in particular, the provincial assembly is in fact local politics on a larger scale. The "provincial" mayors are thus quite different from the mayors who compete at the regional and federal (and European, to a lesser extent) levels. Here we find a perfect split: 14% of the mayors went on to seek positions at the federal level and 14% at the regional level. While most of the

Table 5.3 Political career of mayors in Wallonia who had served in other political levels

Political function held before	Frequency
European MP	1%
Federal MP	13%
European and federal MP	1%
Provincial MP	39%
Provincial and federal MP	8%
Provincial and regional MP	4%
Provincial, regional and European MP	1%
Provincial, regional and federal MP	3%
Provincial, regional, federal and European MP	1%
Regional MP	13%
Regional and European MP	1%
Regional and federal MP	13%
Regional, federal and European MP	1%

Table 5.4 Distribution of Walloon *bourgmestres* by political party

Political affiliations	N	Frequency
Independent list	53	44.9%
Christian Democrats (cdH)	10	8.5%
Ecologists (Ecolo)	1	0.8%
Liberals (MR)	17	14.4%
Socialists (PS)	35	29.7%
Other	2	1.6%

mayors move on to only one other level of government, one third of them nevertheless had prior experience at two or more levels in addition to the local level. Finally, as shown in Table 5.4, 44.9% of them are elected on independent lists, even if quite a few of them have held positions at other levels of government for a given political party. This confirms that at the local level several mayors prefer to water down ideological labels. Nonetheless, a majority of the mayors still show a partisan affiliation, with a distribution that more or less reflects the vote share at the national/regional level.

5 Profiles and careers of mayors: a reflection of the competition and local political identity?

The differences between Quebec and Wallonia call into question the place of the local political scale within a political career that evolves in the context of a multilevel governance. We remind you that our main goal is to be descriptive. However, in this last section of the study, we wish to present elements that could provide insight into certain characteristics of the profiles described above.

Our comparison between Quebec and Wallonia shows deep distinctions in terms of local political competition. Two elements can explain these differences: the nature of the multilevel governance and the political structure of the local scene. As for the nature of the multilevel governance, in Wallonia local officials are considered a valuable pool of people who could eventually serve at other, upper scales, which is likely due to the large number of government offices at those other levels. This possibility of being recruited then influences the political careers of local officials. From a legal point of view, Quebec and Wallonia provide different possibilities of political careers and different opportunity structures for politicians (see Dodeigne in this book). The cumulating of mandates in local, provincial and national politics at the same time (vertical synchronic cumulating) is not possible in Canada, where the Act Respecting Elections and Referendums in Municipalities prohibits a member of parliament (MP) from being mayor at the same time as holding another office (Mévellec 2007: 11). This is entirely different in Wallonia, where, to date, no laws exclude the possibility for a national or regional MP to become mayor of a city. If at all, it is the political parties that may prohibit their members, by means of an ethics code, from engaging in such practices. However, as pointed out by Mévellec, in Quebec it is not prohibited to have mandates or to be active at different levels of government over time (2007: 11). The practical possibilities are also different. There are 1,106 mayors in Quebec for about 200 MPs (75 in the federal parliament, 125 in the provincial parliament).

By contrast, there are 262 mayors in Wallonia for somewhat less than 200 MPs (68 in the federal parliament, 75 in the Walloon parliament, 8 in the European parliament, plus the different mandates of the provincial assemblies). The aspect of the multilevel career in Wallonia corresponds to the general perception of the mayor's role in Wallonia. Valcke explains that the role of lobbyist is considered to be the most important role of the mayor (2009). This means that the larger a mayor's network outside their municipality, the more lobbying they are able to do for their municipality. This is especially important with regard to finding funding for a municipality, as the other levels of government all finance local projects within the remit of their powers. Mayors are therefore keen to build contacts outside the strict arena of their municipality, notably by engaging in provincial, regional and federal politics. Involvement in other levels of government is therefore a particularly important way to solve local problems. Our study of the political careers of the local agents thus provided elements for analysing the intergovernmental relations in the multinational federations from an informal and personal point of view. Our main finding was that Belgium has a strong multilevel governance, unlike Quebec, where the different levels of government are composed of political actors who tend to stick to their level of government.

And as for the political structure of the local scene: it largely diverges. In Wallonia the political parties of the upper echelons are present (sometimes indirectly) at the local scale; while in Quebec the provincial and federal political parties are not present at the local scene. As a result, the mayoral career in Wallonia is realised within a politicised context and in Quebec within an apolitical universe. Moreover, in Quebec the political organisation of the municipal scene is weak. Of the few municipal political parties that exist, most are weakly organised and of a short life span, and the majority of candidates and elected officials are independent candidates. In addition, the potential pool of candidates remains limited. In Quebec, return by acclamation, in other words, being re-elected automatically in the absence of an opponent – which applied to 54.6% of candidates in a position of mayor in 2005 – underlines the difficulty of recruiting candidates who are interested in taking part in local politics while also pointing to a trend to "professionalise" at the local scale. This is compounded with the large number of incumbents who are re-elected. In 2009, for example, the percentage of re-elected incumbent candidates, all offices combined, for the nine biggest cities in Quebec rose to 82.5% (Collin 2011).

This difference between Quebec and Wallonia also questions the traditional presentation of the political career in multilevel polities (Pilet *et al.* 2007). The political career is often considered as one of "successive stages". Many politicians begin at the local level, and the best go step by step to the top, the national level. This dynamic relies on three components: the accessibility of local politics, there being more mandates; the learning process; and the symbolic hierarchy of functions (national is higher than regional is higher than local). But neither in Quebec nor in Wallonia does the data corroborate such a dynamic. As discussed, in Quebec, local politicians tend to remain local politicians, with most never seeking to engage in any other level of government. For them, the municipality is the centre of politics. Yet in Wallonia, where most mayors are engaged in other levels of government, the same applies. This is because the main motivation for mayors to engage in other levels of government is to contribute to their municipality. According to Pilet *et al.*, the careers of the Walloon mayors tally more with an anarchic model (2007: 320) than a hierarchical one. The absence of any clear progression in the different political careers indicates that the municipality is only one among many other possibilities in a politician's career. Mayors are members of a "political class" that tries to remain in local power. Their objective is to remain professional politicians and to find a mandate within that architecture (Borchert and Golsch 1999) in order to strengthen their local position, which then strengthens their other positions.

Lastly, even though the structures of the local scenes in Quebec and Wallonia differ significantly, both have a penchant for apoliticism, seemingly in an effort to disassociate themselves from any ideological stances. In Quebec this situation is more predominant and strongly anchored in the local political landscape, which may be explained by the influence of the Reformists and by the fact that local political parties, when present, are apolitical (Bherer and Breux 2012). Thus, the local scale here is characterised by a levelling of all identity markers. Wallonia, for its part, presents two types of case. On the one hand, the majority (58.4%) of mayors come from national political lists, which explains the continuity between local politics and politics at the other levels of power. It is these same parties, and the same people, who thus compete against each other at the local level – a concept that does not exist in the Quebec framework. Nevertheless, a good portion of the Walloon mayors do present themselves as independent or neutral (41.6%). While many of these clearly have a partisan political affiliation at another level of power, they wish to present themselves as neutral at the local level. In this regard, they share commonalities with the Quebec apolitical and apartisan concept.

It should be underlined that this political independence does not have the same meaning in Belgium as it does in Quebec. In Wallonia this independence, be it real or false, takes place in a strongly politicised context. In Quebec, by contrast, political independence, or non-partisanship, is the norm and also has consequences on the way in which the local democracy and the career of the elected official evolve. Here, the issues at stake are often perceived as being essentially technical or administrative. This non-partisanship could be one explanation for the fact that the career of mayor in Quebec often stops at the local scale.[7] Nevertheless, a tendency to strip the municipal scale of any ideological debate exists in Quebec and Wallonia alike, although less strongly in Wallonia. In Quebec, the absence of partisanship is born from the idea that local democracy is more "managerial" than "existential" (Oliver, Shang and Callen 2012). This notion barely exists in the strongly politicised context of Wallonia, where apoliticism essentially becomes an ideological orientation, as any another, and serves as an electoral strategy.

6 Conclusion

Our research demonstrates that the analysis of the mayoral career provides an interesting angle from which to capture and understand local political dynamics. The cases of Quebec and Wallonia show the importance that the institutional structure of the local scene holds for the definition of the mayoral career and for the political dynamics at work. Both cases show a desire to maintain the local level non-partisan and independent from the other levels of government. The findings also show that this non-partisanship has a specific meaning in each context as well as consequences on the mayoral career and on the way in which a municipal democracy defines itself. As with any research study, our survey has limitations. The main limitation is that we based ourselves exclusively on the functions that the mayors held prior to their election to office as mayor. In future studies, it would thus be interesting to examine what these mayors and *bourgmestres* do after leaving office. Future surveys could also examine the extent to which mayors aspire to run for a political party at the federal or provincial level, particularly in the case of Quebec. We know that this phenomenon does exist in Quebec and that, through activism within a party, mayors are, in fact, brought to discuss with the upper echelons of politics. However, unlike in Wallonia, partisan affiliations of Quebec mayors are only rarely displayed in local electoral campaigns. To summarise, the most important finding of our survey is: first, this demonstrated a willingness to make of the local – in theory at least – a partisan scene that is independent of the other levels of government; and, secondly, that this non-partisanship has a meaning as well as consequences on the way in which a municipal democracy defines itself and on the mayoral career.

Notes

1 With the exception of the work of Bäck, Heinelt and Magnier (2006), which offers a detailed comparison between different European countries.
2 Sec. L1123–1 of the *Code of Local Democracy and Decentralisation* of Wallonia from 22 April 2004.
3 In Quebec, as in the other Canadian provinces, the federal government rarely attempts to intervene in local politics and hardly ever challenges the provincial government's competence on local matters (Rivard and Collin 2006). In Wallonia, by contrast, municipalities are more connected with the federal government through the central figure of the mayor, who is not only a local representative but also the representative of the federal and the regional governments.

4 In addition to these 1,106 municipalities, there are also an additional 23 municipalities in the Nord-du-Québec that are governed according to the *Régime municipal nordique.*
5 For more information, see www.scf.gouv.qc.ca/?id=32 (accessed 1 December 2012),
of the Secrétariat à la Condition féminine pour l'égalité entre les femmes et les
hommes. Site consulted in December 2012.
6 See www.mamrot.gouv.qc.ca/organisation-municipale/democratie-municipale/archives-
des-resultats-des-elections-municipales/elections-municipales-2005/donnees-sur-le-
sexe-et-lage-des-elus/ (accessed 1 December 2012).
7 The fact that the rate of re-election is equally large in Quebec may explain the fact
that the mayors do not compete at other scales, preferring instead to work towards
a new mandate at the local scale (Kushner, Siegel and Stanwick 2001).

References

Alibegovic, Dubravka J., Sliijepecevic, Suncana and Sipic Josip, J. (2013). "The gender
gap among local representatives: a potential for local development?" In *Local
Councillors in Europe*, ed. Björn Egner, David Sweeting and Pieter-Jan Klok, 181–202.
Wiesbaden: Springer VS.
Bäck, Henri (2006). "Does recruitment matter? Selecting path and role definition". In
*The European Mayor. Political Leaders in the Changing Context of Local Democ-
racy*, ed. Henri Bäck, Hubert Heinelt and Annick Magnier, 123–50. Wiesbaden: VS
Verlag für Sozialwissenschaften.
Bäck, Henri, Heinelt, Hubert and Magnier, Annick (2006). *The European Mayor.
Political Leaders in the Changing Context of Local Democracy*, Wiesbaden: VS Verlag
für Sozialwissenschaften.
Becquart-Leclercq, Jeanne (1980). "Local political recruitment in France and in the
United States: a study of mayors", *European Journal of Political Research*, 8(4): 407–22.
Belley, Serge, Bherer, Laurence, Chiasson, Guy, Collin, Jean-Pierre, Hamel, Pierre,
Hamel, Pierre-J., Rivard, Mathieu, with the collaboration of Archambault Julie
(2009). "Québec". In *Foundations of Governance: Municipal's Government in Canada's
Provinces*, ed. Andrew Sancton and Robert Young, 70–137. Toronto: IPAC-University
of Toronto Press.
Bherer, Laurence and Breux, Sandra (2012). "L'apolitisme municipal", *Bulletin d'Histoire
politique*, 21(1): 170–84.
Borchert, Jens and Golsch, Lutz (1999). "Die politische Klasse in westlichen Demokratien: Rekrutierung, Karriereinteressen and institutioneller Wandel". In *Politik as
Beruf*, ed. Jens Borchert, 114–40. Opladen: Leske and Budrich.
Borraz, Olivier and John, Peter (2004). "The transformation of urban political lea-
dership in Western Europe", *International Journal of Urban and Regional Research*,
28(1): 107–20.
Bouvier, Michel (2012). "Local government in Belgium". In *Local governement in the
members states of European Union in a Comparative legal perspective*, ed. Angel-Manuel
Moreno, 45–68. Madrid: Instituto National de Adminsitracio Publica.
Collin, Jean-Pierre (2011). "Quel avenir pour la démocratie municipale québécoise?"
In *Les élections municipales au Québec: enjeux et perspectives*, ed. Sandra Breux and
Laurence Bherer, 311–51. Québec: Presses de l'Université Laval.
Collin, Jean-Pierre, Léveillée, Jacques, Rivard, Mathieu and Robertson, Mélanie (2003).
*L'organisation municipale au Canada: Un régime à géométrie variable, entre tradition
et transformation*, Montréal: Groupe de recherche sur l'innovation municipale.

Dandoy, Régis, Matagne, Geoffroy, Reuchamps, Min and Dodeigne, Jérémy (2013). *Les élections communales de 2012 en Wallonie*, Bruges: Vanden Broele.

Deschouwer, Kris (2009). *Politics of Belgium: Governing a Divided Society*, London: Palgrave Macmillan.

Ferreira, Fernando and Gyourko, Joseph (2007). "Do political parties matter? Evidence from US cities: National Bureau of Economic Research". NBER Working Paper no. 13535. Available from: www.nber.org/papers/w13535 (accessed 28 August 2014).

Flanagan, Richard M (2004). "Opportunities and constraints on mayoral behavior: a historical-institutional approach", *Journal of Urban Affairs*, 26(1): 43–65.

Gerber, Elisabeth and Hopkins, Daniels J. (2011). "When Mayors matter: estimating the impact of mayoral partisanship on city policy", *American Journal of Political Science*, 55(2), 326–39.

Guérin-Lavignotte, Elodie and Kerrouche, Eric (2006). *Les élus locaux en Europe*, Paris: La documentation française.

Heinelt, Hubert and Hlepas, Nikolaos-K. (2006). "Typologies of local governement systems". In *The European Mayor. Political Leaders in the Changing Context of Local Democracy*, ed. Henri Bäck, Hubert Heinelt and Annick Magnier, 23–42. Wiesbaden: VS Verlag für Sozialwissenschaften.

Hesse, Joachim J. and Sharpe, Laurence J. (1991). "Local governement in international perspective: some comparative observations". In *Local Government and Urban Affairs in International Perspective. Analyses of Twenty Western Industrialised Countries*, ed. Joachim J. Hesse and Laurence J. Sharpe, 603–21. Baden-Baden: Nomos.

Johansson, Vicki (2006). "Gendered roads to mayorship in different welfare states". In *The European Mayor. Political Leaders in the Changing Context of Local Democracy*, ed. Henri Bäck, Hubert Heinelt and Annick Magnier, 99–121. Wiesbaden: VS Verlag für Sozialwissenschaften.

Kjaer, Ulrik (2006). "The mayor's political career". In *The European Mayor. Political Leaders in the Changing Context of Local Democracy*, ed. Henri Bäck, Hubert Heinelt and Annick Magnier, 76–98. Wiesbaden: VS Verlag für Sozialwissenschaften.

Kushner, Joseph, Siegel, David and Stanwick, Hannah (2001). "Canadian mayors: a profile and determinants of electoral success", *Canadian Journal of Urban research*, 10(1): 5–22.

Le Bart, Christian (2009). "Les nouveaux registres de légitimation des élus locaux". In *L'élu local aujourd'hui*, ed. Cristian Bidégaray, Stéphane Cadiou and Christine Pina, 201–11. Grenoble: Presses universitaires de Grenoble.

MAMROT (Ministère des Affaires municipales, des Régions et de l'Occupation du territoire) (2005). Archives des résultats des élections municipales. Élections municipales 2005 – Données sur le sexe et l'âge des élus. Available from: www.mamrot.gouv.qc.ca/organisation-municipale/democratie-municipale/archives-des-resultats-des-elections-municipales/elections-municipales-2005/donnees-sur-le-sexe-et-lage-des-elus/ (accessed 28 August 2014).

Manin, Bernard (1996). *Les principes du gouvernement représentatif*, Paris: Flammarion.

Matagne, Geoffroy, Radoux, Eammanuel and Verjans, Pierre (2011). "La composition du collège communal après la réforme du code wallon de la démocratie locale", *Courrier hebdomadaire du CRISP*, 2094: 5–35.

McKenzie, Scott A (2009). "For Mayors, the future is now: the effects of political experience on mayoral reelection and retirement". Paper presented at the Annual Meeting of the American Political Science Association, Toronto, Canada.

McNitt, Andrew D (2011). "Big city mayors: political specialization and business domination in the 19th and 20th centuries", *Journal of Urban Affairs*, 33(4): 431–49.

Mévellec, Anne (2007). "Regarder dans l'angle mort. Le cumul des mandats au Québec". Paper presented at the *Congrès de l'Association française de science politique*, Toulouse, France.

Mourtizen, Poul and Svara, James (2002). *Leadership at the Apex. Politicians and Administrators in Western Local Governments*, Pittsburgh, PA: Pittsburgh University Press.

Muylle, Koen (2012). "Le mode de scrutin". In *Les systèmes électoraux de la Belgique*, ed. Frédéric Bouhon and Min Reuchamps, 307–29. Bruxelles: Bruylant.

Oliver, Eric. J., Shang, E. Ha. and Callen, Zachary (2012). *Local Elections and the Politics of Small Scale Democracy*, Princeton, NJ and Oxford: Princeton University Press.

Pilet, Jean-Benoit, Fiers, Stefaan and Steyvers, Kristof (2007). "Des élus multi-niveaux. Carrière politique et recrutement des élites en Belgique". In *L'action publique à l'épreuve des changements d'échelle*, ed. Alain Faure, Jean-Philippe Leresche, Pierre Muller and Stéphane Nanrath, 309–320. Paris: Presses Universitaires de France.

Reuchamps, Min, Saudmont, Anne, Kravagna, Marine and Jacquet, Vincent (2013). "Le nom des listes". In *Les élections communales de 2012 en Wallonie*, ed. Régis Dandoy, Geoffroy Matagne, Min Reuchamps and Jérémy Dodeigne, 27–45. Bruges: Vanden Broele.

Rivard, Mathieu and Collin, Jean-Pierre (2006). *Le système municipal au Canada en bref*, Montréal: Institut National de la Recherche Scientifique, centre Urbanisation, Culture et Société.

Rysavy, Dan (2013). "European mayors and councillors: similarities". In *Local Councillors in Europe*, ed. Björn Egner, David Sweeting and Pieter-Jan Klok, 161–80. Wiesbaden: Springer VS.

Saltzstein, Alan L., Copus, Colin, Sonenshein, Raphael J. and Skelcher, Chris (2008). "Visions of urban reform: comparing English and U.S. strategies for improving city government", *Urban Affairs Review*, 44(2): 155–81.

Schaap, Linze, Daemen, Harry and Ringelling, Arthur (2009). "Mayors in seven European countries: Part 1. Selection and procedures and statutory position", *Local Governement Studies*, 35(1): 91–108.

Schlesinger, Jospeh (1966). *Ambition and politics*, Chicago, IL: Rand McNally.

Secrétariat à la condition féminine (2010). *Portrait des Québécoises en 8 temps*, Québec: Ministère de la Culture, des Communications et de la Condition féminine.

Sellers, Jeffery M. and Lidström, Anders (2008). "Decentralization, local government and the welfare state", *Governance*, 20: 609–32.

Steyvers, Kristof, Bergström, Tomas, Bäck, Henri, Boogers, Marcel, Ruano de la Fuente, José Manuel and Schaap, Linze (2008). "From princeps to president? Comparing local political leadership transformation", *Local Governement Studies*, 34(2): 131–46.

Steyvers, Kristof and Reynaert, Herwig (2006). "'From the few are chosen the few … ' On the social background of European mayors". In *The European Mayor. Political Leaders in the Changing Context of Local Democracy*, ed. Henri Bäck, Hubert Heinelt and Annick Magnier, 43–73. Wiesbaden: VS Verlag für Sozialwissenschaften.

Sweeting, David (2003). "How strong is the Mayor of London?", *Policy and Politics*, 31(4): 465–78.

Valke, Tony (2009). "Belgian mayors and governors. Leadership in a changing multi-level context". In *Local Political Leadership in Europe*, ed. Herwig Reynaert, Kristof Steyvers, Pascal Delwit and Jean-Benoit Pilet, 247–83. Bruges: Vanden Broele Publishers.

Verhelst, Tom, Reynaert, Herwig and Stevyers, Kristof (2013). "Political Recruitment and career development of local councillors in Europe". In *Local Councillors in Europe*, ed. Björn Egner, David Sweeting and Pieter-Jan Klok, 27–55. Wiesbaden: Springer VS.

Wayenberg, Ellen, De Rynck, Filip, Stevyers, Kristof and Pilet, Jean-Benoit (2011). "Belgium, a table of regional divergence". In *The Oxford Handbook of Local and regional Democracy*, ed. John Loughlin, Frank Hendriks and Anders Lidström, 71–95. Oxford: Oxford University Press.

Wollmann, Hellmut (2004). "Urban leadership in German local politics: the rise, role and performance of the directly electef (chief executive) mayor", *International Journal of urban and Regional Research*, 28(1): 150–65.

Wouter, Jan Verheul and Schaap, Linze (2010). "Srong leaders? The challenges and pitfalls in mayoral leadership", *Public Administration*, 88(2): 439–54.

Part III
Policies in Quebec and Wallonia

6 Québécois and Walloon public administrations

A tool towards autonomy?

Maxime Petit Jean

Over the past 30 years, the landscape of the public sector in many countries has been radically modified, partly due to pressure of theories such as New Public Management (NPM). New Public Management calls, for example, for the use of private-sector techniques and for more competition in the public sector to reduce costs (Hood 1991). In this respect, Québec and Wallonia[1] are no exception: public management reforms have been undertaken in each of these polities to modernise the administration, although NPM has not been as influential as in other Anglo-Saxon countries or Canadian provinces (Facal and Bernier 2009; Pollitt and Bouckaert 2011). As a result, reforms had different scope and pace compared to others provinces in Canada as well as in regard to Flanders in Belgium. Nonetheless they were not insignificant in the development of the studied entities.

This chapter is composed of three main sections. The first two diachronically study the recent reforms of the Québécois and Walloon administrations, and their role in consolidating the autonomy of their respective entities. In this respect, we mostly focus on ministries, giving less attention to agencies and other decentralised public bodies. Moreover, we concentrate our analysis with a focus on the last 15 years, considering, for example, the 2000 Public Administration Act in Quebec, and the creation of a unique central ministry in Wallonia. These two reforms are emblematic of a change in the public management of these substate administrations towards a more efficient and more responsive service delivery. In the last section, we first analyse the different reforms and give some comparative insights, notably on factors supporting or not the administrative reforms. Secondly, we assess how these reforms could contribute or not to an enhancement of the respective autonomy of Quebec and Wallonia.

Before starting to describe reforms in both polities, we should give the reader a few elements related to public-management reforms. A first glance at the international literature clearly highlights a large range of studies and issues related to these reforms, although it seems partly unbalanced as case studies mainly focus on Anglo-Saxon and North European countries (Ongaro 2010). Like Pollitt and Bouckaert (2011), we consider public-management reforms as "deliberate changes to the structures and processes of public-sector organisations with the objective of getting them (in some sense) to run better". As noted by Ongaro:

> The definition proposed is broad enough to encompass both the formulation of the public-management reform packages (the policy decisions in the public-management policy domain) and the implementation of the reform packages, as well as the larger transformations occurring in the running of public-sector organisations.
>
> (Ongaro 2010: 3)

In order to comparatively analyse these changes, Pollitt and Bouckaert (2011: 96–99) proposed a typology of four trajectories of public-management reform. The first one, the maintaining strategy, occurs when a state does not reform its public management, but tightens up traditional controls, diminishes its expenses and fights against corruption. The second one, the modernising strategy, corresponds to reforms aiming at improving the ways of doing through new methods of budgeting, managing, accounting, delivering services to users and strategic planning. It can either be developed in a managerial approach, focusing on procedures or, in a participatory one, considering high-quality services and public participation. The third one, the marketising strategy supports the introduction of more competition within the public sector, with quasi-markets, contracting out, contractual appointments, etc., to reduce the distinction between the public and private sectors. Finally, the minimal state strategy aims at privatising as much as possible and downsizing public-sector organisations.

As a matter of fact, it is obvious that more than one strategy can be used by a single country, that strategies can evolve throughout time and that they are principally patterns that guide our analysis. On a broader note, we should also highlight particular models of reform related to those strategies. Pollitt and Bouckaert (2011) use these models as a general classification, considering again its comparative power. These three models are the Neo-Weberian State (NWS), the well-known New Public Management (NPM) and the New Public Governance (NPG). The first one mainly concerns continental European countries and sees reforms as a renewal of the Weberian bureaucracy mostly through quality, a new professional culture and client orientation. The NPM is, as we have already said, much more market oriented, introducing competition, performance management and practices from the private sector to the public sector. It encompasses Anglo-Saxon countries such as the United States and New Zealand. The last one, NPG, is a new model based on the current evolution and complexity of our societies. Based on network theories, it aims at overtaking the two previous competing models, although it has been theoretically and empirically less developed. In this respect, the maintaining and the modernising strategies are used in the NWS grouping, while the marketising and the minimalising ones exist mainly in the NPM groupings.

We must finally add that the authors classify Belgium in the first group while they set Canada in the second one.

1 Quebec's public administration

1.1 From the Quiet Revolution to the twenty-first century

The current form of Quebec's public administration found its origins in the Quiet Revolution of the 1960s. However, Quebec had already set up an administration after the events of 1837,[2] although it did not receive much attention from the political sphere from 1870 onwards to 1959 (Gow 1990). During this period, Quebec followed the "minimal state" trend of many countries. The tasks assigned to the administration were therefore related to sovereign powers such as police and justice. They were enlarged to economic and social fields throughout time and forced by historical events such as the two world wars and the Quiet Revolution (Baccigalupo 1975; Côté 2004).

In the 1960s, Quebec underwent the Quiet Revolution that symbolised the reformative process marked by a "new and widespread consciousness in favor of the social, cultural, and economic development of Quebec" (Mazouz and Tremblay 2006: 265). The Catholic Church, the dominant institution, was replaced by the state, consequently giving the administration new life.[3] The will of the government – led by Jean Lesage of the *Parti Québécois* (PQ) – was to build a modern and efficient state for Quebec:[4] various changes occurred, notably in terms of structures and means. Structural changes concerned both the central administration and the agencies: a rise of the number of ministries, creation of both vertical and horizontal ones, and the development of new agencies. In terms of means, the number of civil servants rose sharply between 1955 and 1970 (Baccigalupo 1975: 70). This increase was combined with measures to make the public sector more attractive: new statute, training, rationalisation of administrative and budgetary processes, and evolution of selection procedures based on merit and no longer on patronage (Baccigalupo 1975; Pelletier 1992; Montpetit and Rouillard 2001). Moreover, institutions contributing to the socioeconomic development of the province were created, such as state societies and a council of economic orientation (Fortier 2010b). Until the beginning of the 1980s, the public sector knew a period of stabilisation and consolidation, including the adoption in 1971 of the Financial Administration Act by the liberal Robert Bourassa's government. Among other financial management instruments, it created a strong Treasury Board, mainly in charge of budgeting, budgetary control and approbation of organisational plans of ministries (Baccigalupo 1975; Gow 1990). This first period can be seen as exemplary of a maintaining strategy. Once the new administration was set, no fundamental and radical changes were implemented per se. However, in 1976, the PQ won the election and formed a government with René Levesque as prime minister. It opened the possibility of a vast reform: a new act on the public service was adopted in 1983. It instituted wide consultative structures but also reinforced the principle of merit, allowing merit-based salaries for top civil servants and drawing up measures supporting unions (Gow 1984, 1990).

The economic and financial crisis in the 1980s shifted this movement of a continuously expanding administration. The PQ then began to follow a more neo-liberal approach, close to international trends issuing from the NPM. The concept of the role of the state evolved from interventionist to partnership: its role within the society was reduced and cuts in personnel occurred to reduce budgetary deficits (Côté 2004; Mazouz, Tremblay and Facal 2005; Rinfret, Ngo Manguelle and Lortie-Lussier 2010). In 1983, a new act on civil service was adopted, with the objective of reducing centralised controls on managers to give them more autonomy in their competences. It also allowed contractualisation within the public service, although it was not used much by the *péquiste* (PQ) government (Gow 1984; Bourgault and Dion 1989). When they came back to power in 1985, the liberals deepened this vision of a less interventionist state. In 1986, three reports – named after their main editors, i.e. Gobeil, Fortier and Scowen – issued by three different committees, supported the discourse of a state-wide reorganisation that, however, was not as radical as announced (Rouillard and Hudon 2007; Fortier 2010b). The liberals used much more contractualisation than the *Péquistes* and also authorised this alternative for top managers. They reduced the number of agencies but did not substantially modify ministries' structures (Bourgault and Dion 1989; Gow 1990). In this sense, by the end of the 1980s, the reform trajectory taken by Quebec had evolved. Elements from modernising and marketising strategies took over those from the existing one. Indeed, in this neo-liberal approach we can see many more instruments inspired by the NPM such as contractualisation, but also non-managerial mechanisms such as the reduction of agencies.

In 1993, the National Assembly adopted an act on the responsibilities of top civil servants and heads of public agencies to hold them accountable to the assembly, in accordance with their results and management practices. New cuts occurred between 1994 and 1998 to reduce the number of tenured civil servants, mainly through voluntary leave to retirement (Rinfret, Ngo Manguelle and Lortie-Lussier 2010). This was in accordance with the objective of reducing the deficit, for which a bill was enacted in 1996, and which was eliminated in 1999 (Rouillard and Hudon 2007; Rouillard 2008). In parallel, others initiatives took place such as the creation in 1995 of autonomous units of services (*unités autonomes de services* (UAS)) that were based on the principle of results-oriented management instead of administrative controls of means and actions (Roy and Giard 2003). During the 1990s, we can therefore notice some additional elements relying on the marketising strategy, notably this new type of autonomous and results-oriented agency.

1.2 Recent reforms: the modernisation of the Quebec state

The evolution of Quebec's administrative apparatus was given some momentum in 2000 with the adoption of the Public Administration Act by the PQ government led by Lucien Bouchard. This act can be seen as a shift towards a genuine NPM approach. It focuses on the quality of services to citizens and on results-based management, and it set up a frame for the public administration, including values such as flexibility, accountability, efficiency and transparency. One other main objective was the simplification and rationalisation of procedures and methods, taking the path of de-bureaucratisation (Rouillard and Hudon 2007). Various mechanisms were also set to implement the objective in each ministry and agency. They concern the quality of services delivered to citizens and enterprises, strategic planning, performance contracts, annual reports, and the reinforcement of accountability of ministers and top civil servants.

This NPM-inspired reform, however, takes some distance from the neo-liberal model. Accordingly, it does not completely reshape the role of the state, although it is considered as a real turn in Quebec's governance due to its orientation towards market techniques of management (Rouillard *et al.* 2004; Rouillard and Hudon 2007; Facal and Bernier 2009). From the civil servants' point of view, its implementation has improved the quality of services and has instituted a more transparent and efficient public management (Côté and Mazouz 2005). The first strategic plans were published in 2001 and were quite comprehensive (Ministère du Conseil exécutif 2008).

In 2003, when the liberal government led by Jean Charest regained power, it announced a wide reform of the administration: the re-engineering of the state. Deepening the principles set by the Public Administration Act, this reform systematises the previous one, justified by factors such as the budgetary crisis and the aging issue (Fortier 2010b). However, in 2004, this re-engineering became a more modest modernisation both rhetorically and effectively although the orientation remained the same. This was partly due to political errors from the government, notably in terms of social dialogue, but also due to the fundamental core of the reforms that was at odds with the cultural administrative background of the province (Facal and Bernier 2009).

The 2004–7 Modernisation Plan is therefore founded on the distinction between strategic and operational activities, mainly through several mechanisms. For example, these are contractualisation of relationships, the reduction of the role of the state within society, a client approach based on an individualistic vision on society, market mechanisms, and the scale the economies related to the centralisation of services delivery and resources management. Among these projects, there was the creation of three central agencies: *Services Québec* (Quebec Services) (a centralised one-stop desk to ease access for citizens), the *Centre des services administratifs* (Centre for Administrative Services) (support services for human, financial and material resources management) and the A*gence des partenariats public-privé du Québec* (Agency of Public-Private Partnerships of Quebec), renamed *Infrastructure Québec* (Quebec Infrastructure) in 2009 (Secrétariat du Conseil du Trésor 2004a; Fortier 2010b). Moreover, the plan supports a performance management policy, but also the abolition and merging of specific structures. In terms of instruments, agencies, public–private partnerships, the reduction of the civil service by non-replacement and the use of technologies of information and communication are highlighted (Fortier 2010a). Parallel to this plan is the 2004–7 plan for human resources management (Secrétariat du Conseil du Trésor 2004b). In considering human resources as a decisive factor of modernisation, it aims at giving civil servants the tools to implement the modernisation plan (competencies management, training, knowledge transfer and attractive career opportunities).

In this respect, we clearly see in these reforms the extensive use of NPM instruments and principles, such as the distinction between strategy and implementation, contractualisation and performance management. Some elements of a modernising trajectory can also be underlined, notably the emphasis on professionalisation of the civil service and a particular administrative culture.

A second wave of more concise and clear strategic plans took place in 2005, in order to ease their appropriation by the public sector (Ministère du Conseil exécutif 2008). A third wave started in 2007. Finally, in 2012 a new strategic plan on human resources was published, focused on flexibility, motivation, innovation, adequacy between offers and demands, sustainability and expertise (Secrétariat du Conseil du Trésor 2012).

More recently, Pauline Marois took the lead of the government, as the PQ won the elections in 2012. In terms of administrative reforms, the most striking element seems to be the reform of the management of public contracts, fighting corruption and placing transparency at the centre of the public arena (Gouvernement du Québec 2014a). Other smaller reforms concerned administrative simplification for public recruitment (Gouvernement du Québec 2013), and actions for transparency such as open government and online accessibility of data (Gouvernement du Québec 2014b). In 2014, the *Parti libéral du Québec* (PLQ) (Quebec Liberal Party) won the elections and it led Philippe Couillard to become prime minister although it is too early and beyond the scope of this chapter to discuss any further evolution in public-management reforms.

Overall, Quebec's administration has known, over the past 15 years, both managerial and cultural transformations that have led to a more results-oriented approach and has taken into account the cultural values inherited from the Quiet Revolution, such as solidarity and equity. We can underline too that Quebec has followed a trajectory of reform in-between the marketing one and the modernising one, in the sense that instruments and mechanisms instituted can be seen as part of one or the other strategy. However, compared to others Canadian provinces, public-management reforms in Quebec have been much less radical in their managerial orientation.

2 Wallonia's public administration

2.1 The creation and first developments of the Walloon administration

Contrary to Quebec, the Walloon administration per se was legally created in 1980 through the second state reform.[5] It granted the communities and regions specific competences, including the capacity to rule their own functioning. Accordingly, each regional and communitarian executive was given its own administration at its disposal and allowed to organise it in an autonomous manner, although they were restrained by rules set by the federal level. For instance, they were obliged to recruit via the Permanent Secretariat for Recruitment and to apply the federal civil servants statute.[6] At this time, there existed only one single ministry: the Ministry of the Walloon Region (*Ministère de la Région wallonne* (MRW)) that was in charge of competences such as the environment, the economy and employment.

In 1988–89, a new reform was carried out that awarded more managerial and financial autonomy to the federated entities (Mabille 2000). The Walloon government, as in the other federated governments, was given more autonomy to set its own statute for civil servants, in accordance with the general principles of the Belgian civil service listed in a royal decree (Barbeaux and Beumier 1995). For instance, these principles are the tenured position, rights of the civil servants and the evaluation system. Such a royal decree was first adopted in 1991, the latest version being from 2000. Following the 1988 state reform and its transfer of competences and means, a second Walloon ministry, in charge of public works and public transportation, was created in 1989: the Ministry of Equipment and Transportation (MET) (De Brouwer 1982; Beumier 1989). Some other reforms of the state occurred in 1993 and 2001, but their impact on the public administrations have been less remarkable in terms of transfers of competence and personnel.

As a consequence of these institutional reforms, slowly Wallonia started to reform its own administration. A processes analysis project, an audit system and a scoping study of the two ministries took place between 1990 and 1998. The objective was to improve efficiency and quality, and to construct a performance-based auditing method (Stenmans 1999; Vancoppenolle and Legrain 2003). In 1994, a new Walloon statute for civil servants was instituted through a series of governmental decrees. The decrees aimed at clarifying the framework for the civil servants, focusing on a qualitative approach of delivering services rather than on performance measurement. Over the next years, a few changes in the organisational Walloon scheme took place, such as the development of new functions of information, mediation and the centralisation of the financial management of the cabinets (Stenmans 1999).

In terms of financial management, and under the pressure of compliance with European duties, the Walcomfin project was launched in 1999. It aimed to realise a feasibility study on the introduction of the double-entry bookkeeping system. However, as we describe later, this project took a long time to reach maturation, and financial reforms only appeared in the late 2000s.

Thus we can see that the pace of reform in Wallonia has been rather slow during the first 20 years of the administration and no real change has been undertaken within the administration. Accordingly, we can clearly highlight a maintaining strategy during this period.

2.2. The turn of the 2000s

From 1999, a new turn was taken by Wallonia, with the forming of a "rainbow" government,[7] composed by the socialists, the liberals and the greens. One of its first measures, in 2000, was the adoption of the *Contrat d'Avenir pour la Wallonie* (Contract for the Future of Wallonia), aimed at improving socio-economic conditions in the region. This strategic plan was upgraded in 2002 and deepened in 2004 by the next government. This renewed *Contrat d'Avenir* added provisions on e-government and simplification vis-à-vis users and enterprises, and support for economic growth and social inclusion. This was the first time that the Walloon Region had developed such strategic planning methods.

In 2003, the "rainbow" government adopted the Code of civil service (*Code de la fonction publique*). This government decree aimed at simplifying the architecture of the civil service and at modernising some of its features. All the decrees from 1994 are thus codified in a single document. Additional to this rationalisation, the important changes included are a more dynamic approach to human resources (recruitment, selection, evaluation and career management) and a mandate system for the top civil servants. The latter concerned the three highest levels of the administration (Secretary-General, Director-General, Inspector-General) (Daurmont and Schmitz 2005; Petit Jean 2013). Later, in 2004, a specific act was adopted by parliament to give a framework to agencies, stating, for example, the content of management contracts (Cipriano and Van Haeperen 2010b).

In 2005, the various strategic plans related to economic development were integrated into a single document, commonly called the Marshall Plan (*Plan Marshall*). It was designed to guide socioeconomic redeployment in the region for four years, while a specific cell was created to monitor its implementation. In this respect, the successive strategic plans have had a significant impact on the Walloon government and administration: it has rapidly led to a greater awareness of the need to modernise the administrative apparatus (Brunet, Vaessen and Delvenne 2013).

The most important reform that we can highlight occurred in 2006 and is two-fold. First, the Walloon government decided to set up an important plan of modernisation of the structures of its administration, of which the main element was the merger of the two ministries (Service public de Wallonie 2009). In August 2008, the *Service Public de Wallonie* (SPW) was created. Following the matrix approach inspired by the federal Copernicus reform,[8] the objectives were the rationalisation of structures, the simplification of procedures, accessibility, transparency, quality and the motivation of the civil service (De Visscher and Montuelle 2010; Goransson 2010; Petit Jean 2013). Secondly, the government reduced the scope of the mandate system, excluding from it the Inspector-General level. It also changed the term of the mandate from the legislature, while this term was previously congruent. It also rationalised the selection processes with the support of an external actor, the SELOR (Petit Jean 2013).[9]

The legislature that started in 2009 brought a new strategic plan (*Plan Marshall 2. Vert*) and new reforms. These changes mainly focused on the highest positions of the administration. The first one concerned the mandate system: from 2014 onwards, the term of mandate of the senior civil servants is realigned with that of the legislature and starts from 31 December of the year of the regional election. Moreover, the Inspectors-General level is partly re-integrated, according to specific factors, within the mandate system, from which it had been previously removed in 2006. The aim is to give more efficiency, more coherence and more dynamism to this system. The second important reform is closely linked to the first one. It is the creation of the *Ecole d'administration publique* (Walloon School of Public Administration). This institution has three missions, but one of them seems more important so far. Indeed, the new mandate system stipulates that a management certificate from this institution is necessary in order to be designated as a mandated civil servant.[10] The second mission is the organisation of various trainings at the regional level in accordance with the existing structure, while the third mission is similar to the second one, but takes place at the local level (Petit Jean 2013). However, at the time of writing, the implementation of these two missions is still underway.

Finally, a last reform that should be considered is the earlier-mentioned Walcomfin reform. From 1999, several studies on the institution of a double-entry bookkeeping system in Wallonia have been set up. Mostly due to political disinterest, nothing had been achieved until the creation in 2006 of a steering committee in charge of the writing of the bills to propose to parliament. In December 2011, an act concerning the budget and accounting system of the services of the Walloon government was adopted and the project is renamed WBFin. Although the act brings no genuine revolution as it keeps a strong input orientation, it does create new opportunities in terms of performance budgeting and accounting through, for example, non-financial indicators in the budget (Walcomfin 2012).

Overall, the various reforms that we have reviewed in this section allow us to draw on several elements. First, most reforms in Wallonia from 2003 and the Code of civil service are oriented towards efficiency, effectiveness and responsiveness to citizens' needs. Secondly, the role of the administration was also considered within the multiple strategic plans. In this respect, its weaknesses during their implementation played a role in the subsequent reforms. However, the Walloon public administration has not yet disposed of its own strategic plan, as was the case in Quebec. It has lately been the case with the adoption of the AVANTI plan, which has not yet been publicly published.[11] Regarding the different strategies that we highlighted in the Introduction, we clearly see a shift between the first period, between 1980 and 1999, and the current period. During the former one, we identified a maintaining strategy, while new instruments have been brought in during the latter period. Accordingly, the role of the NPM was much less important in Wallonia, and we consider that the region is noticeably part of the NWS grouping, as are other continental Europeans countries.

3 A similar path for divergent reasons?

Comparing the two administrations could seem complicated, especially considering their size and their maturation. A glance at the figures shows that Quebec's public administration is much larger than the Walloon administration. In 2009, the number of full-time equivalents in the Walloon civil servants was 9,310 within the central administration, the SPW, and 15,926 in total (Cipriano and Van Haeperen 2010a). In Quebec in 2009, there were around 67,300 full-time equivalents (Observatoire de l'Administration publique 2012). However, this can be explained by the differences in competences that disposes each of these two polities, and also by the size of the population on which each exerts its power. In terms of distribution of competences, Quebec is responsible in more areas than Wallonia. Indeed, the existence in Belgium of two types of federated entity, namely the communities and the regions, reduces the range of action of each of these entities compared to Canadian provinces. For example, education is a federated matter in both countries, but it is ruled by the communities in Belgium, leaving little room for the Walloon Region to be active in this field, while it is mostly a provincial matter in Quebec (Poirier 2009). The size of the population also plays a role regarding to the number of citizens who are concerned by the public action. While Wallonia counted 3,525,540 inhabitants on 1 January 2011, there were 7,979,663 in Quebec (IWEPS 2012; Institut de la Statistique du Québec n.d.) In addition, in terms of maturation, while Quebec's administration that we currently know had been shaped after the Quiet Revolution of 1960, the Walloon administration was created only in 1980 and only effective around 1985 after several transfers of personnel.

However, although these differences seem to be quite marked, one element strikes us: the path of reform that each of them has followed within their own country. According to both trajectories of reforms, and what we have seen in the two first sections, we can say that both Quebec and Wallonia consider elements that come from the NWS in their own extent in terms of span and intensity. However, the influence of the NPM has also been underlined in Quebec, as it have been influenced by Anglo-Saxon (decentralisation), French (centralisation) and American (administrative culture) contexts (Baccigalupo 1975). We must, however, emphasise that the first reforms had been undertaken much earlier in Quebec – in the beginning of the 1980s – than in Wallonia – in the beginning of the 2000s.

Moreover, maintaining strategies have been used during the building and consolidating phases of each administration, i.e. the first 20 years of the administration, between 1960 and 1980 in Quebec and between 1980 and 2000 in the Walloon Region. In both polities, major reforms only took place around the turn of the 2000s. The maturation factor is thus not the only cause of the several reforms undertaken. In this respect, Pollitt and Bouckaert (2011) also propose several factors that can influence the decision-making process of administrative reforms: socioeconomic elements, the politico-administrative system, diffusion of new ideas for public management, citizens' pressure, political parties, scandals or disaster, and more dynamic elements regarding reforms, such as the content, the implementation and the results of reforms. We emphasise here only those that are most important to us.

In terms of socioeconomic elements, the economic situation of the 1980s and 1990s has weighed on policies and forced many countries, provinces and states to take measures regarding their public management (Bovaird and Löffler 2009). Other important indirect factors are, for example, oil shocks and – for Wallonia only – the Maastricht criteria[12] (Kickert 2011). Specifically, in Quebec, budgetary issues played an important role for sure, but were not decisive in the trajectory of reforms. In similar situations, the provinces of Ontario and Alberta led much more radical reforms than Quebec, a province that has strived to maintain a greater presence of the state within society (Facal and Bernier 2009). Overall, it is difficult here to precisely assess the influence of these pressures on reforms without a thorough analysis, but it seems clear that budgetary constraints played a role in both polities.

Another important factor that has obviously played a role in the development of reforms is the political agenda. In Quebec, during the period from the mid-1980s to the mid-1990s, the constitutional question drew much attention from the elites, while administrative issues were set aside (Facal and Bernier 2009). In Wallonia, the reasoning is quite similar. From the beginning of the 1980s to the 2000s, not much had been done to reform the administrative apparatus as there were many hesitancies on the nature of reform due to a level of uncertainty regarding the institutional status of the Walloon Region and the French-speaking Community (De Visscher and Montuelle 2010). In terms of new ideas, it is interesting to note that both Quebec and Wallonia did not copy or transpose NPM instruments as such and kept their own identity in reforming their public sector. Historical elements have greatly contributed to the evolution of Quebec's administration, as it was influenced by both French and Anglo-Saxon elements. In Wallonia, the reforms concept found its origins in both influences from the French legalist culture and from experiences from the Flemish and federal levels, such as BBB[13] and the Copernicus reforms (De Visscher and Montuelle 2010).

Although it seems that many similar factors of reform exist between Quebec and Wallonia, we must emphasise at least two elements that distinguish the two entities. First, the specific path of reforms that have been taken in Quebec partly relies on the strong national identity of the province. Indeed, in a quite similar context to other Canadian provinces, Quebec has followed its own conception of the role of the state rather than implementing radical reforms in its administrative structures. Moreover, Quebec has a greater sense of provincial identity than the other provinces, which identify more strongly as Canadian. On the contrary, and as mentioned by Caron in this book, a genuine Walloon identity is overcome by the Belgian identity. In fact, there is no consensus among elites on a vision for Wallonia as a state, and this has an impact on the development on the public administration. Accordingly, we see in the first 20 years of the Walloon administration, a prolongation of the former Belgian administration. Second, the type of decision making for the reform is quite different. As we have seen, many stakeholders joined the decision-making process in Quebec while the reforms were much more top-down in Wallonia (De Visscher and Montuelle 2010). According to these elements, it seems clear that the more participatory model of public-management reform in Quebec is closer to participatory modernisation, while the more top-down approach of reform in Wallonia relies more on the managerial modernisation strategy.

Furthermore, as we have mentioned earlier, one of the goals of this chapter is to assess whether these reforms played a role in the development of the two analysed entities as an autonomous polity. In Quebec, as we have seen, the state occupies an important place within the society. This specificity is part of the Québécois identity, which includes values such as solidarity and equity. During these 40 years that we have reviewed, two models of governance are highlighted in the literature (Côté 2004; Mazouz, Tremblay and Facal 2005; Mazouz and Tremblay 2006; Côté, Lévesque and Morneau 2007; Bouchard, Lévesque and St-Pierre 2008). The first period, from the beginning of the 1960s to the beginning of the 1980s, was characterised by the development and consolidation of an interventionist public apparatus. The administration was therefore an instrument of the welfare state to support and implement specific policies. The second period, from the beginning of the 1980s, appeared as a reaction to the former period and to the international economic crisis. However, instead of following the international trend of minimising the structures, Quebec chose to base its governance on cooperation and partnership, acting as a catalyst and animator. The stabilised administration evolved hence towards a more results-oriented management. More recently, the reforms, mainly brought about by the Charest government, has probably led to the development of a new model of a more marketised and managerial governance, superposed on a participatory but individualistic governance. These trends have partly occurred in response to the more and more intrusive federal state within Quebec's competences (Côté, Lévesque and Morneau 2007; Fortier 2010b). Furthermore, as noted by Gow, "the state is not the invader from Ottawa anymore, but an instrument to serve the collectivity" (Gow 1990: 695). In this respect, the evolution of the administration supports the political project of successive governments and has been a tool of the affirmation of the Québécois identity within Canada. Accordingly, it can be seen as one of the instrument used to move towards Quebec autonomy.

In Wallonia, the picture is much blurrier, and the hesitancies of the elites about the institutional future of the region do not give a clear-cut opinion about the role of the administration in the construction of a Walloon autonomy. From its beginning to the mid-2000s, the Walloon administration was a replication of the federal one in terms of ways of doing, adapted to the regional level. There was thus no specific identity or particular culture related to the Walloon administration. However, the creation of the SPW remains, in our opinion, an essential momentum of the affirmation of the autonomy of the Walloon Region as a federated entity of Belgium. Accordingly, such important transformations are a signal that the region has started to appropriate the Belgian federalisation process. One of the main roles of the administration is, therefore, to support the implementation of several strategic plans and to give impetus, with other actors, to the socioeconomic development of the region. For instance, we can cite the new School of Public Administration, the new mandate system and WBFin. There is consequently an ambiguity between these two alternatives for Wallonia, similar to the two currents highlighted by Caron. On the one hand, there is an affirmation of Walloon autonomy through the creation of purely Walloon institutions like the SPW. On the other hand, collaborative projects with the French-speaking Community tend to support the development of a French-speaking administration, whose unique alter ego would be the Flemish one. In the first alternative, the Walloon Region and its administration would be part of a three-player game including Brussels and Flanders. Consequently, forthcoming political and administrative developments will probably give us a clearer idea about the role of the administration in the development of the Walloon autonomy.

4 Conclusion

In this chapter, we focused on the evolution of public administration, both in Quebec and in the Walloon Region. We have seen that both entities have reformed their public sector in their own extent, using different strategies. At the early days of the administration, in the 1960–1970s in Quebec and in the 1980–1990s in the Walloon Region, we identified a maintaining strategy that aims at developing and consolidating the public structures. However, from the 1980s, Quebec used both marketising and modernising strategies, while Wallonia only used the latter one, starting from the 2000s. However, although the instruments were different, the objectives seemed to be quite similar. The Public Administration Act and the modernisation plan, on the one hand, and the Code of civil service and the creation of the SPW on the other, are, among others, recent instruments that all aim at supporting the respective development of the Québécois and Walloon administrations towards more efficiency and more responsiveness for their citizens.

Along these lines, we also determined several factors that have played a role in the development of these reforms. Particularly, the economic situation has probably triggered reforms, although it is difficult to evaluate the exact impact of external budgetary constraints. Next to these, the political agenda also needed to be studied. Indeed, there has been a period of uncertainty and hesitancy in both entities, and reforms have been hampered due to institutional issues related to their future in the federal state. In Quebec, the main institutional issue concerned the independence question, while it was the structures that were stressed in the Walloon Region and in the French-speaking Community.

The work reported in this chapter opens several routes for further research. One of them is, for each case, to deepen the contextual analysis, and to analyse in more specific ways the impact of particular factors such as the role of politico-administrative structures. A second line of research would be comparative, starting from the findings of deepened studies of the public-management reforms, to address more precisely the trajectories of reforms. On a more general note, scholars in Wallonia have much to learn from their colleagues in Quebec, in view of the variety of topics that are considered in Quebec's literature about public administration and public management. Here, we can underline topics such as the relationship of public-management reform with, among others, the evolution of the model of governance, the state–society relationship and the cultural characteristics of reforms. This could help develop a broader spectrum of analysis on Walloon public management. Finally, one must give attention to the future developments in both polities as elections in 2014 will probably modify the political route of public management.

Notes

1 In this chapter, we use without distinction the terms "Wallonia" and "Walloon Region" to qualify what is constitutionally called the Walloon Region.
2 The Lower-Canada Rebellion in 1837 led to the adoption of the Union Act in 1940, which established the United Province of Canada, within the British Colony. It evolved into a federation of four provinces, namely Ontario, Quebec, Nova Scotia and New Brunswick (Watts 2008: 32; Fournier 2009).
3 For more details on the evolution of the Québécois public administration, see Gow (1986).
4 We use here the term "state" as the incarnation of the public power at the Québécois level and not in the sense of any independency.
5 The first one, in 1970, led to the creation of the communities and regions; see the chapter by Turgeon in this book.
6 Art. 87; original version of the special law of institutional reforms of 8 August 1980.
7 It is usual in Belgium to give a particular colour-oriented name to a coalition. In this respect, the term "rainbow" refers to the main colour of the three parties in the coalition, i.e. red (the socialists), blue (the liberals) and green (the ecologists). Previously the coalition in power was composed by the socialists (red) and the Christian democrats (orange), named a "roman red" coalition ("roman" from Roman Catholic and "red" as the colour of the socialist party).
8 This reform at the Belgian federal level took place in the early 2000s and aimed at giving a citizen orientation to the federal's rigid and bureaucratic administration. It led to massive changes in structures and in civil servants status (Brans, de Visscher, and Vancoppenolle 2006).
9 The SELOR was previously the Permanent Secretariat for Recruitment (*Secrétariat permanent pour le recrutement*).
10 The other possibility is to hold a position under mandate before 31 December 2009.
11 This strategic plan, currently under implementation, is supposed to deepen the implementation of new modes of public management within the SPW.

12 These economic criteria were established in 1992 to support the creation of an economic and monetary union within the European Union. They concern, for example, public deficit and inflation.
13 The BBB (*Beter Bestuur Beleid*) reform took place in Flanders in 2000 and redesigned the structure of the ministries to implement principles of the NPM, such as the separation between policy design and policy implementation.

References

Baccigalupo, Alain (1975). "Vie administrative à l'étranger: Le nouveau visage de l'administration publique québecoise", *La Revue administrative*, (163): 68–74.

Barbeaux, Michel and Marc Beumier (1995). "Réforme de l'État et restructuration des administrations et des parastataux (I)", *Courrier hebdomadaire du CRISP*, 1473.

Beumier, Marc (1989). "Des ministères des communautés et des régions ... aux services des exécutifs communautaires et régionaux", *Administration Publique Trimestrielle*, (1): 157–66.

Bouchard, Marie J., Benoît Lévesque and Julie St-Pierre (2008). *Modèle Québécois de développement et gouvernance: entre le partenariat et le néolibéralisme?* Montréal: Chaire de recherche du Canada en économie sociale, Université de Montréal.

Bourgault, Jacques and Stéphane Dion (1989). "Les gouvernements antibureaucratiques face à la haute administration: une comparaison Québec-Canada", *Politiques et management public*, 7(2): 97–118.

Bovaird, Tony and Elke Löffler (2009). "The changing context of public policy". In *Public Management and Governance*, ed. Tony Bovaird and Elke Löffler, 15–26. London and New York: Routledge.

Brans, Marleen, Christian de Visscher and Diederik Vancoppenolle (2006). "Administrative reform in Belgium: maintenance or modernisation?", *West European Politics*, 29(5): 979–98.

Brunet, Sébastien, Alain Vaessen and Pierre Delvenne (2013). "Une politique publique de relance économique et ses impacts sur la transformation de l'administration publique: le Plan Marshall de la Région Wallonne comme incubateur". In *Formes et réformes des administrations publiques*, ed. Geoffrey Joris and Catherine Fallon, 183–96. Laval: Presses de l'Université de Laval.

Cipriano, Sabrine and Béatrice Van Haeperen (2010a). La fonction publique de la Wallonie. Tableau de bord statistique de l'emploi public – septembre. Namur: IWEPS.

Cipriano, Sabrine and Béatrice Van Haeperen (2010b). "Les agences dans le paysage de la fonction publique wallonne", *Discussion papers of l'IWEPS*, (1003): 1–70.

Côté, Louis (2004). "L'étude des modèles nationaux de gouvernance: le cas Québécois", *Economies et Solidarités*, 34(2): 95–117.

Côté, Louis, Benoît Lévesque and Guy Morneau (2007). "L'évolution du modèle Québécois de gouvernance: le point de vue des acteurs", *Politique et sociétés*, 26(1): 3–26.

Côté, Louis and Bachir Mazouz (2005). *Les effets de la Loi sur l'administration publique sur la qualité des services et sur la gestion dans les ministères et les organismes*, Montréal: Ecole nationale d'administration publique.

Daurmont, Odile and Véronique Schmitz (2005). "L'évolution de la carrière des fonctionnaires belges", *Administration Publique Trimestrielle*, 29(3–4): 259–69.

De Brouwer, Jean-Louis (1982). "La mise en place des administrations régionales et communautaires, quelques points de repères", *Courrier hebdomadaire du CRISP*, 967.

De Visscher, Christian and Caroline Montuelle (2010). "Fédéralisme et réorganisations administratives en Belgique: quelles différences de trajectoires entre l'Etat fédéral, les régions et les communautés?", *Pyramides*, (20): 143–72.

Facal, Joseph and Luc Bernier (2009). "Réformes administratives, structures sociales et représentations collectives au Québec", *Revue française d'administration publique*, (3): 493–510.

Fortier, Isabelle (2010a). "Expérience des réformes et transformation de l'ethos de service public dans l'administration publique Québécoise", *Pyramides*, (19): 71–86.

Fortier, Isabelle (2010b). "La modernisation de l'État Québécois: La gouvernance démocratique à l'épreuve des enjeux du managérialisme", *Nouvelles pratiques sociales*, 22(2): 35–50.

Fournier, Bernard (2009). "La Fédération canadienne". In *Le fédéralisme en Belgique et au Canada. Comparaison sociopolitique*, ed. Bernard Fournier and Min Reuchamps, 41–61. Bruxelles: De Boeck Université.

Goransson, Marie (2010). "La responsabilisation des hauts fonctionnaires aux différents niveaux de pouvoir", *Courrier hebdomadaire du CRISP*, 2056–2057.

Gouvernement du Québec (2013). *Adoption du projet de Loi no 41: des changements majeurs au processus d'embauche dans la fonction publique*, Portail Québec. Available from: www.fil-information.gouv.qc.ca/Pages/Article.aspx?idArticle=2111198984 (accessed 20 March 2014).

Gouvernement du Québec (2014a). *Adoption à l'unanimité du projet de loi no 1 – Un grand pas pour rétablir l'intégrité dans les contrats publics*, Portail Québec. Available from: www.fil-information.gouv.qc.ca/Pages/Article.aspx?idArticle=2012077361 (accessed 20 March 2014).

Gouvernement du Québec (2014b). *Portail du gouvernement ouvert – Le gouvernement du Québec choisir la transparence*. Available from: www.fil-information.gouv.qc.ca/Pages/Article.aspx?idArticle=2106117155 (accessed 20 March 2014).

Gow, James Iain (1984). "La réforme institutionnelle de la fonction publique de 1983: contexte, contenu et enjeux", *Politique*, (6): 51–101.

Gow, James Iain (1986). *Histoire de l'administration publique Québécoise 1867–1970*, Montréal: Presses de l'Université de Montreal.

Gow, James Iain (1990). "L'administration publique dans le discours politique au Québec, de Lord Durham à nos jours", *Canadian Journal of Political Science*, 23(04): 685–712.

Hood, Christopher (1991). "A Public Management for All Seasons?", *Public administration*, 69(1): 3–19.

Institut de la Statistique du Québec (n.d.) *Statistiques et publications*, Institut de la Statistique du Québec.) Available from: www.stat.gouv.qc.ca/statistiques/index.html (accessed 20 March 2014).

IWEPS (2012). *Rapport d'activité 2011*, Namur: IWEPS.

Kickert, Walter (2011). "Public Management Reform in Continental Europe: National Distinctiveness". In *The Ashgate Companion to New Public Management*, ed. Tom Christensen and Per Laegreid, 97–112. Farnham: Ashgate.

Mabille, Xavier (2000). *Histoire politique de la Belgique*, 4th edn, Bruxelles: CRISP.

Mazouz, Bachir and Benoît Tremblay (2006). "Toward a postbureaucratic model of governance: how institutional commitment is challenging Quebec's administration", *Public Administration Review*, 66(2): 263–73.

Mazouz, Bachir, Benoît Tremblay and Joseph Facal (2005). "Au coeur du renouveau administratif: l'engagement institutionnel quelques enseignements empiriques tirés de l'expérience québecoise", *Revue française d'administration publique*, (115): 403–19.

Ministère du Conseil exécutif (2008). *La planification stratégique au Gouvernement du Québec. Théorie et pratique*, Québec: Ministère du Conseil exécutif.

Montpetit, Eric and Christian Rouillard (2001). "La Révolution tranquille et le réformisme institutionnel. Pour un dépassement des discours réactionnaires sur l'étatisme Québécois", *Globe: revue internationale d'études Québécoises*, 4(1): 119–39.

Observatoire de l'Administration publique (2012). "La fonction publique Québécoise", *L'État québecois en perspective*, pp. 1–4.

Ongaro, Edoardo (2010). *Public Management Reform and Modernization: Trajectories of Administrative Change in Italy, France, Greece, Portugal and Spain*, Edward Elgar Publishing.

Pelletier, Réjean (1992). "La révolution Tranquille". In *Le Québec en jeu. Comprendre les grands défis.*, ed. Gérard Daigle and Guy Rocher, 609–24. Montréal: Les Presses de l'Université de Montréal.

Petit Jean, Maxime (2013). "Le régime des mandats dans l'administration wallonne", *Courrier hebdomadaire du CRISP*, 2166–2167.

Poirier, Johanne (2009). "Le partage des compétences et les relations intergouvernementales: la situation au Canada". In *Le fédéralisme en Belgique et au Canada. Comparaison sociopolitique*, ed. Bernard Fournier and Min Reuchamps, 107–122. Bruxelles: De Boeck Université.

Pollitt, Christopher and Geert Bouckaert (2011). *Public Management Reform: A Comparative Analysis-New Public Management, Governance, and the Neo-Weberian State*, Oxford: Oxford University Press.

Rinfret, Natalie, Christine Ngo Manguelle and Monique Lortie-Lussier (2010). "L'expérience des <<rescapés>> des réformes néolibérales de la fonction publique au Québec", *Revue française d'administration publique*, (132): 841–53.

Rouillard, Christian and Pierre-André Hudon (2007). "Le partenariat public-privé: un instrument d'action publique au cœur de la reconfiguration l'État Québécois", *Économie et solidarités*, 38(2): 7–26.

Rouillard, Lucie (2008). "Nouvelles stratégies d'action dans le secteur public Québécois: quatre exemples d'innovations financieres", *Canadian Public Administration*, 45(1): 52–69.

Rouillard, Lucie, Jacques Bourgault, Mohamed Charih and Daniel Maltais (2004). "Les Ressources humaines: clé de voûte de la réforme du secteur public au Québec", *Politiques et management public*, 22(3): 81–97.

Roy, Paul-René and Pierre Giard (2003). "Des unités autonomes de service aux agences: un modèle administratif Québécois en émergence", *Coup d'œil*, 9(3): 19–23.

Secrétariat du Conseil du Trésor (2004a). *Moderniser l'État. Pour des services de qualité aux citoyens. Plan de Modernisation 2004–2007*, Québec: Gouvernement du Québec.

Secrétariat du Conseil du Trésor (2004b). *Plan de gestion des ressources humaines 2004–2007. Prendre en main l'avenir de notre fonction publique*, Québec: Gouvernement du Québec.

Secrétariat du Conseil du Trésor (2012). *Une fonction publique moderne au service des Québécois. Stratégie de gestion des ressources humaines 2012–2017*, Québec: Gouvernement du Québec.

Service public de Wallonie (2009). *La modernisation*, Namur: Service public de Wallonie.
Stenmans, Alain (1999). *La transformation de la fonction administration en Belgique. Administration publique et société*, Bruxelles: CRISP.
Vancoppenolle, Diederik and Amaury Legrain (2003). "Le new public management en Belgique: comparaison des réformes en Flandres et en Wallonie", *Administration Publique Mensuel*, (2): 110–26.
Walcomfin (2012). *Rapport d'activités 2011*, Namur: Walcomfin.
Watts, Ronald (2008). *Comparing Federal Systems*, Montréal: McGill-Queen's University Press.

7 Language policy in Quebec and Wallonia

Two French-speaking linguistic minorities, two contrasted political strategies

Philippe Hambye

At first glance, the sociolinguistic situations of Quebec and Wallonia are quite similar. These two regions do indeed share a common language, and each of them is a minority community within a larger political entity where a language from another language family, in both cases a Germanic language, is the majority's language.

However, similarities between Quebec and Wallonia on the sociolinguistic level do not go beyond these rather superficial features. As we shall try to show in this chapter, sociolinguistic differences between the two regions are important and have led to significantly contrasting language policies – a contrast that can be observed at the level of specific political measures set up in each case, and also at the level of principles underlying state action regarding linguistic matters.

We first describe the ways in which the sociolinguistic situations of Quebec and Wallonia are different, and how it has affected the predominant conceptions regarding language, and of its relationship with identity and politics in both cases. It is crucial in this respect to understand how nationalist ideology has been taken up in Quebec and Wallonia. We then use examples of language policies in several domains (linguistic landscape/public communication, education, integration of immigrants and language corpus planning) to show that the contrast between language policies in Quebec and Wallonia can be understood if one relates them to these divergent visions of language and identity. Finally, we discuss the benefits and limits of these language policies in the light of the normative principles of political philosophy in which they are supposed to be grounded.

1 Minority and minoritisation

It is crucial in order to understand the differences between Quebec and Wallonia to make a distinction between the demographic status of a linguistic community in a given state (is it a majority or a minority?) and the social processes conditioning the *value* (in a broad sense) that this community has in this state. For it is this value, notably defined by the relative economic and political power of the community, by its symbolic status and by the prestige of its language, that defines whether the community is a minoritised group or not. Once a group views itself as a minoritised linguistic community – i.e. as a set of individuals sharing a common fate because of a common linguistic and cultural background – a language group may claim more equal treatment, feel its survival threatened, and hence struggle to gain economic and political power as a way to change its situation, notably through certain kinds of (language) policy.

While the French-speaking communities in Belgium and Canada have for a long time been demographic linguistic minorities, it was only Canadian francophones who were in a situation of minoritisation, at least until the Quiet Revolution in the 1960s (Plourde 2000). Conversely, in Belgium, French has never been a low-status language, predominant in low-paid jobs, socially stigmatised as a patois or as a mixture of English and French typical of uneducated people as it was in Quebec (and French Canada) from the end of the eighteenth century onwards. Rather the Flemish (Dutch-speaking) community in Belgium faced very similar economic and symbolic domination to that which francophones in Canada had to endure (see Mabille 2000).

These divergent historical realities explain the strength of linguistic nationalism in Quebec and the very weak symbolic investment in linguistic identity in Wallonia. In Canada, the minority community developed a political strategy to improve its economic situation and used the promotion of the French language within the province of Quebec to dramatically change the power relationships between anglophones and francophones (Heller 2006). The bourgeoisie of Quebec drew upon classical conceptions of cultural and linguistic nationalism to claim and legitimise its right to political and economic power in the name of the nation as a homogenised entity rather than in the name of its own interests. Hence, language policies establishing the predominance of French in several domains of activity (the state and its administration, education and work) became central in the francophone elite's struggle to access better socioeconomic positions. These language policies also came to be viewed as the only way to protect the community against its own tendency towards assimilation, and to affirm the francophones' collective right to exist and maintain as a distinct society (Taylor 1992, 1993).

In Wallonia, improving the status of the community's language has never been an issue. In the second half of the nineteenth century, when the Flemish nationalist movement emerged, its main claim was a fair political representation of the Flemish majority, and the recognition of equal linguistic and cultural rights for Dutch and French speakers. Progressively, the Flemish movement demanded *political autonomy* for cultural political matters, while the Walloon regionalist movement was interested in obtaining more autonomy in economic matters in times when Wallonia was still the most prosperous region of the country (see Mabille 2000; Witte and Van Velthoven 2000). In contrast to what we observed in Quebec, for the left-wing political parties and trade unions that were leading the movement towards regionalisation in Wallonia in the 1960s, protecting their language and culture against assimilation was not the issue, nor was it their intention to Frenchify their economy as a way of gaining positions of power within the economic system. Indeed, French was still the dominant language in Belgium, Walloons had no need to fear assimilation by the majority community, and the economic power in Wallonia was already in the hands of a French-speaking bourgeoisie. Their aim was rather to get rid of the hindrances to socialist progress that were created, in their view, by the conservative forces of the more Catholic-dominated rural Flanders (Erk 2005). For them, regionalisation was a way to look after the interests of industrial workers of Wallonia, as well as a way to strengthen their own power and position within an autonomous political field.

However, it is worth noting that the situation has now changed in both countries. Flanders is now by far the most prosperous region in Belgium and, as a consequence, Dutch–French bilingualism is increasingly viewed as an asset or even as a necessity on the labour market for instance (see Hambye and Richards 2012 for a critical discussion). In Quebec, the francophone population has clearly ensured its future without having to leave the Canadian federation. So one might objectively consider it to be time now for Wallonia to concern itself with the potential minoritisation of French and to develop preventive language policies, whereas Quebec could be in a position to soften its rather coercive language legislation. However, these changes have not put an end to the threat perceived by the Québécois regarding the future of their language, nor to the perceived necessity of monitoring and protecting its predominance in the province through language policies (see e.g. OQLF 2008). In the same vein, the economic decline of Wallonia has not (yet) led to the perception that the status of the French language has to be protected from centrifugal trends. It cannot however be denied that there has been a significant evolution in the Walloons' attitudes towards Dutch, but, as we shall see below (section 2.2), this evolution takes an opposite direction to that usually followed by minoritised communities (see Hambye 2009).

2 The main orientations of language policies in Quebec and Wallonia

Due to its central role in the minoritisation process, language was both a means and a symbol of the awakening of political consciousness in the French-speaking Québécois in the 1960s. Since then, an uninterrupted transverse and proactive language policy has been operating in Quebec, aiming at ensuring the predominance of the French language in Quebec and the symbolic promotion of the national language being viewed as good per se. In Wallonia, on the contrary, we do not observe any structural language policy whose principles could be stated explicitly. At most, one can identify several isolated political measures regarding language, even though they do show some ideological consistency as we shall see later. Let us now examine four areas where this contrast between the two regions regarding language policy is highlighted.

2.1 Public communication and linguistic landscape

In Quebec, the definition of French as the only official language of the state and its precedence in Quebec's linguistic landscape are established by a *provincial* regulation known as Loi/Bill 101 *La charte de la langue française* (Charter of the French Language) which dates from 1977. In Wallonia, French is *de facto* the more prevalent language of public communication – even if freedom of language is constitutionally guaranteed in the private sphere – and its official status is not the product of a specific and voluntary decision made by a Walloon government, but of the application of federal legislation. More generally, there is no founding legal document in Wallonia stating the importance of French for its community. As we suggested earlier, this is mainly due to the fact that the actual status of French in Wallonia is not perceived as threatened by any other language that could encourage politicians to recognise the precedence *de jure* of the majority's language. This threat is all the more remote for Walloons as even in Brussels, official French–Dutch bilingualism does not really undermine the clear predominance of French (95% of the inhabitants in Brussels state that they are able to speak French and only 28% to be able to speak Dutch, see Janssens 2007, 2008). In families with a background in another language and/or culture which have immigrated into Belgium, language shifts are almost always towards French.[1]

As a consequence, the Québécois are much more sensitive to any kind of transgression of the principle of French-language precedence than their Walloon fellows. Very few people in Wallonia feel offended when English instead of French is used in brand or organisation names, advertisement campaigns or state communication. For instance, there was no reaction in the media regarding the fact that three out of the six "competitiveness clusters" created within the framework of the "Marshall Plan for the Future of Wallonia" (a significant plan for economic recovery) in 2005 had English names ("Greenwin", "Logistics in Wallonia", "Skywin"). In Quebec, the *Office québécois de la langue française* (OQLF) has the mission (defined by Loi/Bill 101) to "assist and inform the civil administration, semi-public agencies, enterprises, associations and natural persons as regards the correction and enrichment of spoken and written French in Québec"[2] – the concern regarding the correction and enrichment of French being directly related to endeavours to reduce the frequency of anglicisms in French. Two organisations (the *Conseil de la langue française et de la politique linguistique* (CLFPL) (Council for the French language and language policy) and the *Service de la langue française* (Office for the French Language), attached to the *Fédération Wallonie-Bruxelles* (FWB) (Walloon-Brussels Federation) have a responsibility to guide and apply the language policy of the FWB's government, like their Québécois counterparts (the CLFPL and the OQLF). They have not, however, received equivalent means and power: the CLFPL issues statements for the Minister of Culture, but he/she is free to follow them or not and until now such statements relating to official communication in English (versus French) have seldom had consequences.

It is particularly pertinent to compare the situation of Brussels and Montreal in this respect. Due to Brussels' importance as a source of employment for many inhabitants of Wallonia and as a large proportion of language policies are governed by the FWB and thus shared by Brussels and Wallonia, the way the use of English progresses in Brussels has impacts upon the degree to which English competes with French in Wallonia. In the officially bilingual region of Brussels, English is the second most commonly known language.[3] As a consequence, English is sometimes used in order to bypass the need for official bilingualism in advertising and public communication, since it reduces costs and is viewed as symbolically neutral. This is especially true in the private sector (and above all for services targeting international customers), but it is increasingly the case for official communication too. This tendency can also be observed at the level of federal institutions: in Brussels, but also in Flanders and Wallonia, public railway-service communications are increasingly provided in English. This evolution is also noticeable at the level of individual interactions: while we are not aware of any data that can support such a claim, it is often commented in Belgium that communication between Dutch- and French-speaking individuals is increasingly conducted in English, whereas for a long time French was the default language. In other words, English is competing with French for the role of Brussels' (and Belgium's) *lingua franca*. Yet, because it seems clear that French has still a strong demographic linguistic precedence – which migration movements tend to reinforce – this evolution is not questioned or contested but rather favoured to a degree by political actions, even though several groups and organisations condemn the growing presence of English. Indeed, the lack of bi- or trilingual workers (Dutch, English, French) in Brussels and Wallonia causes much more political concern than the need to protect French (see section 2.2. below and Hambye and Richards 2012).

This situation contrasts sharply with the situation in Montreal. Montreal has long been viewed as the main "battlefield" for ensuring the future of French in Quebec (Lamarre and Lamarre 2009). As a consequence, many provisions of Loi/Bill 101 were directly aimed at changing the balance of power between English and French through the "Frenchification" of the workplace. These policies have partly succeed in making French the default language at work, but OQLF's surveys regularly report that in Montreal only a minority of workers are able to use French exclusively when in the workplace. In addition, the same surveys show that the number of multilingual individuals in Montreal is increasing, especially the number of people who can speak both English and French (plus sometimes a third, home language). These speakers have a very different relationship with their languages – a relationship which values multiplicity, hybridity and complementarity – than that which is somehow expected by the Quebec government's language policy and its quest for the clear predominance of French. A discrepancy is thus appearing between the increasingly bilingual nature of language practices in Montreal and policies and social movements that aim to fight the trend of English and French to sharing the same status and standing on an equal footing.[4] Interestingly enough, language policies in Wallonia mainly try to make the population more bilingual, while in Quebec this bilingualism appears as much a blessing – for many would recognise its necessity in an English-dominant North-American market – as a threat.

2.2 Education

The absence of a political will in Wallonia to ensure the precedence of French can also be observed in its education policy, which contrasts with that of Quebec. In Quebec, since 1977, legislation has limited parents' freedom to choose the linguistic regime of the school where they send their children in order to avoid linguistic shifts towards English by families speaking French or any language other than English. Data from the *Office québécois de la langue française* demonstrates the consequences of such a policy (see OQLF 2008: 79): in 2002, for instance, only 11.7% of Québécois students from kindergarten to secondary school had the right to access an English-speaking school – a right which 92.8% of them used – this is in spite of the fact that 18.3% did not have French as their mother tongue; additionally, 78.9% of the students whose mother tongue was a language other than English or French were enrolled in French-speaking schools.

For a long time in Wallonia, parents had no choice at all regarding the languages used in their children's schools: a federal law renders the use of French as the medium of instruction compulsory in the "linguistic region" comprising Wallonia (outside an eastern officially German-speaking area). However, since 1998, the government of the FWB, which is responsible for cultural and educational matters affecting francophones, has authorised the use of Dutch, English and German as languages of instruction in Wallonia (only Dutch in Brussels) within linguistic immersion programmes, inspired by the model of French-immersion schools for English students in Quebec and Ontario. This is another indication of the fact that francophones in Belgium behave more like the anglophone majority in Canada than the French-speaking minority. So, the monopoly of French on the educational linguistic market in Wallonia has been broken in order to favour children's early foreign language learning, following the increasing demand for multilingualism among parents (see Hambye and Richards 2012). This does not mean that the mastering of French is not regarded as fundamental in Wallonia: on the contrary, it is a constant subject of public debate and concern regarding the potential negative effect of early second language learning on the student's knowledge of a first language is very often invoked in discussions regarding immersion programmes. Yet, these programmes are viewed as compatible with high-level competence in the common language, simply because the learning of English or Dutch is not perceived as a threat to the predominance of French or for the students' proficiency in that language.

In the same vein, programmes in English in the universities of Wallonia and Brussels have been increasing since the 1960s at least. This movement, which is still limited, mainly affects programmes in which many international students are interested (masters in engineering, economics or business affairs), however it could soon concern other types of programme, since offering English courses is a way for universities to attract both local and foreign students within the very competitive European educational market instituted by the Bologna process. What is noteworthy here is the fact that this latent evolution towards a kind of anglicisation of university programmes is not supervised by any state regulation and not even the subject of explicit political debate. A conference debating the topic of the "language for higher education in twenty-first century Europe" was held in Brussels in 2003,[5] but this question has not received the benefit of significant public reflection. The government which represents the Walloon community allows each higher-education institution to establish its own policy regarding the medium of instruction, and does not view it necessary to define a common political vision on a question that might be considered fundamental in other communities.

2.3 Linguistic integration of immigrants

Policies regarding the linguistic integration of immigrants have very recently converged in Quebec and Wallonia. Indeed, in the latter region, a political agreement was reached in December 2012 concerning the establishment of an integration process (*parcours d'intégration*) for newcomers. This agreement (see Walloon Government 2012a) states that newcomers will have to present themselves to a special office dedicated to the integration of immigrants within three months of their arrival. On the basis of an assessment of their level of proficiency in French, French courses might be offered to them, although they would not be compulsory. The measures included in this process aim to "favour the integration of the immigrant" (*"favoriser l'intégration de la personne migrante"*), to "welcome newcomers in a good environment" (*"accueillir les nouveaux arrivants dans de bonnes conditions"*) and to "ensure them a dignified life and equality of opportunities" (*"de leur assurer une vie digne et une égalité des chances"*).

In Quebec, such a "programme for the linguistic integration of immigrants" (*"Programme d'intégration linguistique pour les migrants"*) was established in 2002. Back in 1991, the Law on the Ministry of Cultural Communities and Immigrants (*Loi sur le ministère des Communautés culturelles et de l'Immigration*) had already stated that the minister in charge of immigration matters must establish linguistic integration services accessible for newcomers whose knowledge of French had been assessed as insufficient through a compulsory procedure. While in Wallonia, French is deemed to be important for integration because it is the working language (*langue véhiculaire*), in Quebec it is important because "choosing to live in Québec means choosing to live in a French-speaking society" (*"société francophone"* Quebec Government 2012a). In Wallonia, French is merely, and accidentally, a common means of communication; in Quebec, it is a defining feature of the society. As a consequence, the aim of the linguistic integration programme in Quebec is to allow immigrants to "integrate themselves into Quebec *society*" (Quebec Government 2012b, our emphasis).[6] If French in Quebec is simply the *lingua franca*, as it seems to be viewed in Wallonia, it could not claim any precedence over English, which can clearly play the working-language role as well as French does. This is why those who want to legitimise the precedence of French (over English) promote the establishment of French as an intrinsic feature of Quebec society.

The importance of French in the website presentations of each region for foreigners is very indicative of the role language plays in Quebec and in Wallonia. In the case of the latter, we cannot find any mention of the French-speaking character of Wallonia in the pages entitled "Discover Wallonia" (*"Connaître la Wallonie"*) (Walloon Government 2012b). In Quebec, on the contrary, French appears second in the list of items describing what "living in Quebec" (*"Vivre au Québec"*) looks like (Quebec Government 2012c). Consequently, the measures set up to ensure the mastering of French by new-comers are much more extensive in Quebec than in Wallonia: it is suggested that potential immigrants take French courses in their own country through agreements signed with various language schools around the world, and these courses can be partly reimbursed for those people finally succeeding in their applications to migrate to Quebec. Free online and partly interactive courses of French are also offered to selected candidates for immigration before their arrival in Quebec, and various kinds of French course are available free of charge for immigrant adults settled in Quebec (full-time and part-time and for well- and less well-educated people, specialising in oral/written communication or in management, nursing, engineering, etc.; see Quebec Government 2012d). The study of French is of course also available in Wallonia. However, it is less extensive and not ultimately managed and controlled by a central public authority as is the case in Quebec. Rather, it depends on (sometimes isolated) private initiatives that are nevertheless funded by public money.

The contrast we observe here between policies in Quebec and Wallonia is not only due to a difference in the importance assigned to language but also to a major difference in immigration policies. Immigration policies are fundamental in Quebec, as using selective immigration to maintain its demographic balance has been one of the main tools employed by successive Quebec governments to compensate for the decrease in the birth rate. It is not surprising that Quebec has developed a proactive immigration policy where linguistic integration plays a key role. Indeed, the mastering of French (and English) is a "key selection criterion" (*"principal critère de sélection"*) in the choice of candidates applying to immigrate into Quebec as skilled workers (Quebec Government 2012a). The importance assigned to immigrants' knowledge of French is justified by the fact that not only is it considered "an essential factor in the integration of immigrants in Quebec" (*"un facteur essentiel d'intégration des immigrants au Québec"*) (Quebec Government 2012a), and also by the "desire to ensure the continuity and stability of the

French element in Québec" (*"la volonté d'assurer la continuité et la stabilité du fait français au Québec"*) (Quebec Government 2012e). Such a legal working immigration no longer exists in Belgium. In Wallonia and in Belgium in general, on the contrary, immigration is viewed more as a phenomenon that is passively undergone and for which downstream public bodies, rather than upstream institutions, are responsible. More specifically, Belgium's francophone authorities have long been reluctant to set up policies targeting special-needs groups defined on the basis of language or culture and not on socioeconomic criteria, which potentially cause stigmatisation – and in the same vein they have refused, like the French government, to conduct surveys leading to the publication of statistical data on ethnicity. This explains why, in the education field for instance, schools may get special financial support, depending on the socioeconomic level of their students but not on their cultural and linguistic backgrounds (see Hambye and Lucchini 2005). It also explains why Wallonia decided to set up an integration process eight years after Flanders had established its own programme. Even though there was a global agreement on the idea that newcomers should be accompanied in their integration process – notably at the level of language learning – there was also resistance against policies targeting immigrant communities and being somehow based on an assimilationist approach to immigration.

2.4 Language corpus planning: redefining language norms

We have seen above that policies defining the *status* of French vis-à-vis other languages are dramatically divergent in Quebec and Wallonia. Regarding the concerns of policies aiming at modifying legitimate *norms* of the language itself, convergence is much more important. First, both Quebec and Wallonia have supported and circulated sociolinguistic research questioning the ideological foundations of the vision equating linguistic correction in French with the Parisian variety and rejecting the specificities of regional varieties outside France as if they were improper French. This research presented the consequences of this vision on speakers' linguistic insecurity and its stakes in terms of loyalty towards French (see e.g. Francard 1993; Remysen 2004): the more people in Quebec and Wallonia view themselves as legitimate speakers, the more they will appropriate French, feel that they own their language and be keen to use and promote it. This is why both the Supreme Council for the French language (*Conseil supérieur de la langue française* (CSLF)) in Quebec and the Council for the French Language and Linguistic Policy (*Conseil de la langue française et de la politique linguistique*) in Wallonia (actually in the FWB) have promoted activities and publications describing and highlighting the diversity of French in Quebec and Wallonia, respectively, through the action of the Quebec Board for the French Language (*Office québécois de la langue française* (OQLF)) and of the Service for the French language (*Service de la langue française*).[7] It was also as a way of bringing language norms closer to the speakers' usage and helping citizens to appropriate the French language that these institutions took part in the 1990 orthographic reform of French (Goosse 1991).[8]

However, since such efforts towards *corpus* planning have been subject to vivid polemics (see e.g. Dister and Moreau 2009; Groupe R.O. 2011; Keller 1999; Maurais 2004), governments in both regions have been reluctant to support further reforms, even though some linguists still discuss and propose them. However, certain aspects of corpus planning are still taken up by Quebec authorities as far as they are linked to the definition of the status of the French language. As it is often stated in official discourse, French, since it is Quebec's official language, has to be the normal and usual language of the majority of activities, from the more formal and public to the informal and private, but it is also a "common symbol of belonging to Quebec society" (MICC 2012: 12). Hence, French has to be *particular* and able to express Quebec's specific identity. This is why institutions like the CSLF and the OQLF have always been diligent in ensuring the quality, the correctness, the legitimacy and the specificity of the French language in Quebec. It is therefore essential to promote the particularism of French in Quebec, notably the so-called *québécismes*, and to legitimate *québécois* as an autonomous variety of French. Within this framework it is easy to understand the project, supported by the Quebec government, to publish a *Dictionnaire de la langue française* (Dictionary of the French Language; see Franqus 2012) representing the norm of the French used in Quebec (i.e. containing the words used in Quebec, whether they are also used in France or not) that would be a *reference* for speakers in Quebec and would thus replace traditional dictionaries of French produced in France and based on the specific usage of France and used all over the French-speaking world. The picture illustrating the page dedicated to French on the international portal of the Quebec government is a clear example of this will to highlight the specificity of Quebec French (see Figure 7.1).

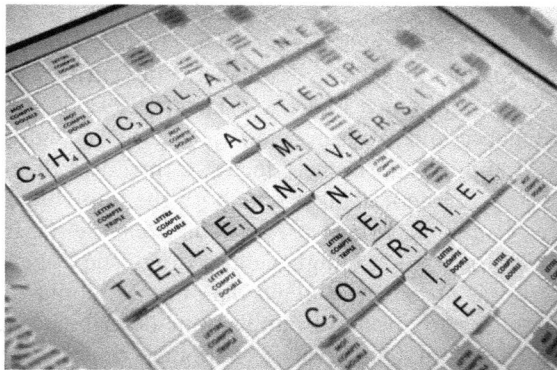

Figure 7.1 Picture illustrating the page "French" on the international portal of the official website of the government of Quebec
Source: Ministère des Relations internationales et de la Francophonie (MRIF), Jean Désy (Quebec Government 2012c).

Indeed, the words on the picture in Figure 7.1 all symbolise the peculiarities of Quebec French: *chocolatine* means "chocolate bread" and is absent in the standard French of France (although it is used in certain French regions), *auteure* illustrates the promotion of professional titles' feminisation in Quebec, *aluminerie* (factory-producing aluminium) and *téléuniversité* (university distance education) are also words that are particular to Quebec French. The latter, like *courriel* (email) (also in used in competition with *mail* in European French), illustrates the efforts of Québécois to use French equivalents to English words borrowed in the rest of the *Francophonie*.

3 Where do we go from here? Assessing language policies in Quebec and Wallonia

Our description of language policies in Quebec and Wallonia highlights the sharp contrast between the heavy symbolic investment in language in Quebec and the very pragmatic attitude of the Walloon authorities regarding linguistic matters. Does Wallonia have an interest in developing a more coherent and structured policy in favour of French in the absence of a real threat towards its predominance?

People in Wallonia could be tempted to take Quebec as an example to be followed for various reasons. Within the context of the conflict between francophone and Flemish Belgians, and in a European context where English plays an increasingly important role, some think francophones should be more active in their defence of French and affirm the value they assign to their language more vigorously. Furthermore, promoting the French language could be considered as part of the effort to build a francophone, Walloon or *wallo-brusseloise* (Walloon-Brussels) identity – regularly called for by politicians – that would ensure the unity of francophones and favour their social and economic development.[9]

Walloons' "deficit of identity" has for long been discussed (see e.g. Francard 1993: 236–37; Klinkenberg 1995: 40–59, see also the contribution of Caron in this book). Although it is not absolutely self-evident, one might believe that developing a kind of national identity in Wallonia, notably grounded on the promotion of French as a common distinctive feature, might be a positive factor for social and cultural cohesion. In this sense, it is possible to believe that Wallonia should follow in Quebec's footsteps. While it undoubtedly has the advantage of being a powerful force for collective mobilisation, the kind of linguistic nationalism Quebec and other communities have developed also causes some serious difficulties.

The struggle for sovereignty in Quebec was based on the idea that Quebec was a distinct nation and that this nation had the right to preserve itself with its defining features, including language, in the first place. The vision of the nation in Quebec then evolved from ethnic nationalism to civic nationalism: what defines belonging to Quebec society is no longer a common ethnic French-Canadian ascendance, but shared "values" that include the French language. However, this is still what one might call a substantive, and potentially essentialist vision of the nation (see Caron, this book), a vision that contradicts the principle of the neutrality of the state that is central to the political philosophy of modern Western states.[10] Indeed, if the will to promote French is one of the main distinctive features of the citizens of Quebec, all the people who can understand this objective but who do not view it as a core value (angophones and newcomers) might see themselves and be seen as second-order citizens. In other words, if the promotion of French is not an objective democratically chosen by the Québécois as they form an actual *demos*, but rather a characteristic of a nation's *essence*, then there will necessarily be people who share this *essence* and are part of this nation, and people who are not – an idea that is, of course, inconsistent with the generally admitted vision of citizenship in our Western societies.

This is why we do not consider it relevant to call for the building of a nation in Wallonia that would rely on a supposed collective identity defined by *substantive* features including language. Does that mean that people in Wallonia should feel very satisfied with the kind of language policy they have? We think there is another reason to call for a policy that would take the political importance of language more seriously. Indeed, the status of French in Wallonia could be consolidated not because of the symbolic role it plays for the definition of a purported collective identity, but for its direct link to questions of equality of access to important material and symbolic resources. Here we can return to the example of higher education: what is at stake in this debate is not (or not only) the symbolic precedence of French in an important area for the building of a collective identity, but rather the question of the costs and benefits for citizens of university courses in English or French, particularly in terms of equality of access to the universities and in terms of quality of education. While we are not asserting that the current movement towards anglicisation implicates more costs than benefits, we think that this question is worthy of political debate. In this sense, the Walloons' reluctance regarding the affirmation of national symbols like language should not necessarily prevent them from thinking about the crucial political questions raised by language issues and calling for a political vision regarding language policies.

4 Conclusion

In this chapter we have examined four areas where one can compare language policies in Quebec and Wallonia (public communication, education, linguistic immigration policies and language corpus planning). Except in the domain of language corpus planning – where efforts to redefine the normative attitudes of speakers and legitimate endogenous linguistic practices have been supported in both regions – policies regarding linguistic matters are rather different in Quebec and Wallonia. In fact, only Quebec has developed a coherent and transversal language policy, specifically with the *La charte de la langue française* (Charter of the French Language), aimed at ensuring the precedence of French in all public domains of language use. This is of course due to the fact that in Quebec, unlike in Wallonia, this precedence is objectively threatened by the attractiveness of English and by the situation of minoritisation in which the French-speaking community lives, in North America in general and in Canada in particular. Even if it has always been a minority, the Belgian French-speaking community has never really suffered from being in a minoritised position. However, Quebec's language policies also have to be understood within the nationalist strategy that French-speaking political and economic elites have pursued in order to gain power in Quebec (Heller 2006).

Since the language policy in Quebec has globally been successful – the status of French is solid nowadays in Quebec and undoubtedly far better than it was before the Quiet Revolution – it might be considered as a model for all those who care about the future of a minority language in a world where globalisation affects the use of local languages in several domains of activity. Yet, we have seen that in Quebec and in many other regions of the world, defence of the minority language is based on a nationalist discourse that is in serious conflict with the democratic citizenship favoured in our societies. That we might have good reasons to reject such nationalist claims about the defence of a community's own language, does not mean that we should lose interest in language policies, as the language globalisation evoked above has many consequences in non-linguistic domains and thus raises many important political issues.

Notes

1 In Janssens' survey, 95% of the respondents who spoke a language other than French or Dutch at home said they use French with the administration (Janssens 2008: 6).
2 See the text of the *La charte de la langue française* (Charter of the French Language).
3 In Janssens' 2005 survey, more than 95% of respondents said they speak French well or perfectly. English was in second position at 35% and Dutch, third at 28% (see Janssens 2008).
4 For instance, the *Mouvement Québec Français* or the *Société Saint-Jean-Baptsiste de Montréal*.
5 The Second University Foundation Ethical Forum (16 October 2003).
6 "Le Programme d'intégration linguistique pour les immigrants (PILI) a été créé pour soutenir les immigrants dans leur démarche d'apprentissage du français langue seconde afin qu'ils puissent s'intégrer à la société québécoise" (The programme of linguistic integration for immigrants has been created in order to support immigrants in their learning of French as a second language and to help them integrate into the Québécois society).
7 See the respective websites of these institutions for an overview of the various initiatives they have taken.
8 The policy, which aims at the feminisation of professional titles, developed in both regions, has other objectives – principally highlighting the place of women in society – but it also contributes to putting forward the idea that the language should be what its users want to make of it, as legitimate owners of their language – French not being the property of the *Académie française*.

9 See, for instance, the interview of Minister Paul Magnette in *Le Soir*, 5 January 2013 and in the newspapers of the Sudpresse group on 1 March 2010.
10 A philosophy that considers that the state should be organised on the basis of a definition of what is *right* and not of what is *good*, the definition of the *good* being always divergent in the different social groups or communities constituting our modern pluralistic societies; see on this subject the important philosophical debate between the liberals and communitarians in, e.g. Berten, Da Silveira and Pourtois (1997) or Taylor (1989).

References

Berten, André, Pablo Da Silveira and Hervé Pourtois (1997). *Libéraux et communautariens*, Paris: Presses universitaires de France.

Dister, Anne and Marie-Louise Moreau (2009). *Féminiser? Vraiment pas sorcier! La féminisation des noms de métiers, fonctions, grades et titres*, Louvain-la-Neuve: De Boeck.

Erk, Jan (2005). "Sub-state nationalism and the left–right divide: critical junctures in the formation of nationalist labour movements in Belgium", *Nations and Nationalism*, 11(4): 551–70.

Francard, Michel (1993). *L'insécurité linguistique en Communauté française de Belgique*, Brussels: Service de la langue française.

Francard, Michel (1997). "Le français en Wallonie". In *Le français en Belgique. Une langue, une communauté*, ed. Daniel Blampain, André Goosse, Jean-Marie Klinkenberg and Marc Wilmet, 229–37. Louvain-la-Neuve: Duculot.

Goosse, André (1991). *La "nouvelle" orthographe. Exposé et commentaires*, Paris and Louvain-la-Neuve: Duculot.

Groupe R.O. (2011). "Faut-il réformer l'orthographe?", *Français et société*, 21.

Hambye, Philippe (2009). "Plurilinguisme et minorisation en Belgique: d'étranges rapports aux langues 'étrangères'", *Langage et société*, (129): 29–46.

Hambye, Philippe and Mary Richards (2012). "The paradoxical visions of multilingualism in education: the ideological dimension of discourses on bilingualism in Belgium and Canada", *International Journal of Multilingualism*, 9(2): 165–88.

Hambye, Philippe and Silvia Lucchini (2005). "Sociolinguistic diversity and shared resources. A critical look at linguistic integration policies in Belgium", *Noves SL*, 6. Available from: www6.gencat.net/llengcat/noves/ (accessed 1 September 2014).

Heller, Monica (2006). *Linguistic minorities and modernity: a sociolinguistic ethnography*, 2nd edn, London: Continuum.

Janssens, Rudi (2007). *Van Brussel gesproken: taalgebruik, taalverschuivingen en taalidentiteit in het Brussels Hoofdstedelijk Gewest*, Brussels: VUB Press.

Janssens, Rudi (2008). "Language use in Brussels and the position of Dutch. Some recent findings", *Brussels Studies*, 13. Available from: www.brusselsstudies.be/ (accessed 1 September 2014).

Keller, Monika (1999). *La réforme de l'orthographe: un siècle de débats et de querelles*, Paris: Conseil international de la langue française.

Klinkenberg, Jean-Marie (1995). "Les blocages dans l'identification wallonne: germes d'une identité postnationale". In *Nationalisme et postnationalisme*, ed. Philippe Destatte, 47–64. Namur: Presses universitaires de Namur.

Lamarre, Patricia and Stéphanie Lamarre (2009). "Montréal 'on the move': pour une approche ethnographique non-statique des pratiques langagières des jeunes multilingues". In *Formes et normes sociolinguistiques. Ségrégations et discriminations urbaines*, ed. Thierry Bulot, 105–34. Paris: L'Harmattan.

Mabille, Xavier (2000). *Histoire politique de la Belgique. Facteurs et acteurs de changement*, Brussels: CRISP.

Maurais, Jacques (2004). *Les rectifications orthographiques de 1990: bilan de la situation au Québec en 2004*, Quebec: Office québécois de la langue française,

Plourde, Michel (2000). *Le Français au Québec. 400 ans d'histoire et de vie*, Quebec: Conseil de la langue française, Gouvernement du Québec.

Remysen, Wim (2004). "La variation linguistique et l'insécurité linguistique: le cas du français québécois". In *La variation dans la langue standard*, ed. Pierre Bouchard, 23–36. Langues et sociétés no. 42. Quebec: Office québécois de la langue française.

Taylor, Charles (1992). "The politics of recognition". In *Multiculturalism and "the politics of recognition"*, ed. Amy Gutmann, 25–73. Princeton, NJ: Princeton University Press.

Taylor, Charles (1993). *Reconciling the Solitudes. Essays on Canadian Federalism and Nationalism*, Montreal: McGill-Queen's University Press.

Taylor, Charles (1989). "Cross-purposes: the liberal–communitarian debate". In *Liberalism and the Moral Life*, ed. Nancy L. Rosenblum, 159–82. Cambridge: Cambridge University Press.

Witte, Els and Harry Van Velthoven (2000). *Language and Politics. The Situation in Belgium in a Historical Perspective*, Brussels: VUB Press.

Official documents

Franqus (2012). "Dictionnaire – accueil". Available from: http://franqus.ca/dictio/accueil.jsp (accessed 20 December 2013).

MICC (Ministère de l'Immigration et des Communautés culturelles) (2012). *Apprendre le Québec. Guide pour réussir votre intégration*, Quebec: Gouvernement du Québec.

OQLF (Office québécois de la langue française) (2008). *Rapport sur l'évolution de la situation linguistique au Québec 2002–2007*, Montreal: Gouvernement du Québec.

Quebec Government (2012a). "Société francophone". Available from: www.gouv.qc.ca/portail/quebec/international/general/immigration/apprendre_le_francais/societe_francophone/ (accessed 20 December 2013).

Quebec Government (2012b). "Apprentissage du français langue seconde". Available from: http://www4.gouv.qc.ca/FR/Portail/Citoyens/Evenements/immigrer-au-quebec/Pages/apprentissage-francais-langue-seconde.aspx (accessed 20 December 2013).

Quebec Government (2012c). "Langue". Available from: www.gouv.qc.ca/portail/quebec/international/general/quebec/langue/ (accessed 20 December 2013).

Quebec Government (2012d). "Migrating to Quebec – French language". Available from: www.immigration-quebec.gouv.qc.ca/en/french-language/index.html (accessed 20 December 2013).

Quebec Government (2012e). "Glossary". Available from: www.immigration-quebec.gouv.qc.ca/en/french-language/glos sary.html (accessed 20 December 2013).

Walloon Government (2012a). "Accord sur le parcours d'accueil en Wallonie". Available from: www.wallonie.be/fr/actualites/accord-sur-le-parcours-daccueil-en-wallonie (accessed 20 December 2013).

Walloon Government (2012b). "Connaitre la Wallonie". Available from: www.wallonie.be/fr/connaitre-la-wallonie (accessed 20 December 2013).

8 International relations of minority nations

Quebec and Wallonia compared

Stéphane Paquin, Marine Kravagna and Min Reuchamps

Today few people deny the existence of regional substate diplomacy (Criekemans 2010). But there is still no common agreement on a region's right to do so and, above all, on their scope of action. This question goes against what used to be the dominant approach in international relations, the state-centric approach that leads to the logic of *speaking with one voice*. Increasingly, a multilevel-governance approach has contested this state-centric view and proposes an alternative logic of multiple actors *speaking with their voice*, nuancing strongly the seminal distinction between "sovereignty-bound" and "sovereignty-free" actors (Rosenau 1990). From the 1970s, the world has seen the growing presence of sovereignty-free actors in international relations. Among these actors, non-central or, better, substate, governments of federal states have developed intensive foreign relations. These governments are using a range of techniques: from shaping the federal government's foreign policy to establishing themselves directly in the international arena (Blatter *et al.* 2008). For minority nation governments this is particularly a challenge, as they have to act internally – where they have developed full-fledged legislative powers within a multinational federation – and externally – where international and national laws are often still reluctant to recognise their right of action (Lejeune 2003).

Yet some minority nations have thrived in developing their own international relations. Bavaria, Catalonia, Flanders, Quebec, Scotland and Wallonia are often seen as successful international players even if they are not fully sovereignty bound (Michelmann 2009; Criekemans 2010). The international actions of these minority nations have been characterised under the umbrella of "identity paradiplomacy" (Paquin 2003); that is, a willingness to use international relations to foster a nation-building process within a multinational state. This observation was particularly prevalent for minority nations strongly in competition with a federal government about their nation-building process, albeit for different reasons, namely Flanders, Quebec and Scotland (Paquin 2004). The case of Wallonia seems to fits less well into the identity paradiplomacy framework, which therefore raises the question of alternative roads to international relations. This is the core question of this chapter: is identity paradiplomacy the only way to go for minority nations?

Quebec and Wallonia are both well known for their active foreign relations. They also share this common feature of being a demographic minority in their federation. But as we move into the question of the nature of the relationship between their minority status and their diplomacy, we ought to qualify the two cases under study, since this is key to understand their international relations. The qualification for the case of Quebec is fairly straightforward. Quebec is the province of Quebec and therefore its government and, in particular, what is today's known as the *Ministère des Relations internationales du Québec et de la Francophonie* (Ministry of International Relations of Quebec and of the Francophonie) that was created in 1965 and whose name and scope changed over time.

By contrast, the definition of the case of Wallonia in the purpose of this chapter is much more of a challenge. If the previous chapters of this book could refer to Wallonia as the Walloon Region, in the field of international relations a more complex qualification is needed as both the community and the regional dimensions are intertwined. This goes back not only to the two-fold structure of the Belgian federation that is made up of communities and regions (Bursens and Massart-Piérard 2009), but also, as noted by Caron in this book, to the very question of the nature of the Walloon/francophone identity. As a consequence, the study of Walloon/francophone international relations has to take into account the institutional architecture they rely on. This means five institutions. First, the French-speaking Community, which has recently been politically, but not constitutionally, renamed the Walloon-Brussels Federation. Second, the Walloon Region for all matters related to regional jurisdiction. Third, the Brussels-Capital Region because of the close connexion with the French-speaking Community. Fourth, the French-speaking Community Commission (Cocof), which is the body of the French-speaking Community in Brussels. Fifth, the German-speaking Community, whose territory for regional matters is part of the Walloon Region (Reuchamps and Onclin 2009)

With this background, this chapter seeks to capture their foreign relations and how they undertake them. To this end, we look more specifically at two dimensions: the *ius tractati* – the right to conclude treaties – and the *ius legationis* – the right to be represented on the international scene, both abroad and within international or subnational organisations. In order to set the stage for this comparative endeavour, we first present the theoretical framework usually used to study the foreign relations of non-central governments that typically refers to paradiplomacy and, in particular, identity paradiplomacy.

1 Foreign relations of non-central governments

With the increasing activities on the international scene of non-central governments in the 1970s, Duchacek followed by Michelmann and Soldatos initiated a conceptualisation in the 1980s around the concept of *paradiplomacy*

(Duchacek 1984, 1986; Michelmann and Soldatos 1990). Paradiplomacy is about "political contacts with distant nations that bring non-central governments into contact not only with trade, industrial, or cultural centres on other continents ... but also with the various branches or agencies of foreign national governments" (Duchacek 1986: 246–47). In other words, paradiplomacy consists in foreign relations that are distinct from those of the central government; it is thus a "parallel" diplomacy (Paquin 2004).

The question of paradiplomacy is more acute in multinational federations where the minority nations may be willing to use their foreign relations to foster a nation-building process within a multinational country. This intense phenomenon has been labelled "identity paradiplomacy" (Paquin 2003). Sub-state governments with a minority status tend to develop their foreign relations in order to obtain resources and support that are lacking at the domestic level. This is even more so in federations where the federal government is antagonistic to their claims, as is striking in the case of Catalonia in Spain, Flanders in Belgium and Quebec in Canada. Nonetheless, comparative-politics literature does not provide a one-fits-all explanation: from one country to another, "identity diplomacy may complete, support, extend, affect or threaten the state foreign policy. It might promote cooperation as well as conflicts" (Paquin 2004: 207, our translation).

This question raises the chief issue in international relations of the sovereignty, or the lack thereof, of non-central governments, and more specifically of substate governments in multinational federations. International law sets the principle of the unity of the federations and thus stresses the need for a coherent foreign policy as well as the responsibility of federations, and therefore of the federal government in particular, to fulfil their international obligations whatever their internal institutional set-up (Lejeune 2003). While federal governments are typically "sovereignty-bound" actors (Rosenau 1990: 36), substate governments have an ambiguous status which is both "sovereignty bound" and "sovereignty free".

On the one hand, their sovereignty-bound status within sovereign countries allows them to have access to the country's foreign-policy decision making. Thus, unlike non-government organisations (NGOs) and other civil-society actors, substate governments enjoy privileged access to the diplomatic networks, international organisations and negotiating forums available only to sovereign states. It is now common for officials of substate governments to attend international forums, and to participate in the drafting of international agreements when the object falls within their constitutional jurisdiction (Paquin 2005).

On the other hand, these actors also enjoy a sovereignty-free status in international relations, which brings both positive and negative effects. On the positive side, Rosenau contends that actors who lack sovereignty are not constrained by responsibilities and obligations that are imposed on sovereignty-bound actors and they can therefore exercise the full measure of their resources to specific goals, which can increase their actions' effectiveness

(1990: 36). But on the negative side, substate governments also face a number of constraints since they are not always recognised as legitimate actors under international law. As a consequence, substate governments have to negotiate with their federal government the terms and the scope of their international relations, such as official missions to foreign countries and to international organisations. This important consequence of their sovereignty-free status is also highly dependent of the federation's internal institutional design and the substate government's position, to which we turn now for Belgium and Canada.

2 International relations of substate governments in Belgium and Canada

Belgium and Canada provide two interesting cases of study for their institutional design in terms of international relations that are quite different, even though they face a similar demand from their constituent units for more international autonomy. Belgium is remarkable not only because of its double structure with regions and communities, but also because these substate governments enjoy full foreign-relations powers for the policy fields they govern domestically, which is known as the *in foro interno, in foro externo* principle (Bursens and Massart-Piérard 2009). Each constituent unit of federal Belgium may act, on its own, in the international area within the remit of its competences. This is the case for Flanders, whose foreign relations is led by the Flemish government and its agencies but also for the French-speaking substate governments, whose foreign relations are, however, more fragmented. Out of this fragmentation emerged initially three distinct administrative structures in charge of foreign relations: the community-based *Commissariat général des relations internationals* (CGRI) (General Commissariat for International Relations) and the two region-based agencies: the *Direction des relations internationales* (DRI) (Office of International Relations) and the *Agence wallonne à l'exportation et aux investissements étrangers* (AWEX) (Walloon Agency for Exportation and Foreign Investments). In 2009, the CGRI and DRI merged into one single structure, *Wallonie-Bruxelles International* (WBI) (Wallonia-Brussels International), while the AWEX remained in charge of external trade and foreign investments.

In Canada, the province of Quebec, as well as the nine other provinces, do not benefit from the principle of *in foro interno, in foro externo* that is prevalent in Belgium. Nonetheless, the government of Quebec has been active on the international scene since the nineteenth century. But it was after the 1960s and the Quiet Revolution that the government of Quebec became increasingly internationally active. One major reason for this is the will to foster Quebec's identity both on the domestic and the international levels. In addition to this nation-building process, the increasing internationalisation of politics and policies also urged the government of Quebec to have a say in the international relations of Canada. In the 1960s, the government of Quebec started complaining that international treaties had a growing effect in provincial fields of jurisdiction. The government of Quebec wanted to have a voice. The next sections of this chapter will investigate how it managed to do so, in comparison with the Walloon/francophone substate governments in Belgium. But in the latter case, there is an important extra independent variable: the European Union (EU). As one of the founding members, Belgium had to adapt its institutional and administrative structure to the European construction that shaped both internal and external politics and policies (Beyers and Bursens 2006, 2013).

To understand these dynamics, formal rules and constitutional assignments of competences are an integral part of the study of power shifts within political administrative systems. They give two kinds of information. First, "they determine to what extent the national executives hold a 'gatekeeper' position within the multilevel government system, which gives them the opportunity of exploiting information asymmetries within both the international and the domestic arena" and, secondly, "they are also strong symbolic representations of the dominant perspective on the appropriate distribution of tasks between the layers of government" (Blatter *et al.* 2008: 466). For both cases we therefore analyse the *ius tractati* – the right to conclude treaties – and the *ius legationis* – the right to be represented on the international scene– that will enable us to discuss afterwards the politics of international relations before concluding this chapter.

3   Quebec's international relations within the Canadian federation

The Constitution Act or the British North America (BNA) Act of 1867 gives little mention of international negotiations. While many federal constitutions assign exclusive power over foreign affairs to the central government, the BNA Act passed by the British parliament in 1867 was silent on the issue. The provisions of the BNA Act enumerating the division of powers – sections 91 and 92 – did not explicitly assign jurisdiction in foreign affairs to either the federal or provincial levels. Nor, importantly, did the BNA Act deny the provinces the possibility of an international role as other federal constitutions tend to do. The silence was entirely understandable, since such an explicit allocation of powers was, in the circumstances, unnecessary. Those who framed Canada's original constitution did not conceive that the new dominion (Canada) might eventually enjoy the same autonomy in foreign policy as it had in domestic affairs. Certainly, as a member of the British Empire, Canada could have no independent international personality. Instead, other states would continue to recognise only one sovereign entity, the British Empire. Correspondingly, the rights and responsibilities of sovereign statehood would be vested in and exercised by the imperial government in London. The constitution was thus framed accordingly.

3.1 *Ius tractati*

The only part of the BNA Act concerned with international law is section 132, which deals with imperial treaties. It specifies that:

> The Parliament and Government of Canada shall have all Powers necessary or proper for performing the Obligations of Canada or of any Province thereof, as Part of the British Empire, towards Foreign Countries, arising under Treaties between the Empire and such Foreign Countries.
>
> (BNA Act 1867: section 132)

Under this provision, while the federal government could not conclude international treaties, it had the capacity to implement imperial treaties, even in provincial fields of jurisdiction. However, with the Statute of Westminster of 1931 and the acquisition of sovereignty in all areas of policy including foreign policy (except for the amendment of the Canadian constitution), the question was rapidly raised in the context of Canadian federalism: does the federal government have the power to force the provinces to implement treaties even when those treaties deal with subjects that fall exclusively within provincial jurisdiction? It was the provincial government of Ontario in the *Labour Conventions* case that challenged the ability of the federal government to legislate in provincial fields of jurisdiction in order to implement international agreements (Patry 1980: 155).

After the 1930 elections, the conservative government of R.B. Bennett ratified three International Labour Organisation conventions. By implementing these conventions, the federal government intruded on the provincial right to legislate in the area of labour (exclusively under provincial jurisdiction). The Judicial Committee of the Privy Council in London (which was still Canada's court of final appeal until 1949), rendered its judgment in 1937. This ruling is of fundamental importance for the legal capacity of the federal government and the rights of the provinces in international relations. The judges recalled that federalism constitutes the foundation of Canada. Furthermore, the principle of the sovereignty of parliament means that the legislature is not obliged to pass measures that might be necessary to implement a treaty concluded by the federal executive. In this case then, it is up to the provinces, where the same principle of parliamentary sovereignty applies to provincial legislatures, to amend their respective laws and regulations to give effect to the said treaty in domestic law. In Canada the power to implement treaties thus follows the distribution of power. According to Richard, the impact of the *Labour Conventions* case "denies Ottawa plenary power in matters relating to treaties.

The *Labour Conventions* case was thus extremely important and would lead to the formulation of the Gérin-Lajoie doctrine in 1965 by the government of Quebec. As the government of Ontario had done in the 1930s, the government of Quebec in 1965 expressed its concern over the effects of internationalisation on provincial jurisdictions. In a speech in 1965, Quebec Deputy Premier and Minister of Education Paul Gérin-Lajoie enunciated what would later become known as the "Gérin-Lajoie doctrine of the international extension of Quebec's domestic jurisdictions" (Paquin 2006). The doctrine asserts that Quebec itself must conclude any conventions in its fields of jurisdiction. Gérin-Lajoie declared:

> There is not, I repeat, any reason for the right to apply an international convention to be separated from the right to conclude the convention. These are two essential stages of a single operation. Nor is it any longer acceptable that the federal state be able to exercise a sort of supervision or control over Quebec's international relations.
>
> (Gérin-Lajoie 1965: 141, our translation)

Gérin-Lajoie suggested overturning the approach then generally taken so that Quebec should itself negotiate and implement international agreements in its areas of jurisdiction. This doctrine is still topical. In 2002 Quebec's National Assembly unanimously adopted an amendment to the *Loi sur le Ministère des Relations internationales* (Act with Regard to the Ministry of International Relations) requiring National Assembly approval for any important international agreement entered into by Canada that concerns Quebec's fields of jurisdiction. The National Assembly has thus become the first parliament of the British model to be closely involved in the process by which a central government undertakes international commitments. Quebec is the only province in this situation and since then has set a number of precedents (Paquin 2006, 2010).

Since the *Labour Conventions* case of 1937, international treaty making in Canada follows two distinct phases: the conclusion of the treaty, that is, its negotiation, signature and ratification, followed by its implementation. The first stage of the operation is the prerogative of the federal executive (a monopoly that has nonetheless been contested by the government of Quebec since the 1965 Gérin-Lajoie doctrine) (Paquin 2006, 2010). The second stage, the passage of the necessary legislation to enforce the treaty, is the prerogative of the legislative branch, federal and provincial. It is therefore necessary to incorporate treaties as a matter of domestic law by legislative action at the appropriate federal or provincial level (Arbour 1997: 160).

In Canada, the *ius tractati* thus remains under the jurisdiction of the federal government, but because the second phase follows the internal distribution of powers, the voice of Quebec is not ignored at the first one. The importance of international treaties, including trade agreements, and the formulation of the Gerin-Lajoie doctrine in 1965, forced the federal government to consult with the provinces where international treaties affected their jurisdiction, since otherwise it risked being denounced. Because the federal government was aware of its limitations, several mechanisms of consultation between the federal government and the provinces have also been established (Zeigel 1988; Turp 2002; Paquin 2006).

However, there is no overall framework agreement in Canada on consultations between the federal government and the provinces in relation to international treaty making, and there is very little consistency in approaches (de Mestral 2005: 319–22). Intergovernmental agreements relating to international treaties on education, private international law and human rights are more institutionalised than environmental and trade negotiations, for example, but, overall, these mechanisms do not concern all international treaties that fall within provincial jurisdiction but rather, sectoral federal–provincial agreements. In other words, the mechanisms do not cover all international negotiations that affect areas of provincial jurisdiction. In addition, they are weakly institutionalised, not binding for the federal government and they leave too much room for federal intervention.

On top of that, since 1965, the government of Quebec has concluded "on its own" more than 700 international agreements (*ententes*) with sovereign or federated states in about 80 different countries. Many of these *ententes* were concluded with sovereign states and, in some cases, with no intervention from the Canadian government. A significant element should be noted: the international agreements concluded by Quebec itself are not called treaties but *ententes* (mutual agreements), which shows the sensitiveness of the national government to the word "treaty" on behalf of Quebec.

3.2 *Ius legationis*

Section 92.4 of the BNA Act gives provinces authority over the "Establishment and Tenure of Provincial Offices". This permits Quebec and other provinces to establish provincial offices abroad if they wish. It is difficult to argue that the opening by Lower Canada (modern-day Quebec) of a representation within the British Empire in 1816 was an international action, since Canada was part of the British Empire. The same is true for when Quebec posted an immigration officer in London in 1869 or opened a delegation in the heart of the British Empire in 1911. The first "real" international delegation was opened in Paris in 1882 when Hector Fabre became the agent general of Quebec. This representation was closed in 1910. It should be noted that this representation was opened before Canada had the right to send representatives abroad. This right would be formally recognised with the Statute of Westminster of 1931. We should also mention that in 1883 the federal government would also appoint Hector Fabre as Canada's Commissioner General in Paris. In 1914, the Quebec government opened an office in Brussels. Importantly, the government of Quebec was not the only one to do so. The government of Ontario, for example, also sent an immigration officer to Britain in 1869 and opened a delegation in London in 1908 (Dyment 2001: 56, 62).

But this early activity was relatively short-lived. Quebec closed its agency in Paris in 1912 because the French business community was so uninterested in Quebec. Both the missions in Brussels and London were closed in the early 1930s in an effort to trim provincial expenditures. When the conservative

Union nationale (National Union) under Maurice Duplessis came to power in 1936, all Quebec's agencies abroad were abolished by law. When the liberals under Adélard Godbout came to power in the 1939 provincial elections, this law was repealed, and legislation authorising the government to appoint agent generals was introduced: Quebec offices were then opened in New York and in Ottawa. When Duplessis and the *Union nationale* were returned to power in 1944, the two offices were left in place, although the budget of the New York office was cut so much that the agent general could do virtually nothing.

It was only after the 1960s that the government of Quebec started to open (and sometimes close and reopen again) international delegations: in Paris (1961), London (1962), Rome and Milan (1965), Chicago (1969), Boston, Lafayette, Dallas and Los Angeles (1970), Munich and Berlin (1971) Brussels (1972), Atlanta (1977), Washington (1978), Mexico and Tokyo (1980), Beijing and Santiago (1998), Shanghai and Barcelona (1999), Mumbai (2007), Sao Paulo (2008) and Moscow (2012).

The right to be represented in international and supranational organisations is typically reserved to the national state. However, Quebec enjoys a particular right of representation in two international organisations: UNESCO and *La Francophonie*. In 2006, after years of demands on behalf of Quebec, the Canadian government recognised officially that "Quebec's peculiarity brings it to play a specific role at the international level". The same agreement also grants Quebec a formal role in UNESCO: it is now officially present in the Canadian permanent representation and has the right to express its interests. The government of Quebec appoints its permanent representative to UNESCO, who is part of the Canadian permanent representation and guarantees Quebec immediate access to all official documents and information of the institution. Moreover, this agreement ensures that the Canadian and the Quebec governments coordinate their positions before every vote, resolution, negotiation and draft international instrument that is put forward or is adopted in the framework of UNESCO (Ministère des Relations internationales et de la Francophonie 2013a). This agreement was a huge step for Quebec: the recognition of its role on the international scene as well as its direct access to the UNESCO decision-making process legitimate Quebec's external actions and grant it direct access to the issues addressed by UNESCO. *La Francophonie* is even more unique: it is the only multilateral governmental organisation in which Quebec is a fully-fledged member. Quebec has seized this opportunity to assert its external aspects (Ministère des Relations internationales et de la Francophonie 2013b).

4 Substates' international relations in the Belgian federation

In Belgium, the dominant perspective on the international relations of subnational governments is not the state-centric approach that would lead to the logic of *speaking with one voice* but rather the multilevel-governance approach that leads to the *recognition of the parallel between one entity's internal and external powers.* Such an approach recognises the right of a substate government to express itself on the international scene and sign treaties falling within its domestic competences (Bursens and Massart-Piérard 2009). It thus prevents the federal government from legislating in subnational entities' areas of competences by means of concluding international agreements in domestic-policy areas (Lejeune 2003). In the Belgian federation, subnational entities have the right to conduct autonomous foreign relations. This was constitutionalised in 1993 with the guiding principle of *in foro interno, in foro externo*, aligning the exercise of external competences with the one of internal competences. This principle mirrors the Belgian internal dual federal system on the international level: each constituent entity has exclusive administrative and legislative powers within its jurisdiction on both the domestic and international level. Thus, unlike Canada, each constituent unit of Belgium must both make and implement international policies falling within its jurisdiction.

4.1 *Ius tractati*

The acquisition of treaty-making powers by the subnational entities follows the main dynamics of the state reforms in Belgium that stress the autonomy of the regions and communities, and the non-hierarchical nature of the system (Jans and Stouthuysen 2007). This right was constitutionally recognised in 1993 for both types of constituent unit, but its establishment has been gradual and first intended for the communities, which acquired it for cultural matters in 1988. Before this date, even if the federal government had full jurisdiction to conduct international relations, the Belgian constituent units were involved in some aspects of foreign affairs through different mechanisms of cooperative federalism. For instance, since 1978, the Cultural Council had to give its consent to treaties dealing with cultural cooperation, and the special law of institutional reforms adopted in 1980 legislated that the substates' governments had to take part in the negotiation of the treaties (Lejeune 1981). These mechanisms combining the autonomy of the substates with the monopoly of the federal state over external relations can be considered as the beginning of the current Belgian system.

Heading VI "On international relations" of the Belgian Constitution, introduced in 1993, defines precisely who does what in international relations in Belgium. Article 167§1 states "The King directs international relations, *notwithstanding* the competence of communities and regions to regulate international cooperation, including the concluding of treaties, for those matters that fall within their competences in pursuance of or by virtue of the Constitution" (our emphasis). What is more, the treaties take effect only after they have received the approval of the parliament or parliaments, depending of which layer of government has the competences. The following articles (168, 168bis and 169) delineate the different scenarios in treaty conclusions.

First, there are treaties that fall exclusively within the competences of the substate governments. Therefore, regions and communities have total freedom in conducting their international activities. Nevertheless, the special law on international reforms of 8 August 1980 was adapted after 1993 to include an obligation for the a substate government to inform the federal government of its intention to start a negotiation, as well as informing it of any legal act that the substate government is willing to perform in order to conclude a treaty (article 81). Even though the possibility exists for the federal government to request the suspension of the negotiations, such a mechanism has never been applied hitherto. Yet, treaties falling exclusively within substates' competences are rare, since international treaties do not take into account the internal distribution of competences and also because the interpretation of the distribution of competences is restrictive.

Therefore the vast majorities of treaties are mixed treaties; that is, most deal with both federal competences and regional and/or community competences. A cooperation agreement had to be concluded between the federal government and the subnational government in order to set the boundaries for such cases. This cooperation agreement was concluded on 8 March 1994 between the federal, regional and community authorities, and approved by the law of 20 August 1996. It requires the use of the Inter-Ministerial Conference on Foreign Policy (CIPE) where the Belgian governments (both federal and substate) meet and negotiate on an equal footing, under the coordination of the federal minister of foreign affairs. Its decisions are adopted by consensus; that is, each constituent unit has a veto right: the mechanism of the CIPE thus prevents any primacy of the federal entity (Bursens and Massart-Piérard 2009).

When the federal government wants to conclude a mixed treaty or it receives a request from a substate government, it has to hold the conference and to inform the members that it wishes to open bilateral or multilateral negotiations for this purpose. The CIPE decides whether it will enter into international negotiations and it can decide to do so even if one of the substate governments does not plan to take part. On this basis, the composition of the Belgian delegation is decided: it comprises representatives of both federal and substate governments. The federal foreign minister or the relevant ambassador exerts a "coordinating leadership", but all parties are on an equal footing (Lejeune 2003). If an agreement is reached, the minister of foreign affairs signs the treaty and each concerned substate parliament has to vote for the act of assent. The final step of ratifying the treaty is ultimately reserved for the King, that is, the federal government. If the CIPE cannot reach a consensus, a Consultation Committee, whose composition respects linguistic parity and equality between the federal and the subnational governments is called on in order to solve the problem by consensus. The procedure introduced by the cooperation agreement of 8 March 1994 prevents the federal government from impinging on the exclusive jurisdiction of the substates through the conclusion of international agreements. The use of the CIPE is therefore a pragmatic solution to ensure the consistency of the Belgian foreign policy as well as the distribution of competences between the federal and the substate governments (Bursens and Massart-Piérard 2009).

In this interconnected multilevel operating system, the federal government holds a gatekeeper position in the articulation between domestic and international law. This gatekeeper position gives the federal government three means of action: the right to be informed and to suspend the concluding procedure of a treaty dealing exclusively with subnational competences; the possibility to denounce treaties concluded before 1993, with the agreement of all concerned governments (article 167§5 of the Belgian Constitution); and a substitution right in the event of non-respect of supranational or international obligations by a substate government and of its condemnation by an international or supranational jurisdiction (article 169 of the Belgian Constitution). This latter mechanism, as well as the first one, has never been used. Bursens and Massart-Piréard (2009) argue that it is even less likely to be used in time of incongruent coalitions: being overruled by a federal government (partly) composed of different political parties would be politically inacceptable for a regional government.

Compared with other federal countries, Belgian federalism has gone one step further in terms of treaty making. Constituent units enjoy fully legitimate and direct legal access to the international stage within the limit of their competences, but with a series of mechanisms designed to ensure the coherence of Belgium's overall foreign policy. At the end of the year 2012, WBI managed no fewer than 145 bilateral agreements (respectively 71 for the French-speaking Community, 58 for the Walloon Region and 16 for the French-speaking Community Commission) and these were part of over 400 mixed treaties. While treaty-making powers are significant, the international relations of Wallonia go much further, as much has to do with political and economic representation.

4.2 *Ius legationis*

The institutional division of powers within Belgium is a purely domestic concern; nevertheless the implementation of the *in foro interno in foro externo* principle has to comply with international law. Even though the principle of the unity of the state does not prevent the development of external relations specific to the substates, it does require a federation to fulfil all its international obligations and to ensure the coherence of its foreign policy (Lejeune 2003; Massart-Piérard 2005). Belgium must therefore always have a single international position, even if substates have the right to decide on this position. The Belgian federation met these requirements through the conclusion of some cooperation agreements with its constituent units.

One of the first of these cooperation agreements was signed on 8 March 1994 on the important question of Belgium's representation within the Council of the European Union, which is the institution representing the member states' governments. The EU requires its member states to act as unitary international actors, but article 16.2 of the Treaty on the European Union allows a substate minister to represent his/her state within the EU council if this minister is empowered to bind his/her whole state. Introduced in 1992, on the demand of Belgium and Germany, this legal provision has enabled Belgium to transpose its internal institutional system to the European level (Lejeune 2003), but it has also forced the Belgian federal government to set coordination mechanisms in order to decide on a single national position to be defended in the EU council.

The cooperation agreement of 8 March 1994 organised the representation within the EU council around three principles: prior internal coordination with a veto right for each government; categories of EU council's configurations determine who holds the seat – whether it is a federal minister or a substate minister; and a rota system between the substate governments on a six-monthly basis when substate ministers have to represent Belgium (Elola Calderon and Van den Abeele 2010). When no agreement can be achieved on the position to be defended in the EU council, Belgium must abstain. However, most of the time, internal – which is also largely informal – coordination works well and consensus is reached.

The procedure and principles set in the cooperation agreement offer the communities and the regions a strong influence on Belgian European policy (Massart-Piérard 2006): the Belgian substate governments are the only ones being completely integrated into the elaboration of the common position of a member state of the EU council (Elola Calderon and Van den Abeele 2010). They make the most of this situation and they also take the lead in promoting a Europe of regions by being very active in formal and informal networks: they take part in interregional, transnational and cross-border cooperation as well as in European bodies representing regional interests such the Committee of the Regions (Bursens and Massart-Piérard 2009).

While European affairs constitute a large part of the substate governments' international activity (Borghetto and Franchino 2010), it is not limited to them. Within international organisations that conduct activities within their fields of competence, the regions and communities do have some rights to represent their interests in such organisations (Massart-Piérard 1999) and they do so by acting within the Belgian representation. In order to ensure the single international position of Belgium, a cooperation agreement concluded on 30 June 1994 has set a permanent structure of dialogue between the Belgian governments. In short, before any ministerial meeting of an international organisation, the Minister of Foreign Affairs has to systematically organise a general information and consultation between the Belgian governments in order to determine Belgium's position. In other words, the federal and the substate governments have to reach by consensus a position that will then be defended as Belgium's position by the Belgian delegation. If no consensus is reached, the same rule applies, as for the EU council, the Belgian representative has to abstain.

What is more, when the issue falls mostly within the substates' competences, Belgium is represented by a minister from a substate government. Substates are thus involved both in the preliminary policy making and in representing Belgium within international conferences and organisations whose activities concern areas that partly fall under their jurisdiction such as UNESCO, the OECD, FAO and WTO (Lejeune 2003). It can even go further for some specific international organisations. For instance, the representation to *La Franco-phonie* is a particular case where WBI is fully engaged: it has its own seat and so does the Belgian federation. The two delegations operate jointly on the basis of a distribution of tasks: the federal delegation works on global political issues while WBI deals with international cooperation issues (Massart-Piérard 2009).

Following this, the cooperation agreement of 18 May 1995 between all the Belgian governments organised the possibility for regions and communities to appoint representatives (*délégués* or *attachés*) in diplomatic or consular posts to foreign states and to international organisations. Integral to the Belgian post, these representatives are subject to the same rights and duties as their federal colleagues and exert their activities under the diplomatic authority of the head of post, but they receive their directions from their own authorities, even if they have to inform the head of post of their activities (Lejeune 2003). Instead of depriving the national state of its means of actions, this system has the benefit of stimulating contacts and mutual knowledge between the Belgian constituent units.

More specifically for commercial and economic matters, a cooperation agreement was concluded on 17 June 1994 between the federal and substate governments. It rules the establishment of regional economic and commercial bureaus within the Belgian consular of diplomatic posts, and sometimes in cities where there is no embassy or consulate. The regions can appoint economic and commercial *attachés* and entrust them with specific tasks and missions. In Wallonia, the regional agency AWEX has been in charge of external trade and foreign investment since 2004. In their contacts with economic partners, its regional *attachés* are completely autonomous. However, they have to work under the "diplomatic" authority of the head of post (a federal representative) in all their contacts with the officials of the hosting state. This emphasises a balance between respecting the exclusive jurisdiction of the Belgian regions and the search for a coherent foreign policy for federal Belgium.

Before the conclusion of this cooperation agreement, there were already similar practices following the signature in 1986 of some protocols between the minister of foreign relations and the constituent units, granting them the right to appoint *attachés*, who were integrated into the Belgian representation, to represent them abroad and in international organisations. However, the Walloon Region could not make use of this right because all the conditions were not met (Massart-Piérard 2005). Therefore, the French-speaking Community and the Walloon Region decided to work in tandem. The French-speaking Community appointed, on the one hand, *attachés* in charge of its representation and, on the other hand, *attachés* in charge of the Walloon Region's representation. It was also agreed that the *attachés* who had to represent the French-speaking Community could also perform activities on behalf of the Walloon Region (Massart-Piérard 2005; Criekemans and Lanneau 2011).

This cooperative practice between the French-speaking subnational entities has become increasingly present, and politically the designation of one single minister in charge of the foreign relations for both the region and the community states this close relationship. Together they act through a network of 17 external delegations, that is, embassies, with diplomatic status and 107 delegates worldwide of whom 73 are in charge of economic representation (Wallonie-Bruxelles international 2012). Together, the Walloon Region and the French-speaking Community are thus among the substate entities with the highest number of trade offices per capita around the world (Paquin 2013).

5 Politics of international relations

Making the most of both their sovereignty-bound and sovereignty-free status, Quebec and the French-speaking constituent units of Belgium have gradually increased their presence on the international level as well as their influence on the conduct of national foreign policy. But the roads they have used are different. While the former actively designed an identity paradiplomacy in order to make its voice heard, the latter enjoys an institutional setting exceptionally prone to foster substates' international relations. In our comparative endeavour we now need, after having discussed the formal rules and constitutional assignments, to discuss the political dynamics that both shape and are shaped by these institutional settings.

To be sure, the institutional setting of Canada was and is much less open to Quebec's international activities than the Belgian system. The nation-building process of Quebec's minority nation and its opposition to the federal level fostered the establishment of such international activities that were justified on the grounds of the principle of the Gérin-Lajoie doctrine and the provinces' right to implement or not treaties concluded by Canada (Michaud and Ramet 2004). Seeking for support and resources lacking at the domestic level, Quebec made use of identity paradiplomacy to affirm its identity on the international scene and, at the same time, strengthen its internal position. These efforts and claims to the rights stated by Gérin-Lajoie in 1965 were at the beginning contested by the Canadian government, and the period that followed matched the development of international relations rather than the formulation of a real foreign policy. The identity and cultural variables were prominent, and the immediate needs took precedence over a view of an overall consistency (Michaud and Ramet 2004).

From the mid-1980s, integrated political guidelines were phased in: Quebec's external actions became increasingly strategy driven and its paradiplomacy more bureaucratised in the planning, optimisation and allocation of resources. As argued above, the internationalisation factor also played a major role in the growing international existence of Quebec: as a small, non-sovereign actor, Quebec benefits from the permeation of the domestic and international fields and its effects on the nation-state system. However, internationalisation also redefined its goals and priorities: the necessity to grasp and control its environment broadened the scope of external actions from cultural interests to economic competitiveness, foreign investment, energy and labour-force mobility, to name but a few fields of action (Michaud 2006). While some particular foreign-policy fields remain exclusively under the jurisdiction of the federal government, Quebec has gone beyond simple international exchanges and managed to affirm itself on the international scene as a well-established actor with its own foreign policy. In the case of Quebec, identity paradiplomacy has been the way to go.

Belgian substate governments are more sovereignty-bound than sovereignty-free actors. This very specific status can be explained by the evolution of Belgium itself, which transformed from a unitary state to a federal, and even confederal, state in less than 40 years. This radical shift is the result of internal pressures for more autonomy. While the initial demands for devolution came from both sides of the linguistic border (Reuchamps 2013), the more recent state reforms were especially pushed by the Flemish political actors in the wake of an internal and external identity paradiplomacy. In this centrifugal federalism, substate actors demanded the international extension of their internal powers as a consequence of their increasing jurisdiction. This makes Belgium more confederal than federal (Philippart 1997) as substates have the right to conclude international treaties, to defend and represent their interests within international organisations and within Belgian diplomatic representations, and to set up their own international networks. In the case of Belgium, even the concept of paradiplomacy seems odd (Massart-Piérard 2009), as it is, in fact, to a large extent real diplomacy.

However, in order to guarantee cohesion, an inter-ministerial conference on foreign affairs and a consultation committee intended to prevent problems that could arise between the federal and substate governments was set up. While the *in foro interno, in foro externo* principle is basically the pure application of dual federalism on foreign relations, some cooperative features were introduced in order to meet the requirement of the international system. This highlights the defining characteristics of the Belgian federal order: autonomous entities, cooperative practices and institutionalised cooperation mechanisms (Beyers and Bursens 2013). The low rate of conflicts can also be explained by the fact that the substate governments are involved in both the negotiations and the implementation of Belgian foreign policy and by the threat of abstention if no consensus is reached. However, the assessment of this system is not entirely positive. It is indeed quite weighty; it requires the involvement of many actors in a back-and-forth process that unavoidably multiplies the number of challenging preferences that have to be aggregated (Borghetto and Franchino 2010), and it suffers from a lack of leadership. When a compromise is reached, it may often affect legal clarity.

Political dynamics not only shape federal–substate relations, but also intra-substate relations. While there are many demonstrations of cooperative and reciprocal practices between the French-speaking Community and the Walloon Region, their degree of closeness has varied over time and in the functions of the political actors. A significant indicator for this is the appointment, or not, of the same minister for international relations in the two governments (Criekemans and Lanneau 2011), which is now the case since 2004 and reflects a joint will to increase international visibility and attractiveness that has also led to the creation of one single structure, WBI. Nonetheless, their interests and visions are neither necessarily the same nor systematically congruent. In the second half of the 1990s, that is, in the beginning of their joint activities, the emphasis was on French-speaking areas and it was clear that the French-speaking Community prevailed (Criekemans and Lanneau 2011). However, the Walloon Region has gradually asserted its concerns for economic and commercial matters and also for international research. Seeking to promote its trade and foreign investments, it has established external relations with close countries and has taken part in interregional, transnational and cross-border cooperation. The region also has given priority to the European process. If the economic reasons are obvious, this engagement with Europe is also based on political grounds: the will to foster the recognition of the regional factor both in Europe and within Belgium. The situation of 1995 is now partly inverted: even if the protection of the French language does remain an important dimension (mainly for internal political reasons), regional priorities have largely come to the forefront.

6 Conclusion

Substate governments, despite their sovereignty-free status – at least theoretically – are now active international players. Their international activities have clearly challenged the federal governments' so-called "monopoly" over foreign policy. But this is not limited to federal states. Any state today faces the opening of international relations to several new sovereignty-free actors: from single individuals to large multinational companies. What is peculiar to substate governments is their mixed sovereignty-bound and sovereignty-free nature. This is especially the case for minority nations which may be willing to use international relations to foster their position both internally and externally.

The comparison of Quebec and Wallonia, and, in this case, the Walloon Region and the French-speaking Community, highlights several common features but also the different roads to achieve an international existence, which are largely shaped by the domestic and supra-regional contexts in which they are acting. On the one hand, in the context of a growing globalisation and of an "antagonistic" national state, the minority nation of Quebec developed an identity paradiplomacy that has gradually evolved into a real foreign policy. On the other hand, in Belgium, a state facing a centrifugal federalism where the equipollency of the norms combined with a shared treaty-making power rather refers to confederalism and acting within the European context, the regions and communities actually support the cooperative dynamic and make major use of internal coordination mechanisms.

This account raises several questions. The current negotiations around the Comprehensive Economic and Trade Agreement (CETA) shed light on questions regarding the involvement of the Canadian provinces and territories in the ratification of any final agreement. For instance, do all the provinces and territories need to agree before there is a deal? Does Alberta have a veto? Or Quebec? And what about the territories? There are precedents with human-rights treaties where a treaty was signed and ratified by the federal government even if only a small number of provinces agreed to comply with the treaty. Can it be the same for an important trade treaty and, above all, for treaties in more conflict-ridden issues such as climate change?

In Belgium, the questions that remain are not so much on legal grounds but rather on practical and political grounds. The implementation of the *in foro interno, in foro externo* principle has led to an interdependency system, based on cooperative features such as permanent consultation and coordination, which works well in practice, partly thanks to the many informal contacts and coordination meetings in addition to those required by the law, and in which the federal government holds a gatekeeping and coordinating position. But is this viable on the longer run, especially now that the regions and communities have received even more autonomy? We have in this chapter focused mainly on the two main groups – Dutch speakers and French speakers – but the smaller partners of the Belgian federation also want to exist internationally and, perhaps as a consequence, foster their internal position. The question of (para)diplomacy of substate governments has therefore not been fully answered yet, quite the contrary indeed.

References

Arbour, Jean-Maurice (1997). *Droit international public*, Cowansville: Éditions Yvon Blais.

Beyers, Jan and Peter Bursens (2006). "The European rescue of the federal state: how Europeanization shapes the Belgian state", *West European Politics*, 29(5): 1057–78.

Beyers, Jan and Peter Bursens (2013). "How Europe shapes the nature of the Belgian Federation: differentiated EU impact triggers both co-operation and decentralization", *Regional and Federal Studies*, 23(3): 271–91.

Blatter, Joachim, Matthias Kreutzer, Michaela Rentl and Jan Thiele (2008). "The foreign relations of European regions: competences and strategies", *West European Politics*, 31(3): 464–90.

Borghetto, Enrico and Fabio Franchino (2010). "The role of subnational authorities in the implementation of EU directives", *Journal of European Public Policy*, 17(6): 759–80.

Bursens, Peter and Françoise Massart-Piérard (2009). "Kingdom of Belgium". In *Foreign Relations in Federal Countries*, ed. Hans Michelmann, 91–113. Montreal and Ithaca, NY: McGill-Queen's University Press.

Criekemans, David (2010). "Regional sub-state diplomacy from a comparative perspective: Quebec, Scotland, Bavaria, Catalonia, Wallonia and Flanders". In

Regional Sub-State Diplomacy Today, ed. David Criekemans, 37–64. Leiden: Martinus Nijhoff Publishers.

Criekemans, David and Catherine Lanneau (2011). "Les relations extérieures de la Flandre, de la Communauté française, de la Région wallonne et de la Région de Bruxelles-Capitale". In *D'une Belgique unitaire à une Belgique fédérale. 40 ans d'évolution politique des communautés et des régions (1971–2011)*, ed. Mark Van den Wijngaert, 201–20. Bruxelles: ASP.

de Mestral, Armand (2005). "The provinces and international relations in Canada". In *Le fédéralisme dans tous ses états : gouvernance, identité et méthodologie/The States and Moods of Federalism: Governance, Identity and Methodology*, ed. Jean-François Gaudreault-DesBiens and Fabien Gélinas, 309–325. Cowansville and Brussels: Éditions Yvon Blais and Bruylant.

Duchacek, Ivo D. (1984). "The International Dimension of Subnational Self-Government", *Publius: the Journal of Federalism*, 14(4): 5–31.

Duchacek, Ivo D. (1986). *The Territorial Dimensions of Politics: Within, Among, and Across Nations*, Boulder, CO and London: Westview Press.

Dyment, David M. (2001). "The Ontario government as an international actor", *Regional and Federal Studies*, 11(1): 55–79.

Elola Calderon, Teresa and Eric Van den Abeele (2010). "La présidence belge de l'Union européenne: organisation et priorités", *Courrier hebdomadaire du CRISP*, (2072): 5–42.

Jans, Maarten Theo and Patrick Stouthuysen (2007). "Federal regions and external relations: the Belgian case", *International Spectator*, 42(2): 209–20.

Lejeune, Yves (1981). "Les Communautés et Régions belges dans les relations internationales", *Revue belge de droit international*, 1(14): 53–80.

Lejeune, Yves (2003). "Participation of sub-national units in the foreign policy of the federation". In *Federalism in a Changing World. Learning from Each Other, Scientific Background, Proceedings and Plenary Speeches of the International Conference on Federalism*, ed. Raoul Blindenbacher and Arnold Koller, 97–114. Montreal and Kingston: McGill-Queen's University Press.

Massart-Piérard, Françoise (1999). "Les entités fédérées de Belgique, acteurs décisionnels au sein de l'Union européenne", *Politique et Sociétés*, 18(1): 3–40.

Massart-Piérard, Françoise (2005). "Une étude comparée des relations entre entités fédérées au sein du système de politique extérieure en Belgique francophone", *Revue internationale de politique comparée*, 12(2): 191–205.

Massart-Piérard, Françoise (2006). "La Belgique, un modèle évolutif et inédit de gestion des relations internationales". In *Les relations internationales du Québec depuis la Doctrine Gérin-Lajoie (1965–2005)*, ed. Stéphane Paquin, 232–50. Québec: Les Presses de l'Université Laval.

Massart-Piérard, Françoise (2009). "Les entités fédérées belges: des relations internationales peu <<paradiplomatiques>>". In *Le fédéralisme en Belgique et au Canada. Comparaison sociopolitique*, ed. Bernard Fournier and Min Reuchamps, 173–83. Bruxelles: De Boeck Université.

Michaud, Nelson (2006). "Canada and Quebec on the world stage: defining new rules?" In *Canada Among Nations*, ed. Andrew F. Cooper and Dane Rowlands, 232–50. Montreal: McGill-Queen's University Press.

Michaud, Nelson and Isabelle Ramet (2004). "Quebéc et politique étrangère: contradiction ou réalité?", *International Journal*, 59(2): 303–24.

Michelmann, Hans (2009). *Foreign Relations in Federal Countries, a Global Dialogue on Federalism*, Montréal and Ithaca, NY: McGill-Queen's University Press.

Michelmann, Hans and Panayotis Soldatos (1990). *Federalism and International Relations: the Role of Subnational Units*, Oxford: Clarendon Press.

Paquin, Stéphane (2003). "Paradiplomatie identitaire et diplomatie en Belgique fédérale: le cas de la Flandre", *Canadian Journal of Political Science/Revue canadienne de science politique*, 36(3): 621–42.

Paquin, Stéphane (2004). "La paradiplomatie identitaire: Le Québec, la Catalogne et la Flandre en relations internationales", *Politique et Sociétés*, 23(2–3): 203–37.

Paquin, Stéphane (2005). "Les actions extérieures des entités subétatiques: quelle signification pour la politique comparée et la théorie des relations internationales?", *Revue internationale de politique comparée*, 12(2): 129–42.

Paquin, Stéphane (2006). *Les relations internationales du Québec depuis la Doctrine Gérin-Lajoie (1965–2005)*, Prisme, Québec: Les Presses de l'Université Laval.

Paquin, Stéphane (2010). "Federalism and compliance with international agreements: Belgium and Canada compared", *The Hague Journal of Diplomacy*, 5(1–2): 173–97.

Paquin, Stéphane (2013). "La politique internationale du Québec". In *Les défis Québécois: conjonctures et transitions*, ed. Robert Bernier, 439–58. Québec: Presses de l'Université du Québec.

Patry, André (1980). *Le Québec dans le monde*, Montréal: Leméac.

Philippart, Eric (1997). "Le Comité des Régions confronté à la 'paradiplomatie' des régions de l'Union européenne". In *Le Comité des Régions de l'Union européenne*, ed. Jacques Bourrinet, 6–13. Paris: Editions économica.

Reuchamps, Min (2013). "The current challenges on the Belgian federalism and the Sixth Reform of the State". In *The Ways of Federalism in Western Countries and the Horizons of Territorial Autonomy in Spain*, ed. Alberto Lopez Basaguren and Leire Escajedo San-Epifanio, 375–92. Berlin: Springer-Verlag.

Reuchamps, Min and François Onclin (2009). "La fédération belge". In *Le fédéralisme en Belgique et au Canada. Comparaison sociopolitique*, ed. Bernard Fournier and Min Reuchamps, 21–40. Bruxelles: De Boeck Université.

Rosenau, James N. (1990). *Turbulence in World Politics: a Theory of Change and Continuity*, Princeton, NJ: Princeton University Press.

Turp, Daniel (2002). *Pour une intensification des relations du Québec avec les institutions internationales*, Quebec: Ministères des relations internationales.

Zeigel, Jacob (1988). "Treaty-making and implementation powers in canada: the continuing dilemma". In *Contemporary Problems of International Law: Essays in Honour of Georg Schwarzenberger on his Eightieth Birthday*, ed. Bin Cheng and E.D. Brown, 319–29. London: Stevens & Sons.

Official documents

BNA Act (Constitution Act, 1867) (2014). *Constitution Acts, 1867 to 1982*. Available from: http://laws-lois.justice.gc.ca/eng/Const/page-1.html (accessed 11 September 2014).

Gérin-Lajoie, Paul (1965). *Texte de l'allocution prononcée par Monsieur Paul Gérin-Lajoie, vice-président du Conseil et ministre de l'Éducation, devant les membres du corps consulaire de Montréal*, Québec: Ministère de l'Éducation du Québec, Service d'information. Available from: www.saic.gouv.qc.ca/publications/Positions/Partie2/PaulGer inLajoie1965.pdf (accessed 4 September 2014).

Ministère des Relations internationales et de la Francophonie (2013a). *Rapport annuel de gestion 2012–2013: Une expertise, un réseau pour le développement du Québec.*

Available   from: www.mrifce.gouv.qc.ca/content/documents/fr/rapportannuel.pdf (accessed 1 March 2014).

Ministère des Relations internationales et de la Francophonie (2013b). *Organisation internationale de la francophonie*. Available from: www.mrifce.gouv.qc.ca/fr/franco phonie (accessed 1 March 2014).

Wallonie-Bruxelles international (WBI) (2012). *Rapport d'activités 2012*. Available from: www.wbi.be/sites/default/files/attachments/publication/rapport_activite_wbi_ 2012.pdf (accessed 1 March 2014).

Conclusion

Minority nations in multinational federations

Michael Burgess

In the early twenty-first century, the comparative study of minority nations in multinational federations has attracted increasing attention from scholars of comparative federalism. In many respects this scholarly interest is a reaction to what Charles Taylor, one of Canada's leading lights in the field of political theory and philosophy, called "an age of identity awakening" of national identities in the new millennium (2001: xiv). And while the specific causes of this new awakening vary widely across the world it clearly has its roots in the post-Cold War years, the collapse of the Soviet Union, the intensification of European integration, enhanced regional international cooperation, and globalisation in telecommunications, information and financial-capital markets. Different combinations of these global factors have merged with historical specificities to trigger a novel revival of old identities and the assertion of new ones. Consequently, it is in this context of complexity that we must situate the comparison in this book between Quebec and Wallonia which share both significant similarities as well as notable differences.

This comparative study is an intriguing and unusual project not simply because it is a relatively neglected one in the mainstream literature (in English), but also because in providing fresh insights into what Min Reuchamps has called the specific "dynamics of minority nations in multinational federations" (see the Introduction) it adds to our understanding of both how and why such minority nations constantly pursue internal self-determination. In a sense, every self-conscious minority nation seeks to achieve what political scientists often call enhanced *autonomy* in a single state. Because by definition the minority identity is not merely a subnational identity that is coterminous with the state, it has to develop strategies to assert its sense of itself in order not simply to survive but also to protect, preserve and promote its own interests. Indeed, it must seek to expand what we might call its cultural–ideological self *within* the larger political nationality, that is, the multinational state. This is precisely what Quebec and Wallonia have achieved so far and it is a never-ending story, with the fate of minority nations always brought into question by their predicament, namely, how to coexist with other minority nations and/or how to co-exist with the majority nation in one state.

This being so, there will always be corrosive tensions, stresses and strains immanent in the body politic. While multinational federations exist today principally to accommodate minority nations, linguistic communities and religious identities which are usually but not always territorially concentrated, they nevertheless confront the sort of challenges that are extremely difficult for political systems to process peacefully. This is because cultural–ideological disputes and controversies are inherently much more intractable and less bargainable than socioeconomic cleavages. In the contemporary parlance of political science they are much "thicker" (or "sticky") conflicts than the relatively "thin" character of socioeconomic conflicts. Clearly it is virtually impossible to entertain trade-offs about identity politics that are deemed existential compared to the compromises that are often reached over socioeconomic public goods.

Given these wide-ranging thoughts and observations about minority nations in single states, it should come as little surprise to learn that this complex relationship between cultural–ideological cleavages, which often spawn zero-sum conflicts and socioeconomic differences and contrasts, and sometimes polarise and sometimes dampen down conflict in equal measure, is a conspicuous thread that runs through many of the chapters in this book. So what do the essays in this book tell us about minority nations in multinational federations? What fresh insights does it provide and what new understandings does it suggest about the relationships between minority and majority national perspectives in a single state? The work is carefully structured in three distinct parts that focus consecutively on polities, politics and policies in two distinct francophone political communities that seek respectively to determine themselves within two quite different federal models.

If we distil the observations and reflections that Reuchamps has sketched in the Introduction, we can see that these broad structural bases of comparison between Quebec-in-Canada and Wallonia-in-Belgium furnish the book with a unifying framework that has enabled us, inter alia, to explore the following analytical dimensions: the major historical and constitutional legacies that reveal both founding and formative moments in their federal evolution; the daunting and enduring issue of identity politics; the federal and subnational arenas of political representation, participation and electoral politics; the role of local bureaucratic politics and the challenges of new public management in the market model of federalism; the lightning rod of language politics and policy; and the increasing para-diplomacy of constituent units of federations in the world of international relations. This chapter will therefore conclude the book by seeking to answer the two questions raised above.

In order to do this I have identified the following broad areas of interest or general themes that have emerged from the contributions made in the book: the nature and evolution of constitutional development in the federal polity; the significance of identity politics related to minority nations in multinational federations; centrifugal and centripetal pressures that determine the character and structure of federations; the role and significance of political parties and party systems in federal states; administrative reform and autonomy; and the increasing prominence of subnational authority in external relations. Together these areas impinge both directly and indirectly on the central focus of the book, namely, minority nations in multinational federations.

It is important, then, to survey these separate but linked areas of interest by keeping in mind their contemporary relevance from the particular standpoint of the minority nation coexisting with other such nations and/or the larger majority nation in the multinational federation. But it is also important to note that the comparative study of Quebec and Wallonia as minority nations in multinational federations is a study that will add yet another layer of complexity to a subject that is already riddled with serious conceptual and theoretical pitfalls and problems that remain highly contested. Consequently, while the recent scholarly interest in multinational states and societies and multinational democracies is undoubtedly a noteworthy development in political science, it remains nonetheless quite striking how few genuine cases exist today in practice. This is because there are multinational states that are not necessarily "democratic" (understood as forms of liberal democracy) and there are multinational democracies that are not formally "federal", at least in constitutional theory, although they may be so in terms of constitutional practice (Burgess and Gagnon 2010). Indeed, if we place empirical reality under the microscope, so to speak, it reveals just how few of the cases popularly referred to in the mainstream literature are actually multinational federations. Spain, for example, is a popular choice to include in this classification, but, while it is clearly multinational (or increasingly *plurinational* in recent scholarly parlance) – including the so-called "historic nationalities" of Catalonia, the Basque Country, Galicia and, more recently, Andalusia – it is not (yet) and may never become one as such, although it may increasingly become a federal political system in practice. In contrast, the Russian Federation is formally a federal state and is also self-evidently multinational, but most informed observers today would be hard-pressed to call it a liberal democracy in the same way that we might describe Belgium and Canada. The same criticism can be levelled at the federal cases of multinational Nigeria and Malaysia where different combinations of deep-rooted corruption, the intrusion of the military in civil society, the fragile basis of citizens' rights, the questionable reality of judicial independence, the level(s) of electoral fraud and intimidation, and the refusal or inability of the state to deliver welfare and/or public goods in general lead us to a verdict that casts serious doubt on the validity of their descriptive credentials.

Clearly we must not take what is often just a descriptive label at face value. But another conceptual problem arises when we refer to multinational federations in form and practice. In a well-known, thought-provoking article titled "Canada and the multinational state", Kenneth McRoberts questioned the word "multinational", which he claimed was "not the most fortuitous of terms" because it had "far too many other meanings" (2001: 683). However, the most relevant point he made for our purposes here is worth more than just a moment's reflection: "while many states are multinational in their composition very few of them actually function as multinational states" (2001: 711). Furthermore, he claimed that to refer to a multinational *state* "in its underlying composition" was actually to infer the sociological reality of a multinational *society* (2001: 712). This clearly suggests that it is one thing to speak about a multinational society, but it is quite another to base "the multinational state itself wholly or in part on the multiple nations it contains" (2001: 686). The conceptual distinction is of course an important one. If there are "sociological nations" (Burgess 2012a), that is, a multinational society within the state, should the state itself be correspondingly multinational? Should the political institutions of the federal state be organised to incorporate the principle of multinationality? If so, minority nations should be represented in different ways both constitutionally, politically and legally, in their collective capacity *as distinct nations* in the larger "political nationality" that is the state.

One question that emerges from these concluding remarks and reflections so far can be posed in the following way: does it matter if the term "multinational" has many meanings? After all, some scholars choose to use it according to so many different nuances and interpretations that it lacks a consistency of meaning and purpose. In the effort to escape from this conundrum, they choose instead to search for conceptual equivalence so that, for example, aboriginal nations (the First Nation(s) or indigenous peoples) in Canada are construed in the same way or in a similar way to Quebec as a nation. This enables them to describe Canada as a multinational rather than a bi-national federation, but it also creates problems for the English-speaking Canadians, widely referred to as the "Rest of Canada" (abbreviated to ROC) and sometimes alluded to as "Canada outside Quebec" (COQ). And these verbal somersaults say nothing at all about Canada itself as a "political nation" and Canadian, including Québécois and aboriginal nations, as a "political nationality". Similarly in Nigeria the ethnic recognition of Hausa-Fulani, Igbo and Yoruba tribal identities as the leading (and largely territorially concentrated) political communities is deemed equivalent to three distinct nations in a multinational federation. Indeed, the tendency to include Switzerland as a multinational federation (which it is not) or at least, in Will Kymlicka's terms, an "historic multination" remains a temptation in the mainstream literature (2001: 92). These examples confirm the conceptual ambiguities that continue to surround and bedevil our general understanding of what it means to be multinational. As we shall see shortly, there is still a certain conceptual fluidity in the comparative study that allows for a language community to be perceived as synonymous with a nation. The main point being made here, then, is that the comparative scope of *all* analytical surveys of multinationalism in formally federal and formally non-federal states is determined by how rigid or flexible the conceptual framework needs to be.

Turning to the first of our general themes, namely, the nature and evolution of constitutional development in Belgium and Canada in so far as it affects the status of Wallonia and Quebec as minority nations, two fresh insights can be identified. These can be encapsulated in the term "process", which refers to the gradual federalisation of Belgium and the growing autonomy of Wallonia and Flanders, and also in the word "visions", which allows us to think about constitutional reform and change from the perspective(s) of Carl Friedrich, who first construed federalism not as a finite end to be attained such as a federal state, but quintessentially as a *process* on a continuum that stretched from loose forms of union to what he called "international federalism" that transcended the state (Burgess 2012b). In this light, the nature of Belgian constitutional reform, as outlined by Turgeon in Chapter 1, can be accurately described as one of federalisation as a process of long-term gradual change, rather than as the result of a carefully negotiated constitutional bargain or founding moment. In contrast, it was actually the by-product of an institutional logic that dates back at least to 1970. The latter word "visions" therefore reinforces this understanding of institutional logic by conveying the sense of enhanced autonomy for Wallonia and Flanders almost as an accident or the unintended long-term consequence of constitutional reform, one that was a response to a specific set of circumstances and lacked a long-term vision of what Belgium should be or become. Constitutional reform in Canada, however, was just the opposite: there were two main competing visions of the future. The first, and successful, vision was Pierre Trudeau's liberal conception of Canada as a multicultural, bilingual federation based on an individualist Canadian Charter of Rights and Freedoms (*la Charte canadienne des droits et libertés*), in contrast to that of Quebec whose principal goal was the constitutional recognition of the province as a nation or a "distinct society" that chimed with its rival vision of Quebec identity as a collective francophone political community. In short, comparing Wallonia and Quebec signify both the absence and the presence of constitutional visions of the federal state.

This broad area of interest brings us conveniently to our second general theme, namely, the question of identity politics. In the specific context of this book the notion of *identity* assumes a central position in the sense of self that determines "who" we are objectively and "who" we think we are subjectively. From the perspective of minority nations in multinational federations, it is self-evidently the case that these two senses of the self – as an individual citizen of the federal state and *simultaneously* as a member of a minority collective identity – interact in powerful ways to shape and determine identity. And it is a "political identity" with which we are concerned here, that is, the sense of "who" I am in the federal polity. This is because minority nations occupy a peculiar position in the larger federal state where they are compelled to determine themselves as a distinct political community that is usually founded on different combinations of cultural–ideological cleavages such as historical specificity, linguistic preferences and religious particularism that are territorially concentrated. Where these people are dispersed across the whole state, it is probably more accurate to label them as "national minorities" rather than minority nations, which today are known as "nested" identities (Miller 2001).

Caron's central theme in his comparative survey of Walloon and Québécois minority nations in this book underlines the pitfalls of identity essentialism that leads to political exclusivism. This dynamic boils down ultimately to one deceptively complex question: who is included and who is excluded from membership of the internal minority nation? Exclusivity based on narrow ethnic, racial or blood ties is relatively easy to determine, but what happens when the minority nation chooses to redefine itself by opening up its culture to a much more pluralistic, civic and territorially nested sense of itself? The twin journeys of Quebec and Wallonia in this respect provide a novel comparison that is both insightful and instructive to those who continue to search for a modus vivendi between majority and minority national communities who live together in a single state. Political constructs such as imagined communities require clear political strategies to achieve their goals. This is abundantly evident in the parallel pathways of the shift from old French-Canadian ethnic-religious nationalism to that of the recent civic pluralist nationalism of contemporary Quebec. It is also evident in the Walloon predicament of choosing between the political strategy of a large francophone community that embraces Wallonia, Brussels and those French-speaking minorities living just outside the perimeters of the capital, and in the idea of Wallonia as the territorial focus of a single emergent new francophone nation with its own distinctive socioeconomic value system, easily distinguishable from that of Flanders.

Clearly these are complex and complicated matters in both multinational states and multinational societies at large. They involve many orders of scale and magnitude that form the basis of local communities via regional, subnational levels of authority, rising up to the multinational arena where, as mentioned above, we enter the world of "political nationality" in the "state-nation". Huge questions of a deeply contested theoretical, philosophical and empirical nature abound here and Alain Gagnon has ably summarised them in his recent thought-provoking and insightful book titled *The Case for Multinational Federalism*, which, while concentrating principally on Quebec and Catalonia, adopts a much wider comparative focus (Gagnon 2010). Finding his way around the essentialism of minority national identity and into the competitive and highly charged arena of political choice, strategy and their consequences has enabled him to construct a powerful normative argument that accurately portrays the world as it is and as he thinks it could and should be. Not surprisingly, the central thrust of his case resides in precisely how to empower minority nations in majority–minority relations within the federation by utilising asymmetrical federalism and creating, protecting and preserving constitutional, legal and political spaces for them to determine themselves within the framework of a single state. The normative "turn" in such intrastate relations appears now to be reaching a measured maturity in intellectual discourse.

Following the two previous themes, it is not difficult to understand why and how the operation of centrifugal and centripetal pressures in federations significantly affects – and is affected by – the character and structure of multi-national federations. Gagnon's recent research has singled out the importance of living historical legacies fossilised in memory and national reconstruction, and it should come as little surprise to learn that there are strong forces inherent in the body politic of the multinational federation that are highly sensitive to the centripetal pressures operating in the direction of centralisation, that is, of the growing power and authority of the federal (central) government, sometimes referred to misleadingly as the "federal centre" (Burgess and Lepine 2012). In these circumstances we may acknowledge that while centralisation might have a positive and/or negative impact on the lives of every citizen in the federation, including all national minorities, its effect on minority nations in terms of their existing and future cultural survival is especially vulnerable to erosion.

This is precisely why it is imperative for minority nations to control the levers of public policy that directly impinge on their identity: education, language, immigration, social-policy projects and fiscal federalism. Here self-rule is pitted against shared rule. Today centripetal pressures that combine to produce centralisation in federations remind us that federal states are not immune to such trends, which can strike at the heart of the constitutional distribution of powers and competences. The general expansion of the federal government due historically to the combined imperatives of welfare and the national economy has in the case of Quebec-in-Canada meant its encroachment into areas of exclusive provincial jurisdiction. By itself, the overall impact might be widely construed as enfeebling constituent units in general, but when minority nationalism and territoriality are coterminous in the federation, its effect is correspondingly magnified. Consequently, the expansion of federal government is regarded not only as inimical to federalism because it undermines local autonomy, but it is also perceived by some minority nations as a direct threat to their capacity to determine themselves and therefore to their cultural survival within the federation.

In Quebec this threat takes the form of an imposition of anglophone public-policy preferences over and above francophone interests. And it is precisely this threat that dogged Canada–Quebec relations in the late 1990s and early 2000s – so well illustrated by the failure of the Social Union Framework Agreement (SUFA) (*l'Entente-cadre sur l'union sociale* (ECUS)) – and still exists today in the background shadows of the recent socioeconomic shift in policy priorities in Quebec (Gagnon and Segal 2000). While identity politics has temporarily taken a step back in deference to Québécois electoral anxieties about general welfare, unemployment and social policy, the federal spending power remains, and still has the capacity to act as a cause for public concern. Small wonder, then, that many Québécois still see in centralisation the extension of anglophone majoritarian thinking and interests at the cost of francophone minoritarian priorities. Both the character and structure of multinational federations are therefore the source of resistance to centralising trends that might serve to undermine minority national identities. As Ronald Watts put it, the more heterogeneous the composition of society in a federal state, the more decentralised the federation tends to be (Watts 2008).

Historical legacies in Wallonia, on the other hand, have furnished a very different basis for reacting to centripetal and centrifugal pressures in Belgium. The case of Wallonia demonstrates, inter alia, that not all putative minority nations – or their cultural equivalent in this case – are destined to resist centralisation in their struggle for internal self-determination. The historical context in which Wallonia evolved as a distinct French-speaking society in the state- and (multi)nation-building processes in Belgium created a very different set of dynamics, as Hambye has noted in Chapter 7, from those peculiar to Quebec-in-Canada, one in which the language question never became a constitutional and political lightning rod of minority identity, for the simple reason that the French language was never seriously threatened, but on the contrary was identified throughout the nineteenth century and the early twentieth century with the powerful francophone economy in the south of the country. Unlike Quebec-in-Canada, the French language in Belgium was therefore strongly identified with economic strength and success.

Moreover, as Caron's chapter has confirmed, the sense of cultural-linguistic vulnerability that Quebec experienced was never replicated in Wallonia because the French language spoken in (bilingual) Brussels dominated the public and political discourse in practice. Wallonia-in-Europe was also surrounded by French-speaking peoples in France and Luxembourg, a francophone zone where the French language was dominant and was eventually elevated in status, first in the European Economic Community (EEC) during the four decades of the 1950s–80s, and then largely perpetuated in the European Union (EU) of the 1990s and 2000s. In short, Wallonia's *visage français* (French face) was firmly embedded in West European economic, political and cultural discourses, thus removing the basis on which it might have been deemed necessary to resist the centripetal forces – especially socioeconomic support from the federal government – that promoted centralist trends in Belgium. As part of the larger francophone community in Belgium (Wallonia and Brussels-Capital), Wallonia sustains its *linguistic* identity while simultaneously preserving its *territorial* identity in terms of its socioeconomic interests as a region in the federal state structure.

Turning to consider the role and significance of political parties and party systems in respect of minority nations in Belgium, we are confronted with a picture that is both fascinating and remarkable. In the mainstream literature on political parties and party systems in federal states, it is customary to refer to William Riker's general dictum about the key role that they play in maintaining or undermining unity and stability in federations (1964). Since then, so much has been written about this relationship that it would not be an exaggeration to regard it as a mini-boom industry in comparative federal studies. We shall not therefore venture very far in this familiar direction but shall instead concentrate on Wallonia and Quebec. Consequently, the three essays included in this section call attention to three particular perspectives that are highly unusual in a book on minority nations, namely, the political uses of metaphors in party manifestos (Mercenier, Perrez and Reuchamps, Chapter 3), the overlapping roles and recruitment of political representatives (Dodeigne, Chapter 4) and some unique comparative insights into the status and activities of local mayors (Breux and Jacquet, Chapter 5). These are analysed and discussed from the standpoint of what they add to our knowledge of Quebec and Walloon identities and how these two minority nations conduct their local affairs. Of special value are the fresh insights that they provide on novel visions, images and profiles of these nations projected through political representation: how they see themselves and how they want to be seen by others both within and without the federation.

What remains remarkable in Belgium has been the metamorphosis of the national party system into two completely separate regional linguistic systems that come together after general elections to form a singular coalition government – a sort of living together by living apart in a single state (Deschouwer 2012: 89–94). While such a development is not entirely unknown in federal states and systems – the Christian Social Union (CSU) in Bavaria and the *Parti Québécois* (PQ) in Quebec bear limited comparison – they have not encompassed the entire state as is the case in Belgium. There is, in other words, no "national" party system in Belgium, but two separate systems in Wallonia and Flanders that work together to hold the federation together. We may therefore regard this as an increasingly loose form of union that could conceivably be construed as a "confederation" within a formally federal state.

In addition to these portrayals, it is also interesting to note the connection made between administrative reform in these two nations in their role as constituent units of government and the aspiration of greater autonomy within each federation. Petit Jean's chapter emphasises the fact that autonomy, if it is to have any real practical implications, must have the "capacity" to use it. Modernisation of public administration and public management in the constituent state apparatus, therefore, is of fundamental importance for minority nations that are territorially concentrated and hence coterminous with such political/governmental authority. These reforms can become, in effect, a tool or instrument of the affirmation of their distinct identity. There is, in short, an extremely interesting insight into the influence and impact of different legal and administrative cultures (French and British in Quebec, and French and Flemish in Wallonia) in the evolution of these two public administrations.

The penultimate Chapter 8 written by Paquin, Kravagna and Reuchamps allows us to view our two minority nations from the standpoint of federated states with constituent governments that have embarked on a long journey in what today is labelled "paradiplomacy", or, in this comparison, "identity paradiplomacy". This development in many federal states and systems has its roots in the written constitutions of some federations and judicial interpretation in others, while membership of the EU for Belgium, Germany, Austria, Italy and Spain has added another layer of political authority that provides another attractive space – or opportunity structure – for minority nations and subnational units to occupy or exploit. In general, paradiplomacy has enabled subnational governments (US states and Canadian provinces) and minority nations (Wallonia and Quebec) to participate directly not only in trade relations, but also to exercise influence in foreign policy and external relations that are normally regarded as the sole preserve of the national (federal) government. When we focus more narrowly on minority nations in multinational federations, however, we must highlight a special feature absent from cases that we find in mono-national territorial federations, namely, nation-building projects. Given the external impact of globalisation today, minority nations are exposed directly to policy pressures that can have a serious impact on their ability to determine themselves. They are vulnerable to a variety of socioeconomic and cultural imperatives that can undermine their identity – such as language, education and cultural erosion – so that it has become increasingly important for them to have an assertive voice in those external relations of the federal government that impinge on their sense of who they are. In this sense, the para-diplomacy that empowers minority nations to promote their own "external" face to the world *outside* the federal state is the logical corollary to their efforts to claim a distinctive presence *within* the federation. Both are part of an overall strategy to achieve internal self-determination. This chapter provides an in-depth analysis of this contemporary phenomenon, and demonstrates how far minority nations can create new institutional spaces to occupy in participatory decision-making, and how, in these two cases, they manage to perpetuate a *visage français* in their dealings with foreign powers.

This fascinating chapter brings the comparison of Quebec and Wallonia to an appropriate close and in so doing has made an important contribution to a subject that requires much more research if we are to understand what the term "multinational" means today. We began this Conclusion by referring to Charles Taylor's "age of identity awakening" and the explorations in our book of essays suggest that the politics and government of identity is, in fact, multifaceted. There are many ways in which minority nations in multinational federations have addressed the question of majority–minority relations, and have successfully expressed themselves – and their identity – in a variety of institutional forms. This book is, in essence, about identity construction, recon-struction, protection, preservation and promotion as a permanent feature of the predicament in which minority nations find themselves in multinational federations. It is the task of such federations to accommodate these nations, as James Tully has argued (2001), by constantly engaging in an equally per-manent public conversation about who they are, what they want and how they can work together with majority mindsets to achieve their goals within rather than outside the state.

References

Burgess, Michael (2012a). "Multinational federalism in multinational federation". In *Multinational Federalism: Problems and Prospects*, ed. Michel Seymour and Alain-G. Gagnon, 23–44. Basingstoke: Palgrave Macmillan.

Burgess, Michael (2012b). *In Search of the Federal Spirit: New Theoretical and Empirical Perspectives in Comparative Federalism*, Oxford: Oxford University Press.

Burgess, Michael and Alain-G. Gagnon (2010). *Federal Democracies*, London: Routledge.

Burgess, Michael and Frederic Lepine (2012). "What is the federal centre?" In *Governing From the Centre: the Influence of the Federal/Central Government on Subnational Governments*, ed. Gisela Farber, 1–20. Speyer: German Research Institute for Public Administration.

Deschouwer, Kris (2012). *The Politics of Belgium: Governing a Divided Society*, 2nd edn, Basingstoke: Palgrave.

Gagnon, Alain-G. (2010). *The Case for Multinational Federalism: Beyond the all-Encompassing Nation*, London: Routledge Macmillan.

Gagnon, Alain-G. and Hugh Segal (2000). *The Canadian Social Union Without Quebec: 8 Critical Essays*, Montreal: Institute for Research on Public Policy.

Kymlicka, Will (2001). *Politics in the Vernacular: Nationalism, Multiculturalism and Citizenship*, Oxford: Oxford University Press.

McRoberts, Kenneth (2001). "Canada and the multinational state", *Canadian Journal of Political Science*, 4(4): 683–713.

Miller, David (2001). "Nationality in divided societies". In *Multinational Democracies*, ed. Alain-G. Gagnon and James Tully, 299–318. Cambridge: Cambridge University Press.

Riker, William H. (1964). *Federalism: Origin, Operation, Significance*, Boston, MA: Little Brown.

Taylor, Charles (2001). "Foreword". In *Multinational Democracies*, ed. Alain-G. Gagnon and James Tully, xiii–xv. Cambridge: Cambridge University Press.

Tully, James (2001). "Introduction". In *Multinational Democracies*, ed. Alain-G. Gagnon and James Tully, 1–33. Cambridge: Cambridge University Press.

Watts, Ronald L. (2008). *Comparing Federal Systems*, 3rd edn, Montreal: McGill-Queen's University Press.

Index

Italic page numbers indicate tables; bold indicate figures.

For Product Safety Concerns and Information please contact our EU
representative GPSR@taylorandfrancis.com
Taylor & Francis Verlag GmbH, Kaufingerstraße 24, 80331 München, Germany

www.ingramcontent.com/pod-product-compliance
Lightning Source LLC
Chambersburg PA
CBHW050439280326
41932CB00013BA/2174